INDIAN GOVERNMENT AND POLITICS

INDIAN GOVERNMENT AND POLITICS

Dr. Archna Chaturvedi

Commonwealth

Indian Government and Politics

Edition 2025

ISBN 81-7169-974-X

Published by :

COMMONWEALTH PUBLISHERS
4831/24, Prahlad Street,
Ansari Road, Darya Ganj,
New Delhi - 110002
Ph. : 23275511, 23257835
e-mail : commonwealthbooks@gmail.com

Typesetting by :

Rishu Computers
Delhi - 110051

Printed at :
Roshan Offset Printers
Delhi

PREFACE

This book aims at tracing the growth and evolution of Indian Government and Politics from colonial rule to the present day. Attempt has been made to make available to our readers material on philosophical and ideological overview of the Indian Political System, Governmental institutions, their structure and working. Social and economic aspects of politics, party system and policy of non-alignment have been included with a view to proper understanding of the subject.

We take this opportunity to thank the authorities on the subject.

Librarians and their staff members have been kind and helpful. They deserve our gratefulness.

Last but not the least my publisher and his staff members rendered every possible co-operation and help. We thank them all.

Dr. Archna Chaturvedi

Contents

1

The Building of a Nation

When the East India Company, chartered in 1600, started its operations in India, establishing factories in Calcutta and Madras, the subcontinent which had known in high degree of unity under the Mauryas, the Guptas, and the Moguls in the times of Akbar, was in a state of dangerous political fragmentation, not unlike Europe after the death of Charlemagne. Rival princes jousted with each other for power and prestige and, as the struggle between the Western nations seeking the wealth of the Indies sharpened, lent their support to one or other of the contending sides. Political and military strife undermined administration, jeopardized economic development, and caused stagnation in cultural activities. Had this process continued, India might suffered the same fate as China in the nineteenth century, when the great powers, intent on obtaining markets and railway concessions, used gunboat diplomacy to achieve their ends, with little or no concern for the interests and welfare of the Chinese people, whom they regarded with contempt, expressing surprise when Chinese leaders who opposed their incursions displayed what Westerners described with hostility as "anti-foreign" sentiment.

India was spread China's ordeal by the success of the East India Company in defeating the attempts of Britain's rivals — France, the Netherlands, and Portugal — to share the trade opportunities which they all envisioned in the subcontinent. The Company's success, it is generally admitted, was due not only to Britain's naval superiority but also to the fact that it operated under a system of free enterprise and decentralization as contrasted with the mercantilist philosophy of France's Prime Minister, Colbert, who established the French East India Company in 1664 as a government-controlled undertaking.

While the French in India had to wait for orders from Paris, which not only took a long time in reaching them but were framed by men with not trading experience, the English were able to make decisions on the spot and to adapt their policies to local circumstances, knowing that the test of their endeavors would not be compliance with governmental rules in London but success measured in monetary terms. When they found that trade could not be effectively carried on under conditions of local disorder, corruption, extortion, and disruption of communications as a result of military skirmishes between princes, the East India Company administrators did not hesitate to wage war on those Indian rulers who challenged it plans, as Clive did at Plassey, or to make compacts with friendly princes, as if the Company were itself a sovereign state. When Clive, who by that time had been honored with the title of Lord Clive of Plassey, returned to India in 1765, to deal with new disorders he said, with what turned out to be a prophetic sense, "tomorrow the whole Mogul power is in our grasp." Yet two years later, at the peak of what he could not but consider merited glory, when he returned to England after establishing a Society of Trade which had a monopoly in betel leaf, salt, and opium, he met with strong public criticism, and was brought before the House of Commons, where he said he was treated like a sheep-stealer rather than like a man who had built an empire. He was so deeply shocked by this sudden turn in his fortunes that after brooding on his downfall, he committed suicide in 1774 at the age of fifty.

The career of his successor, Warren Hastings, was as spectacular and as fraught with sharp contrasts between heights of success and depths of failure. In the wake of a terrible famine that swept India in 170— "the scene shocks humanity too much to bear description," said one official — Warren Hastings was sent to India as Governor of Bengal, the richest agricultural area of India. He was then 40 years old, having risen, like Clive, to the top from the lowly post of writer for the Company, which he had taken at the age of 18. Hastings was primarily not a soldier but a student and administrator. A Persian scholar, he learned Urdu, Bengali, and Arabic, and was deeply interested in the history, art, and culture of India.

Hastings did not think well of the double government system established by Clive, with East India Company administrators operating side by side with local governments, and decided that the Company should rule alone. He settled in Calcutta, which he made the capital of Bengal.

By that time the British government realized that, as Clive had so recently predicted, it was winning a great empire in India through the efforts of the East India Company, and in 1773 the government of Lord North put through Parliament an act regulating the Company's activities in India. This act provided for a civil and military government in the provinces of Bihar, Bengal, and Orissa, and Hastings, as Governor-General, became head of the government, assisted by four councilors. The governor-general and the councilors also had the power to supervise Madras and Bombay, where the Company also had trading centers.

The act, in addition, established a Supreme Court, consisting of a supreme justice and three other judges, which was to deal with all cases involving British subjects in the three provinces. Most important of all for the future development of British rule in India, the directors of the Company were to submit copies of all their correspondence to the government, and every six months were to account for their activities to Parliament. Thus was started the process of transition by which a merchant company with no responsibilities to the government except for the requirement of obtaining its charter was gradually shorn of the political, administrative, and military functions it had assumed, not from choice but from the necessity of maintaining conditions of order favourable to trade, and was increasingly made responsible to the legislature, which in turn was responsible to the British people.

A further step in this evolution was taken by Prime Minister William Pitt who in 1984 introduced the India Act. Under this act Indian affairs were placed under a committee of three senior directors of the East India Company, which in turn was to be supervised by Board of Control whose members were appointed by the Crown. The office of President of the Board of Control was the forerunner of what eventually became in the nineteenth century the office of the Secretary of State for India. Hastings, who had already experienced many clashes about his authority with the Supreme Court, was alarmed by the India Act, and returned to Britain, where a storm of criticism awaited him. His enemies—Pit, Fox, and particularly Edmund Burke—who had increasingly condemned Hastings' activities, notably his alleged mistreatment of India rulers that was said to include torture and extortion for purposes of personal enrichment—obtained his impeachment by the House of Commons. When he was brought to the bar of the House, amid scenes of colourful splendor vividly described by the historian Macaulay in his essay, *Warren Hastings,* he was subjected to the most eloquent denunciation by Burke of which this distinguished and often vitriolic orator was capable. Although Hastings was finally, acquitted, he retired from political life with a sense of grim failure.

Yet, in retrospect, Hastings laid the basis for orderly and just rule by the British through three principal contributions. First, he contended that power should always be accompanied by a sense of responsibility, this respect continuing the philosophy of the Hindu Asoka and the Muslim Akbar. Second, he urged the officials and employees of the East India Company to observe principles of good conduct in their relations with the Indians, declaring that it was in the interests of Britain, as well as India, that the peasants should be assured orderly rule, justice and freedom from outside attack. And, most significant of all for a future understanding between the British and the Indians, he respected the traditions and culture of the subcontinent. He based a new civil and penal code on Indian customs, arranged for translations of ancient Hindu books by Indian scholars, thereby introducing the treasures of Indian literature to Europe, and in many other way sought to preserve and promote India's cultural values, which the Indians themselves had tended to neglect during the turbulent centuries of disintegration of the Mogul empire. Thoughtful Indians, among them Raja Ram Mohan Roy, and even Dadabhay Naoroji, who first used the word *swaraj* (self-rule) to describe India's goal, recognized the benefits of British rule for India. In fact, when Naroroji attacked Indian rulers, he did it in book entitled *Poverty and Un-British Rule in India*.

The experience of Clive and Hastings epitomized two basic problems of Britain's relationship with India for nearly three hundred and fifty years. On the one hand, the British could and repeatedly did, claim that their arrival in the subcontinent, although admittedly inspired by motives of private profit-making, had the twofold result of safeguarding India from invasions by other powers while restoring law and order within the continent, and of serving the strategic and economic interests of Britain and the empire it built around the world during that period. On the other hand, both British critics of this relationship and Indian nationalists could and repeatedly did contend that, however true these claims might be, the price paid for the achievements first of the East India Company and subsequently of the British Crown, which in 1857 took over the administrative functions the company had previously exercised, was too high, both in moral terms and in economic terms.

British critics—Burke among them - again and again were conscience-stricken at what they heard about the ruthlessness of Company-appointed administrators toward the Indians, their contempt for people of colour, their enrichment through methods which would have been condemned in Britain, such as bribery, extortion, and torture of persons form who funds were sought, as well as the sale of opium, and the violation of Christian principles which the British working in India claimed to support and propagate. What troubled British critics most was the use of a double standards of moral conduct—depending on whether a man acted in Britain or in India. The Indian nationalists, who could heartily subscribe to the views of the British critics, increasingly argued as the struggle for independence from Britain gained momentum after 1858, that the presence of the British, whatever its advantages for India, was an obstacle to the modernization and development which the subcontinent might have been able to experience in the absence of foreign rule, no matter how benevolent.

This clash between two aspects of British life—what seemed good and useful to merchants and administrators, an what seemed evil and ineffectual to British critics and to Indian nationalists—is a familiar feature of the colonial relationship between a Western nation and a non-Western people. Colonialism, whatever its initial motivation—whether military or political or economic or ideological — is bound to have the appearance of the Roman god Janus with two faces booking in opposite directions. The colonizer genuinely believes, or rationalizes its actions into believing, that it is conferring benefits on the colonized people from whom it expects at least gratitude and at most uncritical co-operation in the policies it regards as necessary.

The colonial people, for its part, even when, as proved to be the case in India, it acknowledges its indebtedness to the colonizing power in some respects, resents and all means at its disposal opposes the foreign ruler and is willing to risk the possible dangers of disorder and misrule as a results of independence on the ground that "good government is not a substitute for self-government." What makes the argument between the two invariability confused, and when resistance is allowed to reach the stage of armed uprising, dangerous for both, is that the colonizing power does not regard it necessary to observe, in its colonial possessions, the moral rules of conduct to which it would be held at home, justifying this double standard by arguments such as that its overseas subject are either backward or inferior, and therefore unprepared for self-government. Meanwhile, the colonial peoples having been repeatedly told of the superior advantages of democracy and Christianity as contrasted with their authoritarian regimes and their own faiths, are led to except form the Western ruler higher standards of relations between human beings than those to which they have been traditionally accustomed.

Here too a two-faced picture emerges—with the colonial power showing at home the noble mien of respect for representative government, for individual liberty, for free enterprise, and for the equality of man; and in the colonial possession the less appealing features of administrators, traders, and even educators and missionaries. These, for whatever reason, believe it proper to restrict political liberties, to limit free speech, to extol the advantages of what amounts to benevolent dictatorship by the colonial power, to discourage the growth of economic activities which might complete with those of the metropolitan country, and to discriminate against the natives in social life. They inculcate religious and educational values which, however suitable they may be in the West, are often ill-adapted, and in any case often opposed, to the needs of the non-Western lands, and often arouse deep-seated opposition to values imposed by the outsiders, which in turn nurtures nationalism and anti-Westernism.

It is the this context of mixed experience with Western colonialism—or, to use the Indian formula of "this and that" rather than "this or that" — that the impact of British rule on India, must be judged and the alternatives that might have occurred had the British never come to India must be evaluated.

On the credit side of the ledger, an outside observer would have to put down at least five major contributions made by Britain.

First, the British, through the East India Company, checked the political and economic disintegration of the subcontinent that had set in as a result of the breakdown of administrative control by the Mogul empire with it capital in Delhi.

Second, after eliminating their Western competitors for influence and control in India, they henceforth protected the subcontinent against intervention or incursion from outside — not only by the West, but in the nineteenth century also by the Russian Empire under the Tsars.

Third, they introduced order and security in the areas over which they had control, eventually extending this control over the entire subcontinent, which the British Crown, after 1858, administered in two separate sectors—British India, ruled directly from London and 562 princely states, where the local rulers remained in power, but made bilateral pacts with the British Crown.

Fourth, they introduced the rule of law, familiar to the English people, with equal treatment for individuals, irrespective of color, race, or religion.

And, fifth, in the contrast to the Dutch in Indonesia and the French in Indo-China, they gave an opportunity, after 1858, to a small but significant number of Indians of high intellectual quality to be trained for civil service, at home and in English universities, and entrusted them with high-level jobs, thereby preparing a select group for the administrative tasks they might have to perform in an independent country.

In a subcontinent menaced by chaos, the British gradually constructed the skeleton of a unified area where they instilled, within limits they themselves determined, some of the basic principles of law and government which they had evolved in their own society.

What the British had not yet done by 1947, when they decided it was wise to withdraw form India before their task, as they had previously seen it, had been completed, was to clothe this skeleton with adequate flesh and to articulate it in all the parts necessary for a modern state. Whether or not they would have succeeded in completing this task had they found it possible to remain in India for further, undefined period of time must remain one of the unanswerable questions of history, but is seems doubtful that they could have done so, given the growing strength and impatience of Indian nationalism.

Assuming that the British, by 1947, had gone as far as they could, an outside observer would have to set down a major charge on the debit side of the ledger, which must be broken down into several separate items. This major charge is that the British, once they had introduced order and security against outside attack, the rule of law, and a core Indian civil service—all of which were necessary for the safe operation of British administration in India—they either did little to change the patterns of Indian life or, when they changed these patterns, gave little thought to the consequences of their actions. They thus created serious problems for the future, which were left as a harsh inheritance for independent India.

The British abolished certain practices which they found repugnant to Western customs, such as suttee, infanticide, and thuggee (banditry), but they carefully avoided tampering with the caste system, choosing, like their Mogul predecessors, to leave it alone. While it is understandable that the British preferred not to challenge head-on a social and economic system deeply entrenched in Hindu life, the result was that the political structure they slowly erected in India stood apart from, and did not merge with the Hindu structure. It has remained for the government of the Republic of India to start dismantling the caste system and to forge a political, social, and economic framework within which new human relations could be developed without undue shock to public order and to the sensitivities of the people.

Meanwhile, the changes the British did make had far-reaching consequences which they either did not or could not foresee at the time, but whose impact is now having serious results for India. First, as already indicated, by reducing the death rate through public health measures and increased internal security without taking steps to decrease the birthrate the British, like other colonial rulers, unwittingly set the state for an explosive growth of population which has proved a tremendous obstacle to India's economic development.

Second, under the governorship of Lord Cornwallis (1786-1798) the British, though the "Permanent Settlement," created a new group of middleman, the *zamindars* (holders of land) , who had previously served as tax collectors for the British, and now were made landlords. They had the obligation to pay the Company a fixed or "permanent" sum on taxes which they collected, keeping the rest for themselves. This "Permanent Settlement" which, Lord Cornwallis believed, would introduce in India the way of life of England's landed gentry, proved to have an effect the British had not anticipated. For one thing, since the *zamindars* had to pay a fixed sum in perpetuity, whatever the amount of the taxes they collected, the Company, and ultimately the British government, was deprived of additional revenue in days of prosperity. For another, whenever the *zamindars* were unable to pay the sum set for them, they lost their land, with a consequently disruptive effect on land ownership. The most serious and disastrous effect of the *zamindari* system, however, was its effect on the peasants, who were left pretty much at the mercy of the *zamindars*. The peasant had to pay heavier rents, often risk or lose his land to the *zamindar*, owe the zamindars forced labour duty, and so on. The social effect of creating a landed and often absentee landlord class, which has political repercussions in India today, is another very important and direct effect of the *zamindari* system of former days.

Third, the British introduced in India the system of education they found desirable in Britain, as proposed in the *Minute on Education* draw up in 1835 by Macaulay, who regarded Indian ideas and literature as barbaric ("a single shelf of a good European library," he said "was worth the whole native literature of India and Arabia"), and believed that the English should bring light to "the children of darkness." English was made the medium of instruction in institutions of higher learning. This in itself proved useful to India when it achieved independent, although only 10 to 15 per cent of the Indian population speak English today, and the teaching of English has markedly deteriorated since 1947. But the question which now confronts India is whether British education, based until 1945 on the concept of training an elite in exclusive schools and colleges, Eton and Harrow, Oxford and Cambridge, primarily in the humanities with little emphasis on science and technology, was suited for Indian needs. In India, with a vast and growing population, the masses must receive at least a modicum of education if they are to create democratic society and to satisfy their newly aroused aspirations for advancement; and urgent tasks of modernizing agriculture and creating new industries call for more and more young men and women trained in modern technical skills rather then for those who seek white-collar jobs as government clerks or as writers.

Fourth, while the British continued the construction of irrigation facilities and built communications—railways, posts and telegraphs, and telephones, all of which were necessary for their civilian and military administration—they did little to encourage the development of India's economy and in some important respects actually discouraged it. From the point of view of the Indians, the lack of British initiative in the economic sphere seemed to be an evil design to destroy their opportunities for ultimate independence and to keep them in thrall to the British Empire. It must be borne in mind, however, that the British at that time, and until the rise of socialism in Britain during the 1930s, were firm believers in free enterprise, free trade, *laissez faire*, and an unplanned economy. They could thus justify to themselves their lack of alacrity in examining India's potential resources and devising methods for their most effective use.

At the same time, it is clear that the British saw in India a source of cotton for their Lancashire mills, then the most advanced in the world, and as an outlet for their finished cotton goods. Their economic policy was calculated to achieve both objectives. By abolishing India's customs tariff in 1882, and refusing to establish another tariff until 1923, after World War I, they made it impossible for India either to keep out British cotton goods, or to establish under at least temporary protection, some of those "infant" industries which other countries had created at a comparable stage of economic development, to replace their heavy dependence on cotton. Although a revenue tariff of 5 per cent was imposed on imports in 1894, the Lancashire cotton interests protested against it. British goods were therefore admitted at 3½ per cent but, to offset this, a countervailing excise duty of 3½ per cent was imposed on goods made out of cloth produced in India which competed with that made in Lancashire— an instance of Britain's capacity to combine its belief in *laissez faire* with a measure of planning. Meanwhile, by insisting on importation of their cotton good into India on preferential terms, the British caused the decline of cottage industries in the villages, which had provided a subsidiary source of employment and income for the peasants.

Britain's refusal to recognize the double problem its cotton good policy was creating for India aroused the vigorous opposition of Gandhi, who urged his supporters to symbolize their resistance by devoting some time each day to work at the spinning wheel, and to refuse to wear garments made of British-manufactured cloth, using instead homemade goods (*swadeshi*, or made in one's own country) produced by the cottage industries. Here, again, the British failed to see the consequences and inter-connectedness of their policies. A population rapidly increasing as a result of lower death rates but unchecked by lower birth rates needed employment, yet the British government did not face the need to encourage corresponding growth in productivity.

The peasants either had to find increased employment in handicrafts in the villages, or seek work in newly created industries as peasants had once done in Western Europe at the end of the Middle Ages. But the British showed little inclination to diversify the Indian economy by the creation of new industries which might have competed with those of the metropolitan country — although they did provide technicians to improve the productivity of India's cotton mills. When the well-known and highly respected Parsee industrialist, J.R. Tata, decided to build the first (and until after independence the only) steel mill in India, and sought capital in Britain, the president of the Federation of British Industries, expressing profound disbelief in the capacity of the Indians to create such an enterprise, is said to have exclaimed: "I'll eat every ton of steel they make!" Although this gentleman was presumably spread the ordeal of eating 1,200,000 tons of steel a year — the eventual output of the Tata mill — the required capital had to be raised in the United States.

The net result of Britain's lack of economic policy, or the use of economic policy to discourage local initiative, is that independent India found it had to modernize and reorganize its primarily background agrarian economy and, at the same time, do what it could toward diversifying its production thorough the creation of essential industries, among them an antibiotics plant, three fertilizer factories, a locomotive works, and three new steel mills, before it could hope to make a start on the output of consumer goods sufficient to fill even the minimal needs of the population. Moreover, it had to undertake this gigantic task with only a handful of scientists, technical experts, and responsible entrepreneurs, since the British had not encouraged technological education or a climate favourable to the emergence of enterprising businessmen, as distinguished from speculators in commodities who are characteristic of underdeveloped countries, and in India deal largely in such commodities as sugar, cotton, or jute.

And fifth, but perhaps most unfortunate for India's immediate future, foreign rule impeded the country's social and cultural development. At this time in its history India, having made contact through Britain with the West after centuries of isolation, could have benefited by the application of modern science and technology to modernize not only its economy but also its education, its social structure, and its political system. Yet the energies and creative faculties of its intelligent and enterprising people were diverted for a century to the struggle for independence, which for long periods removed some of its most prominent leaders to jail and, no sooner had Britain withdrawn, to the devastating Muslim-Hindu riots which sapped the vitality of both new nations when they were most in need of strength for new undertakings and of cooperation in common problems.

2

India in the 1940s: A Great Divide?

Indian public life in the 1940s was dominated by the Second World War II, which affected the subcontinent far more closely and deeply than that of 1914-18, and by the escalation of communal hostilities which cost thousands of lives and resulted in the country's partition when the British withdrew in August 1947. Obviously a case can be made out that the decade was a great dividing line in the Indian experience, and that 1947 marked the end of an era. That year saw the end of the *raj* and the coming of the political independence India's politicians had demanded for over half a century. This had major domestic consequences, but also far-reaching international effects. It heralded the obvious decline of British world influence and the contraction of the British empire, particularly in Africa where colonies lost much of their significance once they were no longer needed as guarantees of the routes to India. India's independence was also a powerful symbol and a practical example to other colonial nationalist movements in the empires of various European nations. 1947 also seems at first sight to be an obvious dividing-line because of the subcontinent's partition into India and a curious two-winged Pakistan in the north-western and north-eastern parts of the former empire; and because of the demolition of the princely order which was older than the *raj* itself and had been so cosseted by the British in their need for allies. Undoubtedly, too 1947 was symbol of a brave new world for some Indians. Gandhi was burdened with despair at the shattering of his vision for a new India; but Nehru's famous speech at independence was passionately hopeful, claiming the end had come of 'a period of ill fortune' and that India was about to rediscover her true self.

> Long years ago we made a tryst with destiny, and now the time comes when we shall redeem out pledge... At the stroke of the midnight hour, when the world sleeps, India will awake to life and freedom. A moment comes, which comes but rarely in history, when we step out from the old to the new, when an age ends, and when the soul of a nation, long suppressed, finds utterance. It is fitting that at this solemn moment we take the pledge of dedication to the service of India and her people and to the still larger cause of humanity.[1]

Yet this very speech was made at midnight because independence had to occur on an auspicious day for Hindus, and the British had not considered this when they fixed their departure date—a symbol of continuities in Indian life, despite the decade's political upheavals! It can be argued powerfully that there was really far more continuity than change in the 1940s. 1947 is more important to the historian searching for tidy demarcations than a deeply critical point of division in the Indian experience—not just in the realm of traditions, ideas, life-styles and the land's basic economic and social structures and problems, but in government and politics, too. Even the apparently dramatic changes of the 1940s were often the culmination of long-term trends, though some of them were intensified by the war's impact. (The end of *raj* itself was hardly unexpected, though the actual British exit was more precipitate than anyone could have imagined even six months before it occurred.) Therefore it is more accurate to describe the 1940s as a significant middle passage in along saga of a people's experience. Consequently this chapter focuses on the continuities as much as the changes, as both were vital in making India into an Asian democracy, and in generating the tensions and contradictions which were to beset its consolidation and operation. This chapter is therefore thematic, not chronological: nor does it give a detailed account of the abortive offers and negotiations which preceded independence, because these seem less important in introducing the real forces making modern Indian than longer-term trends. For the reader's convenience, a chronological appendix a the end of the chapter sets out the main moves in the tortuous politics of 1930-47 in the context of major changes in British politics and the war situation which impinged on Indian affairs.[2]

The most obvious change on the subcontinent was the end of the British *raj*—the formal transfer of ultimate authority from the British Parliament to an Indian legislature, and the departure of British troops and the majority of Britons in the civilian services. Why did the British choose to resolve their imperial crisis by total exit rather than by techniques similar to those they had used since the Great War? The impact of the Second World War on Britain and on India was obviously crucial in determining the timing of their departure, and in making it essential to solve the imperial crisis—outstanding from the late 1930s—in months rather years after the war. But the end of formal *raj* can only be understood in relation to the long-term character of the empire. Its precise nature and strength at any particular time was always the end-product of a balance between the basic British interests at stake in India, and the cheapest, most ideologically acceptable methods they could contrive to secure those interest. For nearly two centuries the Indian empire had rested on a fine balance of actual force, whether deployed or in reserve, the attraction of allies within India, and the creation of a public image of prestige and legitimacy in the eyes of its subjects, so that the majority of them acquiesced in its presence as an unquestioned if remote authority in their lives. The degree of force shifted a times, as did the people on whom the British relied as active friends: the interests at stake also changed over time. But an equilibrium was maintained. However, by 1947 the balance of interests and viable modes of control had disintegrated, and the British had no option but to go.

Changing British stakes in India were a significant aspect of this new plunge into disequilibrium. In the last hundred years they had included various kinds of economic profit, expatriates' civil and military careers, and the subcontinent's crucial position in imperial defence. These interests were altering significantly in the decade before the 1939-45 war. During the World War II the erosion of British interests in India was dramatically halted. She became a vital source of men, money, and war materials; and a major base for operations in the Middle East and against the invading Japanese in South-East Asia. The army increased in size from 205,058 in October 1939 to 2,251,050 in July 1945. Defence expenditure ran at its highest in 1944-45, when the grand total was Rs. 896.16 crores; over half of which was actually chargeable to India. Between 1941 and 1946 India provided £286.5 million worth of materials for the war, mainly textiles, clothing, and ordnance.[3]

However when the emergency of world war ended the longer-term trends reasserted themselves. Demobilization, a pervading desire to get 'home' after the war, and the contraction of the ICS meant that fewer Britons looked on India as a place for a career. But more significantly, for economic and political reasons Britain could even less than in the 1930s assume that India's economy would balance metropolitan trading books with other parts of the world, or provide a protected market for British goods. Tariff policy had been controlled in India and made subject to the pressures of Indian political opinion before the war. This could not be reversed a decade later; and furthermore, under the terms of the Cripps Offer of 1942. Britain had promised independence after the war. It seemed that the remaining, and still significant, trading and investment connections between the two countries could best be maintained through friendship between equal nations. Some British business firms were selling out to Indian buyers. Many of the successful 'new' British entrepreneurs needed as the context for their operations an administration set on planning and post-war reconstruction: they required no imperial protection and patronage—unlike older, expatriate enterprises. At the level of international exchange transactions India's relationship with Britain had been transformed by her expenditure in the war. It was no longer for Britain a question of ensuring that India paid her debts in sterling. She had now piled up sterling balances in London, and by 1946 Britain owed India more than £1,300 million. Britain's last significant stake in India was imperial defence. Before the war it had become clear that India could no longer be forced to contribute anything more than a strictly limited and agreed amount; and once global conflict ended Britain, as India's debtor, faced the fact that it would be more prudent and effective to base future imperial defence on treaties with a friendly independent state or on Commonwealth co-operation. At that stage the worst thing for British defence interests would be a subcontinent in turmoil, fighting an imperial regime or engaged in inter-necine conflicts. Rarely did the British openly discuss what India meant to them. But in times of crisis the role of the subcontinent was articulated. Reflecting on the prospects for British interests in 1946, Wavell sent a note London which concluded that, provided power could be transferred in an orderly manner to a friendly and united India, and arrangements could be made for defence, 'The general conclusion is that on the whole Great Britain should not lose, but on the contrary, may gain in prestige and even in power, by handing over to Indians'; while Britain ought to profit naturally because of her established links with subcontinent from any expansion in Indian trade and industry.[4] After the war long-term changes in British interests, combined with the Cripps Offer, dictated that a profitable and peaceful connection with India could best be maintained by friendship and treaties with an independent member of the Commonwealth.

Yet this was not the whole picture—as the existence of the Cripps Offer indicated. The situation was more complex than a simple calculation of the cost effectiveness, in maintaining current stakes of friendship as against control of a reluctant empire. By 1946 it was manifest that the old methods of formal empire were actually unworkable. Before inquiring into the final decay of those older methods of imperial control it must be underlined that the British were never pushed physically out of India by the strength of a mass, nationalist movement: though such claims have been made for Gandhi's final, most famous but most 'un-Gandhian' all-India campaign, the 1942 'Quit India movement'. The Congress leadership decided to embark on 'Quit India' after their rejection of the Cripps Offer earlier that year, not because they felt the country was on the brink of mass revolution or readiness for non-violent resistance to the *raj*, nor because they were assured of sufficiently widespread support to force the British to leave. The prospect of another major conflict with the *raj* was not in fact appealing to many of them. Rather it was a policy which achieved a compromise within the Congress leadership and enabled them to deal as united body with the interlocking questions which divided them—non-violence as a principle, the possibility of a Japanese invasion if the British remained in India, whether in the *raj*'s hour of crisis to assist the opponents of its imperialism who were also opposed to so much of what the Congress itself stood for, and if not, how to maintain a nationalist movement and a national demand in relation to a *raj* which refused to offer immediate power in such crucial areas as defence to Indians, such was its preoccupation with winning the war.[5]

When the AICC launched the movement in August control of it slipped out of the hands of the Congress leadership far more rapidly than in 1920-21 or 1930-31, because the leaders were promptly jailed and the Congress organization disrupted by swift government reprisals. So the 'Quit India movement' became the enterprise of lower-level leaders and those who, as in Bihar, had been pushed out of power in Congress because of their factional loyalties, left-wing leanings and connections with economic groups such as the Kisans whose demands embarrassed the main leadership. Students also played prominent parts in organizing resistance, particularly in towns. While in some areas there was substantial rural upheaval. There was little co-ordination of the movement (and considerable controversy about the extent to which it had been pre-planned). Each local leadership or group acted on its own authority, issuing its own instructions, forced to work underground and in isolation by government suppression. Not surprisingly the result was often violent, extremely patchy and followed no over-all plan. But its main manifestations were assaults on obvious aspects of and key links in the *raj*'s hold over India, particularly government property and communications. Police stations and post offices, railway stations, track, and rolling-stock were prime targets (By the end of 1943, 332 stations and 945 post offices had been destroyed or severely damaged, and it was virtually impossible to estimate damage to track.) From the *raj*'s point of view this was the worst rebellion it had encountered since 1857, and one which it tried to conceal for reasons of military security: but the worst was over in weeks. The storm-centres had been Bihar, eastern UP, and Bombay. At its height breakdown in communications followed by widespread looting led to local losses of government control. For brief periods whole district administrations collapsed, as in Billia (UP), while Bengal and Assam were isolated from the rest of India by disturbances and disruption of communications in Bihar. (The Bihar administration resorted to Tiger Moths of the Bihar Flying Club to keep communications open with one of its districts!) [See Table A for detailed evidence of the nature and regional variations of the movement.][6]

Yet very rapidly the British were able to bring 'Quit India' under control. Not only had they a well-prepared plan for immediate incarceration of the Congress leadership and a preemptive stike against Congress. Now under pressure of war and with an expanded army on the spot they had both the motivation and the man-power to smash the movement hard, and first, in a way they could not have contemplated in 1920 or 1930. 'Quit India' was pathetically like a flotilla of rafts colliding with a battleship. Well over fifty battalions of troops were deployed in the early suppression of the movement, and by the end of 1943 troops had fired sixty-eight times inflicting nearly 300 fatal and over 200 non-fatal casualties. Despite temporary losses of control the over-all security of the *raj* was never endangered by the movement. After its destruction the British proved capable of putting Indian politics 'on ice' until the end of the war, not least by the device of locking up the major Congress leaders, and leaving at liberty only those politicians, including 'Moderates' and Muslims, who were disposed to collaborate in the wartime administration or to refrain from disrupting it. Within a year of the August eruption the Secretary of State could write, 'it looks as if India had never been so quiet politically as it is at this moment.' Not surprisingly this demonstration of imperial power irked wide range of the politically aware, including those who would never have countenanced or participated in the actions taken in the name of 'Quit India', though they were staunch supporters of eventual Indian independence. One southern politician who had been in Liberal and Congress politics for years said this to the new Viceroy's face in 1944. Wavell reported to London his informant's view that 'the present regime could carry on quite comfortably till the end of the war... it was this knowledge and the fear that we should do so which was making the intellectuals so bitter.'[7] Yet 'Quit India' was a lesson the British could not forget: for it demonstrated the frailty of their local administrative structures and warned them of the possible strength of any future Congress-led movement which was well co-ordinated, particularly if it occurred after the war when the *raj* was no longer so well equipped psychologically or materially for ruthless suppression.

Although neither *satyagraha* nor violent upheaval pushed the British into the Indian Ocean there accumulated during the 1940s indisputable evidence of the weakening of the network of collaboration on which the British had relied from imperial stability and the routine functioning of their administration. Two major strands in the network had been the services, and the politicians who since 1919 had been increasingly incorporated into the formal support structure of the *raj* and by 1939 were far more significant than the great landlords who half a century earlier had been the most valued of British buttresses. Both strands in the network were by 1946 either broker or badly stretched.

The army and police were the *raj*'s main instruments of coercion, and they had always been predominantly manned, though not officered, by Indians. During the war there was no lack of recruits for either service; and very few disaffection even during 'Quit India'. [See Table A. The 'Indian National Army', those Indian soldiers who defected to the Japanese, was a special case. Their disaffection occurred not in India but when they were captured by the Japanese. Many prisoners remained loyal to the British despite pressure and hardship.] The chronic weakness of the police in some areas had long been a source of concern to government. This problem remained unsolved and war exacerbated it because considerable numbers resigned to join the army. Moreover in some places, notable Bihar, there were ominous signs that this combined with declining morale was leading to a breakdown in the *raj*'s intelligence network. The Governor of Bihar admitted that his province's intelligence system was probably 'badly at fault' in failing to report the possibility of severe local disturbances in 1942, and that he had 'had very poor reports of the ordinary constabulary and in some places of the armed police: their hearts are not in the job.' Confused loyalties among officials and a breakdown in intelligence were notorious signs of the end-game of empire, as the Moguls has found out two centuries before.

It was after the war that the loyalty of the police and troops came to be seriously doubted or displayed. In April 1946 some

Table A. Evidence of the regional incidence of the *'Quit movement'*

Category	*Madras*	*Bombay*	*Bengal*	*United Provinces*	*punjab*
Government servants (excluding) those of the central governments					
Police					
No. of occasions on which police fired	21	226	63	116	1
No. of casualties inflicted, non-fatal	39	112	87	207	-
No. of casualties suffered, non-fatal	86	406	149	458	-
No. of casualties suffered, fatal,	-	6	5	16	-
No. of casualties suffered, non-fatal	91	563	180	333	-
No. of defections from police	1	6	6	2	-
Other government servants					
No. of attacks on other government servants, fatal	-	1	-	3	-
No. of attacks on other government servants, non-fatal	19	50	14	141	-
No. of defections from other government service	-	3	-	9	-
Damage to property (excluding central government property)					
No. of police stations or outposts ect. destroyed or severely damaged	5	46	4	42	-
No. of other government building destroyed or serverly damaged	50	318	95	45	2
No. of public buildings other than government buildings, e.g., municipal property, schools, hospitals, etc., destroyed or serverly damaged	57	152	58	37	4
No. of important private buildings destroyed or severely damaged	11	34	29	3	5
Estimated loss to governmentRs.	225192	945410	171876	363366	1000
Estimated loss to other partiesRs.	916025	563581	55391	102778	105000
Cases of sabotage					
No. of bomb explosions	17	447	51	60	-
No. of bombs or explosives discovered without damage	35	738	106	157	1

and its suppression, for the period ending 31 December, 1943

Bihar	*Central Provinces*	*Assam*	*North-west Frontiner Province*	*Orissa*	*Sindh*	*Delhi*	*Coorg*	*Total*
96	42	4	1	9	-	22	-	601
166	45	15	3	69	-	20	-	763
508	181	19	13	111	-	10	-	1941
26	8	-	-	1	1	-	-	63
342	256	17	52	26	90	62	-	2012
205	2	-	-	-	9	-	-	216
4	2	-	-	-	-	-	-	10
87	39	-	-	13	-	1	-	364
4	-	-	5	-	-	-	1	22
72	29	4	-	5	-	1	-	208
103	41	64	1	25	-	4	1	749
92	45	66	-	8	2	4	-	525
119	2	61	-	2	1	2	-	273
354720	424840	284582	200	46459	1904	15456	120	2735125
495231	167270	194847	-	33598	2932	370376	245	3007274
8	10	10	1	-	50	-	10	664
218	18	9	1	-	13	11	12	1319

Table A. Contd. . .

Category	*Madras*	*Bombay*	*Bengal*	*United Provinces*	*punjab*
No. of case of sabotage to roads	32	78	57	84	-
No. of case in which collective fines imposed	41	73	20	7	-
Amount of collective fines imposed	Rs. 1034359	817950	605503	3176973	-
No. of sentences of whipping indicted	295	17	2	1252	-
No. of arrests made	5859	24416	4818	16796	2501
No. of local authorities superseded under defence Rule 38B or otherwise	27	19	11	7	-

Source: Home Political File 3/52/43(1); quoted in Hutchins, *Inida's Revolution,*

of the Malabar Special Police (crack armed companies) went on strike over conditions of service and pay, though the Madras government suspected political influence at work. Four companies were disbanded and nearly 1,000 men were dismissed. Bihar also experienced a police strike in 1946. By September 1946 Wavell was reporting to London that they could not rely implicitly on the police (or other provincial services) to carry out the orders of a British government. Earlier that year there had been mutinies in the Indian navy, in which politics and services conditions were sources of discontent: again, an occurrence for which the government had practically no warning . But the real threat now to the dependability of the police and troops was not political propaganda from a Congress which acted a counter focus and possible successor to the *raj*, but the pressure of communal strife. By the close of 1946 Wavell and his advisers believed that the army was still dependable despite escalating communal violence, but that communalism had undermined the loyalty of some of the police.[9]

But how reliable was the ICS, the 'steel-frame' of empire into which Indians had been recruited rapidly in the 1920s and 1930s? Even before the war its capacity to respond to a major crisis had worried the Viceroy. In 1943 Indian recruitment to the

Bihar	*Central Provinces*	*Assam*	*North-west Frontiner Province*	*Orissa*	*Sindh*	*Delhi*	*Coorg*	*Total*
169	7	43	-	4	-	-	-	474
16	3	1	-	-	5	-	7	173
2660765	3444595	339487	-	27750	-	-	-	9007382
340	282	-	-	9	-	-	-	2562
16202	8753	2707	2339	2806	3689	90	860	91836
3	35	-	-	5	-	1	-	108

pp. 230-1.

ICS was stopped because European recruitment had dried up as Britain mobilized her man-power in the fight for her own survival. As a result of this and secondment to other work in wartime, the ICS was badly understaffed just at the point where it was stretched to limits inconceivable before the war. The economic effects of the conflict and India's contribution to the war effort soon took their toll of the Indian economy, bringing inflation and food shortages. Government became involved in a wide range of new activities, from air-raid precautions and civil defence, to food procurement: and these burdens were laid on the ICS man over the above his ordinary and heavy work load. Late in 1943 Wavell told the Secretary of State that the Governors believed the services were stretched to breaking-point and pointed to the horror of the Bengal famine to warn what could happen when an administration proved incompetent in the face of a major disaster. In July the Governor of CP had painted a vivid picture of an administrative machine stretched beyond its limits by the demands of war; when the basic problem of food supplies consumed the energies of all administrative staff from the Deputy Commissioners downwards, and wen the province's ICS cadre has been absorbed by the Government of India to an extent which was never dreamt of in the calculation on which the strength of that service is based.[10]

Of longer term significance than the physical strain on the civilian services, and their spearhead, the ICS, was the fact that by 1940 there were for the first time more Indians than Europeans in the ICS (614 as opposed to 587): at the beginning of 1947 there were 510 Indians and only 429 Europeans. Indians were also by this time in very senior administrative posts. They were known to sympathize with political aspirations of their compatriots and to want independence as strongly as any Congressman. Naturally, too, they began to wonder what their future would be and to look to Congress as the new locus of authority, despite their understandably ambivalent attitudes to its. Although the loyalty of Indian ICS men was never in doubt, their possible reaction if government decided to crush Congress rather than transfer power in India after the war was a crucial consideration in British appreciation of their options. In December 1946 Wavell told the Cabinet that Indian ICS men could not be expected to carry out 'a firm policy' unless they knew the British would be there for at least a decade afterwards to protect their interests.[11]

By 1946 the British knew their network of Indian allies in their various services was a fast-weakening support and instrument of their rule. The strains of war, the prospect of transferred power, and the communal conflict had eroded efficiency and morale, and now threatened ultimately loyalty to the *raj* itself. Wavell was in no doubt that he was not only presiding over an imperial edifice which must be dismantled or collapse. He was also head of a government whose very mechanisms for daily administration were breaking down. In September he argued that simply on administrative grounds the *raj* could not last more than 18 months; and looking back over 1946 he noted in late October, 'Our time in India is limited and our power to control events almost gone. We have only prestige and previous momentum to trade on and they will not last long.' On the last day of the year he confided to his journal, 'And while the British are still legally and morally responsible for what happens in India, we have lost nearly all power to control events; we are simply running on the momentum of our previous prestige.'[12]

The *raj* had always relied heavily on the 'informal' part of its collaborative network of support—those Indians who were not paid in hard cash to serve it but chose for a variety of reasons to give it informal support, advice, and information, and to guarantee it the backing of their own followers. For thirty years the British had responded to changes in the distribution of power and influence in Indian society and had remodelled their methods of attracting such support, particularly to enlist in new constitutional structures the growing numbers of educated and other aware of the potential of new styles of politics. Now during the early stages of the war this enterprise was severely weakened by the decision of Congress to withdraw from co-operation. Its first step was withdrawal from the provincial ministries late in 1939. But for two years thereafter at local level Congressmen continued to contest local board elections and support the political system by participation in it. Gandhi's 1940—41 civil disobedience campaign, in which individuals spoke against the war, was a holding operation, to demonstrate Congress's claim to status as national spokesman, and to mask the fact that the leadership could contrive no alternative policy and was sitting on the fence rather than split Congress apart. Individual civil disobedience barely inconvenienced the government; and the campaign began to flag early in 1941. Meantime the British were content to administer the former Congress-controlled provinces through their governors exercising their special powers, and to keep the 1935 constitution in operation in those provinces where non-Congress ministries had carried on co-operating.

The real breakdown of co-operation between Congress and government occurred early in 1942. By then the attack on Pear Harbour and American entry into the war, followed by the fall of Singapore and Rangoon, convinced the Cabinet in London that a new attempt must be made to get Congress collaborating in government and the prosecution of the war which was now reaching India's borders as the Japanese swept north; or at least that an attempt to do so must be seen publicly, to soothe American, British Labour, and Indian Moderate opinion. The result was the mission of Sir Stafford Cripps, Lord Privy Seal and Leader of the Commons, to offer India full Dominion status at the end of the war, or the chance to secede from the Commonwealth and go for total independence, with the proviso that no part of India could be forced to join the new state. In the short term there was to be no constitutional change, but

Indians were to be urged to put their full weight into the urgent war effort, and were to be given more places on the Viceroy's Executive Council to facilitate such collaboration. The device failed to weld Congress into the collaborative enterprise, and its rejection by the leadership led to open confrontation with government in 'Quit India'. Much controversy surrounded the mission at the time, and has continued among historians—on the actual terms Cripps was empowered to offer, his conduct of negotiations with Indian leaders, the hostility of the Viceroy and Churchill to his endeavours, the role of Gandhi, and the precise reasons why Congress rejected the offer.[13] It seems from the official records now open that Cripps' brief was never fully clarified before he left London, and that the Cabinet was much divided on the whole matter. It was therefore quite possible for Linlithgow to jerk Churchill into restraining action when he felt that Cripps' discussions and proffered concession to Congress leaders, together with the intervention of Louis Johnson, a peripatetic envoy of Roosevelt, were imperilling Viceregal powers over his Executive Council. The breakdown with Congress amid consequent accusations of bad faith, was probably the compound of Congress leaders' dislike of the 'opting out' provision in the long-term plan, and their understanding that whatever Cripps might say his political masters had no intention of allowing complete Indianization of the Viceroy's Executive Council, its functioning with collective responsibility like a Cabinet, a or Indian control over defence in wartime.

The failure to achieve a formula for wartime co-operation with India's main Hindu political group did not prevent the *raj* from administering India for the rest of the war, with officials where politicians could not be found to work the constitution, or form suppressing 'Quit India.' Yet the Cripps Offer was the point at which the British departure after the war became inevitable. As even Churchill recognized, there could be no retraction of offer of independence.[14] So ironically, a hasty and ill-conceived attempt in large part designed to placate opinion outside India as well as to attract Indian politicians' co-operation at one of the war's darkest hours became the charter of India's freedom. The decision was made by a handful of British politicians as a by-product of war, not as a result of any prolonged discussion among India's rulers or the Parliamentary representatives of the British people about ultimate goals and priorities. After the war the attraction of political co-operation was still necessary, but for a different reason. Indian leaders no longer had too be incorporated into the foundations of imperial power, but built into a bridge or India's passage from one *raj* to another. They had to be persuaded to participate in provincial and central government until power could be transferred to legal successors of the British. The politicians, including Congressmen, readily formed provincial governments after the elections of winter 1945-46. When their collaboration was not forthcoming it was not because of hostility to the British but because of communal strife and the tactics of Congress and League in bargaining for position as heirs of empire as in 1945 when Wavell vainly conferred with political leaders at Simla to achieve agreement on the reconstruction of his Executive Council, or in 1946 when he formed an Interim Government. Yet these final years of the *raj* showed conclusively that British rule had lost legitimacy and that among the vast majority of Hindus Congress had become the *raj*'s legitimate successor. Tangible proof came in the 1945-46 elections to the central and provincial legislatures. In the former Congress won 91 per cent of the votes cast in non-Muslim constituencies; and in the latter gained and absolute majority and became the provincial *raj* in eight provinces. The acquiescence of the politically aware (though possibly not of many villagers even at this point) would have been seriously in doubt if the British had displayed any intention of staying in India. This in turn reacted on all those who had been the *raj*'s 'friends' or paid servants, making their position highly ambiguous, and, in the case of latter, eroding their morale and efficiency. European ICS men sensed that support for them was dropping away, and were aware that increasingly where Congress politicians had gained power their own ability to carry on the administration depended on Congress goodwill and co-operation. The trends evident in the late 1930s was now virtually complete. Wavell was bluntly realistic when landed gentry waited on him, asking what they should do as 'loyalists' and 'friends' of the *raj*. He felt that many of them had actually done little to help the *raj* and were loyal only because they could draw their rents while the British kept order. Now in a series of painful interviews with such he reminded them of the plain facts of political life.

> I always feel it is better to honest and to say that we are going to hand over power; that it is right that we should do so and leave Indians to govern themselves; that while the Congress is not a body one would have chosen as the representatives of the great mass of the Indian people, it is the body that the Indian people have chosen for themselves and we have to do business with the men of their choice.[15]

So far the end of the *raj* has been explained in terms of changing British interests in India and the erosion of older methods of imperial control. Both trends originated far earlier than the 1940s but were intensified by the experience and pressures of war. A final element in demolition of empire was the subjective one of British commitment to formal rule. It is significant, because by 1946 it had become plain that only a massive injection of men and money over at least two decades could have re-established the *raj* on anything like its old foundations. Even after the crucial Cripps declaration some British politicians concerned with India still envisaged a form of long-term British presence on the subcontinent, to provide unity and defence. R.A. Butler was among them. Amery and Linlithgow, despite their realism about anit-imperial sentiment among Indian politicians, found it hard to envisage an end to the British presence and lamented apparent British loss of a sense of world mission, and were loth to 'lie back and let ourselves be pushed off the map by the Americans.'[16] Churchill was bitterly hostile to Indian aspirations and given to tirades in Cabinet about the maintenance of empire. His ignorance of India, yet the reluctance of his Cabinet colleagues to challenge him, made realistic assessment of the British position and prospects in India, extremely difficult. His priority anyway was winning the war. Implicit in this was keeping the Americans' good will, however. Churchill only deigned to consider India when, as in 1942, a policy shift seemed necessary to serve his main task. He was essentially a maverick in British political thinking; and when war ended, bringing Labour to office, their tradition of sympathy for Indian aspirations, and for Congress in particular, meant there was chance of a new Cabinet realism on Indian affairs. Despite very real ignorance of India, still, in government circles, it was accepted that Britain must quit—and soon.

It was not just Labour's landslide victory which weakened British politicians' hankering after a modified British presence in India. American hostility to British imperialism was another crucial factor as it had been during the war when even Churchill felt the need to 'prove' to the Americans that Congress 'recalcitrance' rather than continuing imperial aspirations prevented political advance in India. In a real sense the *raj* was losing international legitimacy, just as its prestige and authority within India were draining away.[17] Furthermore, at 'home', beneath the level of India Office and Cabinet it was increasingly clear that the British public and consequently their Parliamentary representatives had other priorities than keeping up the *raj*. Jobs, coal, electricity, and housing were the political and practical agenda in the immediate post-war period. India had always been a minority interest in British public life; no great body of public opinion now emerged to argue that war-weary and impoverished Britain should send troops and money to hold it against its will in an empire of doubtful value. By late 1946 both Prime Minister and Secretary of State for India recognized that neither international opinion nor their own voters would stand for any reassertion of *raj*, even if there had been the men, money, and administrative machinery with which to do so.[18]

This compound crisis of empire proved amenable to the simple solution of British withdrawal. The crisis of Indian nationhood, on the contrary, deepened as the British made clear their intention to leave, and it became increasingly urgent to decide who constituted the Indian nation which would inherit imperial power. The ingredients of the problem of national identity were becoming clear in the 1930s, most strikingly in relations between British and princely India, and between Congress and British India's minorities. Although the most obvious dimension of the latter was Congress's fraught relations with Muslim groups, there were also the Sikhs' growing fears about their future as a minority in Muslim-dominated Punjab, the unease of linguistic areas and backward castes about their likely position under an Indian government, and the claims of the more militant Hindu nationalists who wanted independent India to be a homeland for 'pure Hinduism' in contrast to the secular concept of nationhood promulgated by Congress.

Although the Muslim dimension of India's deepening crisis of political identity culminated in Pakistan, one should remember that there was no historical 'inevitability' about the 'Great Divide' despite the almost mythic proportions partition gained in the historical self-imagining of post-independent India and Pakistan, and in many historical accounts of the 1940s. Muslims had found cross-communal alliances viable political strategies for decades at different levels of political life, in UP district board politics for example, or at provincial level in the Punjab under the 1919 and 1935 constitutions. As late as 1947 there was serious thought about the viability of a united Bengal where Hindus and Muslims might co-operate as Bengalis rather than seeing their Bengali homeland partitioned. Even some of the Muslim clerisy, notable those of the deeply conservative seminary at Deoband (UP), opposed the idea of Pakistan, believing it would not serve the interests of orthodox Islam, despite the League's claims that it would be a land where Islamic purity would be secure. Clearly although Muslims saw themselves as a distinct religious community, and increasingly as community whose interests needed political protection as the British devolved power to Indians, they were divided over the nature of that political protection (depending on their local strength and status), and had no common commitment to the idea of religious identity fusing with territorial national identity as found in Europe. Moreover throughout the 1940s it was not at all clear that Muslims in general or their politicians had any clear idea of what clear that Muslims in general or their politicians had any clear idea of what Pakistan might mean in practical geographical or constitutional terms—the whole of north-west India (which would include large Hindu and Sikh groups in Punjab), north-west and north-east India, the north-west and east with Bengal and Punjab partitioned, a totally separate state, or a Muslim bloc in a loose continental confederation? H.V. Hodson, a Government of India Reforms Commissioner, touring south and north-east India late in 1941, noted that virtually all Muslim League politicians he met saw Pakistan in the context of a federation with Hindu India, not as separate successor state. In April 1943 Jinnah specifically advised the League's Working Committee against producing 'a cut and dried scheme for Pakistan' because this would only create division among Muslims. Furthermore, in May 1946 Jinnah for the League offered the visiting Cabinet Mission as a 'minimum demand' the plan for six Muslim provinces (Punjab, North-West Frontier Province, Baluchistan, Sind, Bengal, and Assam) to be group within a loose continental federation which would deal with foreign affairs and defence, and later accepted the Mission's own plan which would have given Muslim areas their own 'groups' within an Indian federation for certain subjects, and would have avoided any territorial division of the subcontinent.[19] But if 'Pakistan' was neither *inevitable* nor even an unambiguous claim in the 1940s, what made it *possible* was the almost total integration of Indian Muslims' politics for the first time behind the claims of the Muslim League under Jinnah's autocratic leadership. His leadership, the emotive Pakistan claim and the League's organization strengthened it to a degree inconceivable even in 1937—in relation to Indian Muslims (including jealousy autonomous provincial groups), to Congress and the British. By 1946 the League had gained legitimacy among Muslims as Congress had among Hindus over a longer period.

The basis of the leverage Jinnah and the League increasingly exerted over the British, and consequently over congress in negotiations, was the famous Lahore Resolution of the League in March 1940, just days after Congress has called for complete independence and a constituent assembly to frame India's new constitution. Jinnah, presiding at the Lahore session, claimed that Muslims, too, called for India's freedom; but a freedom in which the Muslim nation as one of the major nations on the subcontinent had its own homeland and state and was not subject to government by a permanent Hindu majority. Just what he had in mind is suggested by his article published in the London magazine, *Time and Tide*, in January 1940, where he wrote of a new constitution which would recognize that in India there were two nations which must share the governance of their common motherland. The League rejected the 1935 federation scheme and resolved

> that no constitutional plan would be workable in this country or acceptable to the Muslims unless it is designed on the following basic principle, viz., that geographically contiguous units are demarcated into regions which should be so constituted with such territorial readjustments as may be

> necessary that the areas in which the Muslims are numerically in a majority, as in the north-western and eastern zones of India, should be grouped to constitute 'independent State' in which the constituent units shall be autonomous and sovereign. . . .

Significantly this resolution was not only vague on details but nowhere mentioned 'Pakistan'; and indeed Jinnah later complained that other (Hindus and the British) had foisted that name on the Lahore Resolution. It seems increasingly likely from the evidence of recent scholarship that Jinnah in fact did not want the sort of partition which occurred in 1947. It was not a popular Muslim demand at the time, made little sense to Muslims secure in provincial majorities, and offered nothing to the millions of Muslims scattered as minorities throughout the subcontinent. Furthermore, it made little sense in terms of economics and defence. It probably therefore was designed as bargaining-counter, vague enough to unite Indian Muslims behind it, in order to achieve recognition for Muslims as a 'nation' and therefore as equal with congress in negotiations about the future, and possibly in the longer term to situate Muslims as a distinct and autonomous element in a larger all-India federation. This reading of Jinnah's intentions would explain why later he refused to define 'Pakistan' more clearly and seemed prepared to countenance solutions which fell short of absolute partition. It also suggests an underlying continuity in his political career as an all-India politician searching for assured status for Muslims within India, rather than a dramatic and unproven conversion to 'communalism' and religiously based nationalism.[20]

The Viceroy was neither impresses nor unduly perturbed by the Lahore resolution. He commented that it was not a serious claim but a bargaining counter.[21] Despite its ambiguities it became highly significant in negotiations for the post-imperial dispositions of power. There is no evidence that the British encouraged the Pakistan demand as a device to divide Indians so deeply that they could maintain their *raj*. Rather, in war time they could not afford to antagonize Muslims who were valuable recruits to the army, and in particular would not risk disturbing the Punjab—that traditionally great recruiting ground for the Indian army. So they reassured the Muslims that they would not be forced live under any future government against their will. In the 1940 'August Offer' minorities were told that their views would be given weight in any policy revision, and that power would not be transferred to any system of government whose authority was denied by large and powerful elements in India's national life. The assurance was sharpened by the 1942 Cripps Offer of total post-war independence, when it was categorically stated that no part of India would be forced to join the new state.[22] Henceforth the League and its claim had a powerful blocking veto in any British attempts to contrive means for devolving power and departing. Congress implicitly recognized this when in July-October 1944 Gandhi met and corresponded with Jinnah on the Pakistan issue. This raised the status of the Pakistan idea and of Jinnah as the only Muslim leader Congress felt it necessary to deal with, though their contact proved fruitless in terms of a settlement between Congress and the League. Congress's earlier withdrawal from constitutional co-operation with the British had also contributed to the League's growing stature. By going into the political wilderness viz 'Quit India' Congress left Jinnah and the League a clear field, not only to build up local strength unchallenged by Congress counter appeals to the masses, but also to insert their politicians into the formal institutions of political consultation and control if forming provincial governments in Bengal (1943), Sind (1942), Assam, and even the North-East Frontier Province which was the one Congress Muslim stronghold (1943). Only in Punjab did the provincial Muslim leadership pursue an independent line and hold office without the League's name.

Jinnah was perfectly ready to use the leverage Congress and the British had given him, and to exercise his power of veto. For the League he proved a highly skilled spokesman negotiating virtually single-handed with the Congress leadership and the government. Wavell felt himself utterly checkmated by three elderly politicians and complained to his journal, 'I wonder if we shall ever have any chance of a solution till the three intransigent, obstinate, uncompromising principals are out of the way; Gandhi (just on 75), Jinnha (68), Winston (nearing 70).[23] Jinnah's steady persistence in pursuing the League's claim to speak for all Muslims wrecked the 1945 Simla Conference convened by Wavell a as post-war move to break the political deadlock between the politicians, and to begin a new phase of co-operation between the political leaders and government. His hope had been to form a far more representative and almost entirely Indian Executive Council under the existing constitution, to defeat Japan, govern Indian until a new constitution could be achieved, and to make such an ultimate achievement easier. The Conference broke down when Jinnah insisted that the League must nominate all the Muslim members. 'He said that it suited the Congress to come into the scheme for they stood for a united India, and once they came in they would strangle Pakistan. In the circumstances it would not be in the interest of the Muslim League to accept the offer.'[24] A year later, when the Cabinet Mission visited India in the hope of breaking the deadlock and extracting Britain from the uncomfortable role of declining *raj*, Jinnah's negotiating position was even stronger because the results of the elections in the intervening months had proved his point that the League was undisputed representative of Indian Muslims. The Mission put forward its own plan for a three-tiered constitution of a federation, groups of provinces which chose to act together for agreed topics, and provinces at the base, after Indian leaders failed to agree upon a plan themselves. It also suggested the formation of an interim Government in Delhi representing the main political organizations of British India. This second enterprise foundered on the rock of Muslim representation, as Jinnah refused to co-operate in any Interim Government unless the League nominated all the Muslim members. This Congress could not concede because it would have undermined its own claim to speak for the nation, including Muslims, and would have denied the representative character of its own Nationalist Muslims. The complex longer term plan for India's future ran into the sand after initial hopes that Congress and League would work it. Nehru as Congress President made it plain that Congress believed that once the Constituent Assembly was in being it would be a sovereign body not bound by the Cabinet Mission plan, particularly on the issue of voluntary grouping by provinces. The League thereupon rejected the plan, because it felt sure that Congress would use its weight of numbers in the Assembly to jettison the safeguards proposed in the plan for the Muslim areas. Simultaneously the League called on Muslims to resort to 'direct action' to achieve

Pakistan. The communal breakdown occurred amidst bitter recriminations and accusations by the League of British and Congress bad faith, and triggered a wave of communal violence which only deepened the deadlock.[25]

Although Jinnah and the League could create a negotiating deadlock, in the early stages it was far from obvious that their support among Muslims could give 'Pakistan' content and viability. Detailed evidence is still lacking on the League's support in many areas. But it is abundantly clear that during the 1940s the League 'took off' politically. It is increased its hold over Muslims dramatically; and consequently strengthened its hand against Congress and its small group of Nationalist Muslims. The build-up of strength in turn had a 'band-wagon' effect which was evident as early as the closing months of 1941. Muslims in politics feared to appear un-Muslim, or to rend Muslim solidarity which seemed increasingly important as Congress manifestly achieved strength and status among Hindus and claimed immediate independence; and the League increasingly appeared a valuable name and resource at election time.[26] Under Jinnah's guidance the League continued to build up its local organization, to enrol members in large numbers, to train 'Muslim national guards', and to create a publicity network which included trained and paid speakers, production of pamphlets and tracts, and even popular songs performed by professional musicians. In 1942 with the help of a Muslim businessman, M.A.H. Ispahani, Jinnah converted the weekly, *Dawn,* into an English language daily and an invaluable Muslim forum and mouthpiece. Among the crucial groups tied into the League's support and propaganda structure were students as communicators, and businessmen as financial backers and planners for the economic construction of Pakistan. In some provinces such as UP there was also evidence that local Leaguers were deliberately courting *maulvis* and *imams,* local Muslim clergy in touch with the grass roots of Muslim opinion and able influence it through the mosques and Friday prayers.[27]

However, the League's initial success was in Muslim minority areas where Muslims felt most threatened, first by Congress accession to provincial *raj* in 1937, and then by the spectre of British withdrawal. But if Pakistan was to be viable the League had to win over the Muslim leaders or the Muslim population in the majority provinces, which would eventually become Pakistan. At first the Muslim politicians of these provinces were content to rely on their local majorities which had served them well as the franchise was extended, and they kept Jinnah and the League at a safe distance. But increasingly the realities of the all-India political situation made them recognize the importance of having an all-India political voice in decisions about the future: and this need became the more vital once the war ended and it was clear that the British were set on departure and would no longer be guarantors of Muslim political identity and status on the subcontinent. The very ambiguity of the 'Pakistan' claim enabled a degree of all-India Muslim co-operation behind Jinnah and the League. Moreover, in areas of Muslim numerical dominance the League was gaining support particularly form 1943, at the grass-roots level. By May 1944 the Sind Provincial League claimed 300,000 member—23 per cent of the province's adult Muslim male population actually enrolled in the League. This growth of support, extending even into the countryside, did not reflect any radical new politicization, or a clear understanding of and commitment to a new 'Pakistan'. It was largely the result of the shifting attitudes of influential Muslim religious and landowning notables, particularly the *Pirs*, who began to recognize that in the changing political situation alliance with the League would buttress their local influence rather than the alliance with the *raj* which had served them well in the century since the British annexation of Sind. When they changed their allegiance, so did their many followers: and 'League' strength was consequently not genuinely new and institutionalized support. By contrast in Bengal the League did manage to build the beginning of a mass organization in some areas, claiming 550,000 members by 1944. Here a significant factor was clearly the division between Muslim peasants and Hindu landlords and moneylenders, and the way agrarian tensions, exacerbated by the war, were stretching the province's socio-economic fabric to breaking-point. The swing to the League in the crucial Muslim majority areas has been most clearly documented and analysed in the Punjab, where the League completely undermined the Unionist Party between 1944 and 1946 and won over the bulk of Muslim politicians. Its success in the Punjab was partly the result of a direct and concerted attempt to appeal to and organize ordinary rural Muslims, appealing not only on the Pakistan issue, but playing on a range of other grievances resulting from the war's deep inroads into the provincial economy. Students worked hard in the vacations to rouse popular support, and were specifically trained to use Islam's appeal. But the League's main strategy was to win the support of elite Muslim groups who would then bring their followers with them. Most significant of these were the landlords and many of the Muslim Pirs who, as in Sind, wielded significantly more influence than mosque-based *ulema*, through their networks of followers. These groups began to desert the Unionist Party in large number from 1945, undermining that Party's strength in the Legislature and depriving it of its rural support networks.[28]

This swing began to show in elections. Between 1937 and 1945 the League won 55/57 provincial by-elections in Muslim seats: independent Muslims won 18 and Congress only 4. In the winter elections of 19145-6 the League won all the Muslim seats in the Central Legislative Assembly and 439 of the 494 seats reserved for Muslims in the provincial legislatures. This included a stunning 113/119 in Bengal: and 75 in Punjab, compared with the Unionist Party's 10- whereas in 1937 it had only fielded 7 candidates for the 85 seats and won 2. In Bombay and Madras it won all the Muslim seats contested, and in UP 54/64 Muslim seats. So by early 1946 the League could legitimately claim to speak for virtually all Indian Muslims. Only on the North-West Frontier did the League fail to change its local standing: there many Pathans stuck with their Congress alliance until the imminent departure of the British forced them to consider all-India issues and particularly whether they wished to be part of Hindu dominated India or a Muslim Pakistan. So it seemed for the first time that Muslim politics on the subcontinent were almost to completely integrated and channelled into one organization, and that provincial strategies had been laid aside to pursue an all-India claim. However, the content of that claim was still profoundly ambiguous; and as the new state of Pakistan was to find to its cost, support for the League was rarely deeply rooted, and reflected the calculation and strategies of provincial Muslim elites who were concerned more with their own standing the interests than the creation of a new nation state.

However, there was a darker and wilder aspect of the breakdown of political relations between Hindus and Muslims, and the divergence of their political identities, than the canny negotiations of high politics, or the building of political organizations. The political use of religion is a potentially inflammable strategy in any society which has not become deeply secular, the more so at a time of extreme social stress, as in India in the 1940s, when war was straining the economy and the very fabric of society. 'The overtly 'communal' violence which erupted in terrifying proportions in the last year of the *raj* was totally beyond the politicians' control, though their strategies, accusations, and claims often triggered it. It brought India to the brink of civil war. We know comparatively little about the dynamics of communal violence, for it leaves few records but dead, injured, and frightened people and shattered buildings. Observers could only attempt to assess the relative roles of national and local leadership, of new issues and long-standing antagonisms, of rumour, mass panic and fear, and of roving bands of armed thugs. The first wave started with the 'Great Calcutta Killing' which lasted for nearly a week from 16 August 1946, the day designed for 'direct action' (*hartals*, strikes, rallies, and meetings) by the Muslim League Council. About 4,000 people were killed and an unknown number—possibly up to 15,000—injured, and 100,000 made homeless. Muslim actions triggered the violence but as a minority in the city they were its main victims. The weakness and communalism of the police and the lack of proper intelligence made the situation even graver; and the Governor felt that only the presence of three battalions of British troops 'prevented a complete collapse of the administration', He was sickened by what he saw and heard of the mob 'bestiality', and told the Viceroy, 'I observed very great damage of property and streets littered with corpses. I can honestly say that parts of the city . . . were as bad as anything I saw when I was with the Guards on the Somme.[29] Trouble then spread to Noakhali district in East Bengal, where Muslims were the aggressors and Hindus the victims; and to Bihar on a far larger scale, where possibly as many as 7,000 Muslims were butchered. Bombay and UP saw some communal disturbances, but elsewhere there was little trouble. Early in 1947 Punjab became the worst scene of communal tension and at times what amounted to carnage, though disorder was chronic in Calcutta and in parts of Bengal and Bihar. In Punjab the Muslim majority was now fanatically pro-Pakistan, and the problem was compounded by the fears of the Hindu minority and the Sikhs, who became increasingly belligerent as they saw the real possibility of their Sikh homelands in central Punjab being divided in the event of Pakistan. The worst violence in Punjab and Delhi did not occur until the actual time of partition, when train loads of refugees crossed the frontier in each direction and were exposed to hostile gangs from other communities who descended on the passengers and engaged in mass slaughter. As one Delhi Muslim commented of the summer of 1947, the old city where many Muslims lived became a living nightmare of stabbing, where even the main roads dangerous and few ventured out at night. But even before partition, by the end of July, around 5,000 had been killed in Punjab, mainly in rural areas. At this stage Hindus and Sikhs were the main victims, but they took their revenge in the following months.[30]

As India seemed increasingly ungovernable and in danger of plunging into wide-scale civil war, all the major political groups involved realized that the deadlock must be broken lest all of them lose in disorder and devastation what they had been aiming for—the British an orderly devolution of power to a competent and friendly successor state, Congress rapid independence for a strong and unified polity, and the League the equal status it claimed with Congress in deciding India's future mode of governance to protect Muslim's status and security, symbolized in the idea of 'Pakistan'. Attlee's government sacked Wavell, whom it increasingly (and unfairly) judged as politically incompetent, and sent the flamboyant Earl Mountbatten to do with speed and style what Wavell had failed to achieve. Mountbatten's task was made easier in a sense by the communal violence because it pressed Indian leaders into compromise at last: and also by the fact that he had a far freer hand than his viceregal predecessor, ensuring his own terms on accepting office. He was particularly insistent that Britain should set a precise time-limit for its *raj* to force the Indian parties into realism. On 20 February Attlee announced Mountbatten's appointment and June 1948 as the latest possible date for British withdrawal. In the event independence came in August 1947. Mountbatten saw within a month of his arrival in India that there could be no rescue-operation on the Cabinet Mission Plan, for even though League and Congress were co-operating by this time in the Interim Government the League's representatives were not participating in the Constituent Assembly. He also realized what Wavell had tried to impress on London for so long, that unless a final solution was rapidly achieved there would be civil war and administrative breakdown. The result of his deliberations with the politicians, his hand-picked staff and the Cabinet in London, was the 3 June Plan for swift British withdrawal and the transfer of power to two successor dominions, India and a 'two-winged' Pakistan in the north west and north east of the subcontinent, the exact boundary being drawn by an independent boundary commission after provincial legislators in Bengal and Punjab had voted on whether their provinces should be partitioned. Voting mechanisms were also provided to register the wishes of the other Muslims majority areas.[31]

The partition of the subcontinent and of two of its major provincial units, Punjab and Bengal, was bitter resolution of the problem of national identity which had developed in the previous decades. For Jinnah it was the wreckage of his all-India plans, and gave Muslims a 'solution' which left the remaining Muslim minority in Indian unprotected, divided the major Muslim provinces, and produced not only a 'moth-eaten' Pakistan', in Jinnah's words, but one divided by a thousand miles of Indian territory. By treating as a real demand what had almost certainly been a bargaining-counter, and calling his bluff, Congress and the British demolished Jinnah's strategy, which had depended on British willingness to stay on until they had imposed a solution, and Congress's wish to maintain Indian unity. But by early 1947 the British would not and could not adopt such a role and were looking for strong an stable successors. Moreover, the Congress leaders themselves, as Gandhi's political influence receded, had come to feel that freedom for a strong new nation state was their priority, even at the expense of the unity they had so long claimed. Quite when this shift in Congress thinking occurred is unclear; but almost certainly well before Mountbatten launched his plan the main leader, including Nehru and Patel, backed by some of their business allies such as Birla, had concluded that a Muslim element in a federation with an inevitably weak centre would fatally undermine the strong and unified India which they considered essential if India was to plan its economy and launch its people on a path of modernization. Muslims in Congress such as A.K. Azad were deeply distressed what they saw as the sacrifice of their co-religionists and the partition of the country in effect by Congress itself.[32] For the inhabitants of the two divided provinces, and Punjab in particular, it meant fear, disruption, violence, and a huge transfer of population, as Muslims and Hindus trekked to the 'safe' side of the border. It is impossible to compute the magnitude of migration and disruption. Possibly a million died; and with a year five and a half million refugees had moved each way across the border of West Pakistan India, while one and a quarter million moved from East Pakistan to the part of Bengal remaining in India.

The problem of nationhood was thus in part made into an international question. In this guise it has remained with India ever since, flaring at time into open warfare between the two countries. But India also retained a large Muslim minority—over thirty million, near 10 per cent of the population after partition. They were scattered after the major majority areas had become party of Pakistan, but there were still locally significant clusters of Muslims in some areas such as Delhi, UP and Hyderabad in the south, once a princely state. This minority understandably fearful, and vulnerable to communal violence, despite the possible 'safeguard' of the likelihood of Pakistani retaliation on Hindus left in Pakistan if Indian Muslims were persecuted. The integration of the Muslims into the new Indian nation remained one of the tasks of India's secular and democratic political system. Despite the 'Great Divide' Congress leaders still had to face the problem they had failed to resolve thus far, and to make their political organization the accepted political environment of Muslims within India's own border.

Other minorities' apprehensions and aspirations were a further dimension of the problem of national identity, and a continuing part of Indian public life. They were less dramatic than the Muslim dimension because no other group had the numerical weight to force territorial or political concessions in the process of the transfer of power. Yet the unease and demands of many of the subcontinent's groups and areas caused concern to Congress before 1947 and threatened considerable problems of governance thereafter.

The Sikhs were a major case.[33] Clustered in central Punjab they were a substantial provincial minority. But even in the Punjabi heartland they were not a local majority, and in the west Muslims were over 60 per cent of the population while in eastern Punjab Hindus were a comparable majority. Yet the Sikhs had vivid sense of their distinctiveness as a community, and of the role of political power in maintaining their communal identity and integrity. This sense of separation was fostered by the religious reform movements of the later nineteenth and twentieth centuries and by their special relationship with the British as a source of valuable military recruits who had their community regiments. The succession of constitutional discussions and reforms as the British sought to devolve power to the provinces confirmed their political identity and claim for particular consideration in the Punjabi and all-India contexts. Special Sikh seats in the Punjab legislature and the Central Legislature were first created under the Montagu-Chelmsford Reforms. In the preparation and aftermath of the Nehru and Simon Reports Sikhs claimed separate political identity, and many of them called for continuing separate electorates: and at the Round Table Conference in London their representatives pressed for reserved seats and for separate electorates if other minorities were to have them. The Communal Award rejected their demand of 30 per cent of seats in the Punjab legislature and gave them only thirty-two seats, leaving Muslims in a permanent majority However despite their separate religious and political identity the Sikhs split politically into numerous groups—'Moderates', those who joined Congress, and the Akali Dal with a distinctive religious orientation, led by Master Tara Singh, which was itself divided politically. In the later 1930s and early 1940s the Akali Dal was in uneasy relationship with Congress and gradually broke with its former ally. Sikhs could not agree among themselves either on provincial political issues, or on-operation with the British in the war. The absence of an undisputed leadership had tragic consequences as the British prepared to leave. It bred what Punjab's Governor called 'a kind of competitive intemperance among the Sikh leader which I have always found it very difficult to deal with.' It also left local Sikh populations outside the control of any central leadership which might have helped curb the violence and carnage which accompanied partition.

In the 1940s the Muslim demand for Pakistan precipitate a crisis for the Sikhs. Increasingly in looked as if Pakistan would mean the partition of the Punjab, with the new border cutting through the Sikh homelands in the centre of the province furthermore it would lose the Sikhs their leverage in Punjabi politics as a substantial minority with strategic importance in political coalitions, given the Hindu-Muslim-Sikh balance of the population and political representation. Instead it would, they feared, deliver them into the hands of either a Muslim or a Hindu majority. Under the threat of partition Sikhs drew nearer together politically in concerted opposition to the idea. When in 1944 it looked as if some of the Congress leaders including Gandhi, would ultimately agree to Pakistan, a meeting of Sikh politicians from all parties gathered in protest and empowered Tara Singh to organize 3 September as 'protest day'. The new Sikh unity was further displayed in the post-war elections when an all-parties Sikh board was constituted to fight the elections in opposition to Pakistan. The resulting Panthic Party won twenty-two seats and the Sikh Communists, who were the only Sikhs to support Pakistan, were eliminated. Sikh politicians attempted to deal and negotiate with the British, Congress and the League in attempts to protect their future when it became clear their British patrons were really going. The latter, though sympathetic, felt they could do little except urge the Sikhs not to make trouble and to use their strategic position as protection, because of their dispersed demographic and geographical position. The Congress leaders were prepared to accept partition as the price of independence and peace; while the League was not willing to compromise over power, as the Unionists with their provincial political orientation had been.

As Sikhs looked about in vain for protectors or allies they turned increasingly to the slogan of 'Azad Punjab', though the 'Pakistan' in its early stages the practicalities of the idea were vague. The idea of a 'free Punjab' where Sikhs would be political master, or of a 'Sikhistan' (land of the Sikhs), had been mooted by Akali Dal leaders even in the 1930s. By 1946 it was the Akali

Dal's declared political objective, and the claim made by Sikh representatives to the Cabinet Mission as an alternative to permanent subjection to either Hindu or a Muslim majority. Tara Singh, for the Sikhs, said the preferred the future to be within a united India in which Sikhs had bargaining power because of differences between Hindus and Muslims; but if partition occurred he wanted a separate Sikh state with the right to federate with Pakistan or Hindustan.[35] Not surprisingly Sikh politicians were angered and frightened by the Cabinet Mission's own proposals for voting on the future in three 'groups', because Punjabi Sikhs were in the predominantly Muslim Group B (Punjab, North-West Frontier Province, Sind and Baluchistan), even though the idea of partitioning Punjab appeared to have been rejected. As one of the more moderate Sikh leaders, a member of the provincial government, Baldev Singh, put it, 'The seeds of Pakistan are . . . already there in the Group system and as the Constitution of the Groups and their ultimate disposition is to be decided by force of numbers, the Sikhs cannot but contemplate their future with grave misgivings.[36]

The demand for political recognition of a distinctive Sikh homeland came to nothing, and Sikh fears were not allayed as the main communal conflict pressed all-India leadership and the British into the final plan for rapid independence and partition. The result was open Sikh violence against their Muslim neighbours and Muslim refugees leaving India, and large-scale Sikh migration across the border into Indian Punjab. The refugees' future caused administrative problems for India's government for many months after independence. Furthermore, the Sikh claim to be a distinct nation with its own state was renewed almost immediately. As early as September 1947 Mountbatten's Press Attache was writing of the burgeoning of a Sikh 'nationalism' which would not be satisfied even with an Indian province of Sikhistan. Early in 1948 Tara Singh began to call for a Sikh province where the community would be able to protect its identity, tradition, and culture by self-determination in religious, social and political affairs. The difference between this demand and the pre-partition call for 'Azad Punjab' was that now it was both viable and cogent. Sikh migration to India had meanwhile produced a Sikh majority in the north-western part of Punjab and thereby removed the argument that there was no Sikh majority areas to which political power could be devoted. Furthermore Punjab was now a border province with Pakistan, giving its politicians advantages of bargaining power over a central government anxious to keep its border populations loyal; while it remained as it had been under the British *raj* a highly significant recruiting ground for the Indian army.

The Sikh campaign for regional autonomy continued for nearly two decades to concern a central government bent on welding together a new nation. (It received in a more extreme form with escalating violence in the 1980s.) Somewhat similar fissiparous tendencies occurred in several linguistic areas, though demands for linguistic states within the Indian Union rarely had the reinforcing religious dimensions which made the Sikh demand so powerful. Unease among linguistic minorities who felt educationally and politically disadvantaged had for decades been an aspect of the new perceptions of group identity which developed as the sources and distribution of power shifted in public life. Telugu-speakers had demanded an Andhra Province and Oriya-speakers an Orissa free from Bengal, for example, long before the imminent transfer of power. Similar proposals had come from Kannada and Malayalam speakers and reached the Bombay and Madras provincial legislatures in the late 1930s. the British were reluctant to tamper with provincial boundaries after their disastrous attempt to divide Bengal in 1905 unless there were clear administrative grounds. The only two new provinces created between the wars were Sind and Orissa in 1935. Congress, however, implicitly encouraged the idea of redrawing provincial boundaries on linguistic lines by recognizing the principle within its own organization from 1920, and explicitly endorsed the principle in a Working Committee resolution of 1938 and in its 1946 election manifesto. But when Congress came to govern an independent state the principle it could so easily uphold as a movement trying to incorporate as many regions and groups as possible proved a divisive threat. The Dar Commission set up in 1948 to consider the cases of potential provinces of Andhra, Karnataka, Kerala, and Maharashtra rejected the notion of linguistic provinces as an obstacle to the growth of nationalism. So widespread was opposition to this conclusion that Congress set up its own committee of Nehru, Patel, and P. Sitaramayya. They proved almost as hostile under the new pressures of building a nation state.

> Taking a broad and practical view . . . we feel that the present is not an opportune time for the formation of new Provinces. It would unmistakably retard the process of consolidation of our gains, dislocate our administrative, economic and financial structure, let loose, while we are still in a formative state, forces of disruption and disintegration, and seriously interfere with the progressive solution of our economic and political difficulties. . .

Yet they conceded that as democrats they might have in the future to accept linguistic redistribution 'if public sentiment is insistent and overwhelming'. Thus they ensured the continuity of yet another problem in the governance of India and another hindrance to the growth of national identity, though their intention was the reverse.[38]

The claims of the Sikhs and linguistic groups could be shelved, if not permanently ignored. The future of the princely states could not, as their link with British India was the British, and they were going. The fate of these blocks of territory, with their rulers and peoples, who were politically and culturally apart yet geographically inextricable from the rest of the subcontinent was one of the most formidable problems facing both the departing rulers and those who wished to construct and govern an inheriting nation state. Ironically it was tackled seriously very late in the process of imperial withdrawal, and earlier planning for the states' future proved of little use because it had been based on the assumption of a united, federal India as posited in 1935. The demise of the princely order, like the emergence of Pakistan, had generated historical controversy: particularly over the difficult relations between Mountbatten and the Political Department the who had different sympathies and priorities, over the methods used to 'persuade' princes to join an Indian Union, and the long-term intentions of British India's politicians and administrators towards the states, despite their conciliatory moves in the threatened chaos of mid-1947.[39] This complex of questions needs more historical investigation. But for our purposes the crucial point is the continuing problem posed by the states in the 1940s and thereafter. It was not disposed of in 1947, but was deepened by Britain's determination on a hasty withdrawal.

Cripps' Mission and Offer in 1942 marked the final collapse of the federal plan on which the British had pinned their hopes for the whole of India. In the new political situation, with total independence on offer to British India after the war, the princes would be far more vulnerable, and would have to come to terms directly with politicians of British India, though Cripps assured them that the British would not transfer Paramountcy to any other body, would not force any state to join an independent India, and that they would retain both Paramountcy and their obligations in relation to those states which did not join. The British, however, had been far too successful in their policy of buttressing the states as a conservative counterweight to the escalating demands of British India's politicians. Because they had merely encouraged reform rather than coercing the princes into radical change they had left their client-allies ill-equipped to cope with the new situation. Basically the states were anachronistic political and administrative structures built on ideals fast losing legitimacy. Yet in wartime imperialists needed their loyalty and material contributions too much to force reform. Even after the war British policy-makers assumed that there was a considerable time during which they could chivvy the princes to face the new world realistically. The alternative to this gentle approach was to offer protection if any princes tried to 'go it alone'. This they could not have done, though probably some members of the Political Department would have liked to encourage their 'charges' in such an enterprise. The British in fact lacked the physical resources and would not have wished to embitter their relations with the new India by such a move. Instead they spoke vaguely about fulfilling their treaty obligations. The blunt Wavell felt that they ought to be more open and tough with the princes about their predicament. As he told the Cabinet's India Committee as early as 1945, 'We knew that we could not in certain circumstances implement our formal obligations and the States were well aware of that. He thought that there was everything to be said for frankly warning them that in face of the changes that had taken place there were very definite limits to the extent to which we could honour obligations given in quite different circumstances.[40]

With justification the princes were becoming increasingly apprehensive. They demonstrated this when the whole Standing Committee of the Chamber of Princes resigned late in 1944 in protest against what they termed the deterioration of their position and disregard of their interests. They were only pacified six months later when Wavell assured them that their relationship with the crown would not be transferred to any other body without their consent, provided they themselves did not unreasonably veto any constitutional changes. Their predicament became really acute when the British made precise proposals for a swift departure. When the Cabinet Mission visited India in 1946 it told the princes bluntly that when independent Indian came into being the British would no longer be able to exercise paramountcy and did not intend to keep British troops on the subcontinent for that purpose. Paramountcy would lapse, states would regain all the rights they had surrendered to the crown, and would have to make their own arrangements with the successor authority (or authorities) in British India.[41] Eventually the princes accepted the Cabinet Mission Plan as a basis for further negotiation, and as containing the machinery for independence, and set up a negotiating committee to work with the corresponding committee of the Constituent Assembly. While they were pressurized by their patron's explicit statement of their unprotected future the princes were simultaneously harassed by the belligerent stance of some Congressmen, particularly Nehru, who said publicly that no state could hold out against India once the princes lost British support, and that any state which did not join in the Constituent Assembly would be treated as hostile state. Under pressure the princes could not agree whether to sit on the fence or plunge into the Constituent Assembly.

Mountbatten's June pronouncement that there were but weeks to independence forced decisions on to the princes. The Viceroys saw this and from then on relied on the new States Department rather than the existing Political Service to conduct relations with the states. Its key men were Vallabhbhai Patel, the Minister, and his chief aide, V.P. Menon, who had long been in government service with particular expertise in the details of constitutional changes. All three man realized both the short time at their disposal to solve the problem of the states' futures, and the thin line between the country and chaos. Together they achieved a policy to 'stop the gap', as Menon put it. Its essence was the states' accession to the new India (or Pakistan) on three fundamentals—Defence, Foreign Affairs, and Communications. Later negotiations could take place with each state on other matters which were covered in the meantime by stand-still agreements.' Patel and Menon combined conciliation and toughness (at times amounting to threats and blackmail), and were reinforced by Mountbatten's charm and moral pressure as he threw the weight of his personality and office behind the new policy. By the moment of independence only three states had withstood their efforts and declined to accede. After independence the Hindu ruler of Muslim Kashmir acceded to India rather than Pakistan in circumstances which led to acute international tension between the two countries and counter-accusations which continued for decades. The remaining states, tiny Junagadh and vast Hyderabad, were ultimately subdued by armed actions of dubious legality. Thereafter administrative and political arrangements were made to weld the former states into a uniform all-India structure. Some smaller states were merged into surrounding provinces. Others were grouped to form state unions equivalent to provinces. While eight, including Kashmir, Hyderabad, and Mysore, retained their separate, identity. All now were equipped with democratic institutions like those of the provinces of former British India. However, ex-rulers were granted privy purses, some private property, and personal dignities and privileges, including their former titles. In units developed from ex-princely states, as in Rajasthan and Travancore, princes also received a constitutional position of leadership in the new democratic context with the title of *Rajpramukh*. Details varied from state to state, and often the process of integration was smooth and amicable.[42] But the truth was that within a short time after independence the new Government of India was the paramount power on the subcontinent, whatever the pre-independence assurances of the British and of Vallabhbhai Patel himself.

The integration of the states into the new India's political and administrative structures was complex, but at least concrete. More subtle, but equally vital for India's future a democracy, was the integration of the states' peoples into an all-India political environment, and their political education to value and use the new sources of political power and the novel pathways to power through elections, parties, and legislatures. The task confronting politicians and administrators was to create a political culture and inculcate patterns of activity similar to those which had developed unevenly through the previous century in British India. This is another area where much research still needs to be done. Rajasthan has been studied in depth, and the integration of the former princely subjects into a new political arena as participant citizens explored.[43] There was nothing there like the PCCs and DCCs which became vital organizational units in the provinces of British India and the structure through which most political activity was channeled, but there existed a range of urban protest movements, *Praja Mandals*. They were often tenuously connected, but their leaders were often in touch with Congress in British India. There were also peasant movements, very different in origin and aims, many of which grew out of the social reform movement of the Jat caste. Both types of movement were bases on which a new Rajasthan Congress could draw for support and local leadership and which provided stepping-stones for local men to move from the political styles and concerns of the princely world to those of a democratic state. Not surprisingly it was the urban-based *Praja Mandals* which first joined as a unit in the All India States Peoples Conference and in 1948 became the Rajputana Pradesh Congress Committee. Since then the resulting Rajasthan Congress Party has reflected the segmented character of the older order. But it has adapted to the local environment with its particular past and social structure. It has proved a means of integrating Rajasthan's people into a new democratic order, by drawing in men from small towns and rural areas and catering for the needs of the new recruits to politics within a Congress frame word, so channelling their interests through new political institutions and behavioural conventions.

However it was not only groups clearly distinguishable by their minority status or their separate historical development which raised the issue of national identity. Others who were deeply committed to independent India had a very different vision of the essence of Indian nationhood from that of the Congress leadership. To sustain its inclusive nature in a plural society Congress had felt it essential to present the ideal of nationhood in secular terms, the nation's members being bound by common citizenship in a democracy where religious identity should not be a barrier to full participation. Though Gandhi was distressed by the 'unspiritual' basis of Congress politics and ideals of nationhood, he too rejected the idea that India was solely for the Hindu majority and envisaged adherents of all religions pouring their spiritual resources into the new India. Yet this was a difficult sense of nationhood to publicize and for which to generate a genuine loyalty. Even Gandhi had found that support accrued to him because he was seen in 'Hindu' terms, not as the apostle of an inclusive national unity. But there were Hindus who deplored the attitudes of Congress and Gandhi alike. Like the Mahatma, they also had a spiritual, almost mystical, vision of Indian nationhood. The second leader of RSS expounded this in 1939 in his book *We or Our Nationhood Defined.* Hinduism was to be the land of the Hindus where they could practice their all-prevailing religious tradition without contamination from European or Muslim culture. Any non-Hindus in India 'must learn to respect and hold in reverence Hindu religion, must entertain no idea but those of glorification of the Hindu race and culture', and could only stay in the country wholly subordinated to the Hindu nation, claiming nothing, deserving no privileges, far less any preferential treatment'. After independence this vision led Hindu Communalists into bitter diatribes against Pakistan and condemnation of legislative reform of aspects of Hindu society according to secular criteria. But in the early 1940s that main Communalist cry was hostility to the idea of partition and to the Congress leadership who appeared willing to barter away the Hindus' birthright. Partition was 'vivisection' of the Holy Motherland, and Congress leaders, including Gandhi, traitors in their eyes.[44]

It is impossible to enumerate precisely the number of activists in such communal organizations as the Hindu Mahasabha or the RSS, let alone those who formed a penumbra of sympathizers, attracted less by a coherent ideology than by fear of communal violence and hope of some protection form the bands of activists who were given uniforms and para-military training. Support for the Mahasabha and RSS expanded in the 1940s; initially while Congress was politically inoperative and its leadership in jail, leaving a free run for communist politicians, and later when communal bitterness and violence escalated in the months before and after partition. The RSS always remained strongest in the north where communal tension was sharpest, though efforts were made to extend it in the south at the start of the decade. In contrast to Congress which had been putting down increasingly deep and broad-spreading rural roots, it remained an urban movement, attracting students, lowly placed government servants, some business and professional people, and—predictably—refugees from Pakistan. Communal groups could not hope to challenge Congress as the legitimate successor of the *raj* in most Indians' eyes. But their dangerous potential in public life was demonstrated in January 1948 when a young man who had connections with both Mahasabha and RSS shot Gandhi at one of his regular public prayer meetings in Delhi. A wave of emotional hostility to communal groups engulfed horrified country. The RSS was banned, while the Mahasabha voluntarily withdrew from political activity.

At the time of Gandhi's assassination it looked as if the force of communalism had struck a grievous blow at the Indian nation at a crucial phase of its consolidation. A desolate Nehru spoke of a light going out of their lies with Gandhi's death, thousands flocked to Delhi to watch with grief and awe the passage of his frail old body to the cremation grounds, and even beyond the subcontinent millions moured one who had embodied the Indian claim to a new order, who had made non-violence a living political reality, and who had in the previous months by his physical presence in Bangal, Calcutta, and Delhi helped to stem the tide of communal killing.[45] Yet Gandhi martyred proved even more powerful a bond for Indians than he had been when alive, particularly in his last years when he had been isolated from the main stream of Congress politics and weakened by the escalation of Muslim nationalism. He became a national symbol, and in time almost a myth; his name invoked in times of national crisis and disunity, and his career part of the historical picture of their country and their political education received by Indian schoolchildren as future citizens and patriots. But though Gandhi's death cast a slur on the most overt forms of Hindu communalism, communal bodies re-emerged in public life in 1949. The RSS was only permitted because it submitted a new constitution to the government which stated that it was a non-political cultural organization and would preach religious tolerance. Yet militant Hindus' persistent concern to protect the Hindu religious and cultural heritage, and their complaints against 'secularization', have remained a potentially explosive element in public life. To the Congress leadership they proved embarrassing and ambiguous in their implications, for India's new rulers had to walk a tightrope between the Hindus and India's minorities as they tried both to weld a new country and embark on major social reforms.

When the historian shifts his focus from the most urgent questions of national identity in the 1940s and from the dramas of independence and partition to the mundane business of actually welding and governing the new nation state, continuity rather than striking change is again a dominant motif in India's experience. It is unusual to stress the continuity of the problems facing the old and new government, and the resources at their disposal. But realism about what was little changed, however out of tune with the heady aspiration of Indians in August 1947, is essential for an understanding of the achievements and limitations of India as a democratic state in subsequent decades. The institutions of government, the structure of society, and the fundamental beliefs of most Indians did not change just because the Union Jack was lowered and the last British troops marched to the Gateway of India to board ship in Bombay harbour, or even because a new constitution in 1950 laid down ideals and institutional frameworks which were intended to be new basis for the nation's public life.

Independence and partition caused a range of very specific problems which India had solve immediately to avoid chaos. The government confronted them with remarkable speed and success. One was the virtually unprecedented division of the resources of central government between two inheriting authorities, including civil servants, the armed forces and their equipment, and the paraphernalia of government down to office furniture. India had the advantage of being the 'setting tenant', whereas Pakistan had to construct a new capital city and central government. The other administrative crisis was the influx of refugees in continuing circumstances of communal bitterness and fear. Patel and Nehru were so appalled by the gravity of the situation in Delhi in September 1947 that they consulted Mountbatten, by then Governor-General, and when he proposed an Emergency Committee they asked him to chair it. It dealt with the transport and settlement of refugees, harvesting crops in deserted Punjabi villages, keeping some newspapers and the Delhi telephone service going, bringing government servants of to work and burying the dead left on the streets by communal strife. By the end of November its work was done. In UP which faced similar problems because of its communal composition and geographical position the premier, Pandit Pant, a leading Congress politician experienced in government. Just over half the refugees eventually settled in towns, particularly in UP and the great cities of Delhi and Calcutta. But he ultimate fortunes of these new Indian citizens, their relative prosperity compared with their previous lives, and their contribution to the new country, have been little studied, so sensitive is the topic.

By far the greater range of matters concerning the new government were of far longer standing. Chief among them was the country's economic base and the poverty of so many of her people. Poverty had not left an imperial government unmoved, but given its limited resources and the magnitude of the problem, and its basic rationale, it only took steps to alleviate distress when it seemed so acute as to threaten disorder. The 1939-45 war, for example, had sharply focused government attention on the problem because of its inflationary impact on India.[46] But far more significant than any short-run inflation produced by exceptional circumstances was the grindingly low standard of living of the vast majority, which was unacceptable to a government which was committed to a new order for its people and also realized that the low level of income, and consequently of demand and potential investment, was a drag on development in every part of the economy, whether agriculture, industry or the service sector. In 1949 a National Income Committee was established to discover the dimensions of Indian poverty. Its report in 1950/1 showed that average annual income per person was Rs. 260 or $55. Some fell below this level, particularly those engaged in domestic service and in agriculture, where families did not own land from which to feed themselves. A decade later (by which time prices had risen further) 38 per cent of the rural poor lived on less than Rs. 180 a year, or about ten cents a day;

and roughly half the urban population earned less than the Rs. 270 which was required in towns to maintain an officially recognized minimum daily intake of calories (2,250). Such poverty where there is little state welfare provision, is of a degree never seen in the west in the late twentieth century. It means almost perpetual hunger, a monotonous and unbalanced diet at the best of times, cramped and squalid housing, perhaps one change of meagre clothes, insufficient bedding to prevent deaths from cold in northern Indian winter, children's absence from school for lack of clothes or books or the need to earn to feed the family and no money for doctors or medicines. Poverty and malnutrition produce a vicious spiral of ill-health, vulnerability to infection, and inability to maintain minimum standards of cleanliness and sanitation. Moreover, given the patriarchal nature of Indian society and the high value placed on males for economic and cultural reasons, women are even more disadvantaged than men in conditions of poverty, and have less access to food, medicine, and education.

India's economic problems were not amenable to easy solutions. What progress was made was rapidly swallowed by a rising population, though the upward trend only became a frightening explosion from the 1950s. (In 1951 the population was c.360 million). In rural areas life went on much as it had for centuries. Much farming was still for subsistence on tiny plots, and only in certain areas did farmers produce for the market and consequently have the profits to invest in even more efficient agriculture. By 1950 agricultural technology was still very limited. A tiny proportion of farmers had tractors or tube wells and less fertilizer was used per acre than in any other country. New equipment, new seed producing sturdier and more abundant crops, secure water supplies, cheaper and accessible credit to the poorer farmers, and redistribution of land were all important ingredients of any reform of the country's agricultural base.

Unlike most African countries at independence in the 1960s India did have substantial and well-established industrial sector in 1947, with the financial networks to support it. Her involvement in the Second World War encouraged industrial expansion, though much of the increased production was for armaments or was drawn off for other military requirements, and was therefore not available for civilian consumption. For example, all mill production of wool textiles, all factory production of leather and footwear, nearly three-quarters of steel and cement production and over two-fifths of paper production was directed away from the civilian economy. Only certain industries really boomed—steel, chemicals, paper, paint, and cement, for example. But shortages in capital goods and skilled manpower prevented major new industrial ventures, as did government policy of restricting non-food production of consumer goods.[47] A further reflection of wartime industrial growth was the increase in the urban percentage of the population (from nearly 13 per cent in 1941 to jest over 16 per cent in 1951). But still in 1950/1 factories produced only 6.5 per cent of the national income, and less than 3 per cent of the labour force was employed in factories and mining, compared with nearly 75 per cent in agriculture.[48] The limited nature of industrial development and its restricted geographical distribution could only be overcome by major investment. That meant the generation of resources in rural as well as industrial sectors of the economy, and their direction into industry, either by market forces or by government through such instruments as taxation and licensing.

Economics always were, and still are, at the root of many of India's social problems. Her resources have long been both absolutely scarce and very unevenly distributed among her peoples. Whole regions are poor, particularly where agriculture is precarious and population density high, Bihar, Orissa, and Rajasthan are at the bottom of the heap; fertile Punjab and parts of western Indian like Gujarat have a far higher *per capita* income. A National Survey soon after independence showed up the inequalities between families. Fourteen to fifteen million households (22 per cent of rural households) owned no land at all. Just under half of the country's rural household owned 1.5 per cent of India's cultivated land, whereas the remaining half were incomparably better placed, particularly the top 25.5 per cent who owned over 83 per cent of all the cultivated land, in parcels of at least five acres, though some of the holding of this wealthiest group were well over ten acres.[49] Great distinctions of wealth have also meant uneven access to services such as medical care and education. Provision of doctors, nurses, rural clinics, hospitals, colleges, and schools were an urgent priority for the new government, for despite developments in medicine and education through the century these had not been areas of massive government expenditure, even when they had been handed over to Indian control. Educational standards varied from region to region, reflecting each region's past history, its degree of urbanization, and its *per capita* income. In 1951 literacy was still very low, particularly among country women (See Table B). Without improvement here there could be little hope of significant change in attitudes, in the economy, or an end to the deprivation of so many who had no resources of land or skills other than their manual labour.

Table B. Literacy in 1951

	Men	Women
All areas	23.54	6.62
Rural areas	19.02	4.87
Urban areas	45.05	12.34

Source: Census of India, 1951, quoted in J.N. Sinha, 'India: A Demographic Profile', in S.C. Dube (ed.), *India since Independence. Social Report on India* 1947-1972 (New Delhi, 1977), p. 32.

The social problems generated by uneven access to opportunities in the environment of absolute scarcity which the new government inherited were particularly sharply focused in the plight of certain groups whose deprivation was reinforced by their ritual status in Hindu society. Despite advance in female education and the participation of some women in political life through *satayagrahas* and the enlarged franchise, the vast majority of women still had no choice over their destinies. Neither the limited movement for social reform nor the ways in which women had participated in politics had challenged the fundamental assumptions and institutions of patriarchal society. Consequently women's marriages were arranged, often in childhood or early adolescence, and from that time tending husband, children, and crops was their lot. Divorce or even separation were neither legal nor sanctioned by society. Restrictions on inheritance and ownership of property curtailed women's chances of a livelihood other than through dependence on men; low educational standards similarly deprived them of a viable alternative by barring their entry it a range of service jobs such as those of secretary, clerk, nurse, or teacher. Hindu ideals of womanhood and ritual prescriptions powerfully reinforced these economic and social restrictions. For most Untouchables, too, their deprived and isolated position in Hindu society remained unchanged. Despite Gandhi's campaigns, abject, poverty, ritual degradation, and a consequential barring of them from access to resources which might have changed their position, such as land, education or skilled work, all ground them down. The new government recognized the burden of its inheritance in these areas of society and the 1950 constitution stated its commitment to fundamental change and a denial of Hindu conventions which an alien government had not dared to initiate, the Directive Principles laid down in the constitution that the state's duty was 'to promote the welfare of the people by securing and promoting . . . a social order in which justice, social, economic and political, shall inform all the institutions of the national life.' Among the Fundamental Rights laid down as enforceable by the courts were rights of equality, freedom, ownership of property, and protection against exploitation. Accordingly Untouchability was now abolished. But it was clear that further legislation, administrative engineering in society, and economic change would be needed if Untouchables or women were to attain a status reflecting their constitutional rights, or if India was to be the secular state founded on the equality of its citizens which it claimed to be.

Hindu ideas of inequality and ritual status were deeply rooted in the minds of millions. Even the deprived and exploited—in non-Hindu eyes—often subscribed to the ideals which were the rationale of the society in which their roles were so circumscribed. However, economic developments in previous decades had shown that Hindu beliefs and ritual status were in themselves no bar to indusrialization, responsiveness to market forces and occupational and geographical mobility. Even caste identities and practices had proved flexible and able to accommodate change, although the social and ritual (as opposed to the public, work) context of people's behaviour was slow to change. Despite the constitution's brave claims and the genuine convictions of many of India's new leaders, traditional identities, values, and patterns of behaviour were so strong that they were a dead weight against social change. Yet the very stability of society in the 1940s was in another way a valuable inheritance for the new regime as it sought to weld and govern the nation state. Its reverse, major economic and social instability, would have generated other dilemmas which might well have destroyed the government and the new state's precarious unity.

Ironically, too, the new Congress governments in Delhi and the former provinces faced political problems of attracting collaboration similar to those of their imperial predecessors, though they had themselves as the main opposition to the *raj* constituted one its major dilemmas. Like any other government they had to gain allies and reward them with the knowledge that their interests would be considered in the processes of decision-making and government. Now the ground rules for attracting allies were changed, and universal suffrage created a comprehensive framework for soliciting support at all political levels. However, the Congress Triumph in the 1946 elections and the legitimacy it had gained among Hindus as the natural heir to the British was not a guarantee of unlimited support from the electorate. Congress governments would have to keep on proving their responsiveness to the needs of those crucial to the functioning of the economy, and to those who by virtue of their economic or social position could act as vote-banks, promising the votes of their caste groups, followers, clients or allies. In a land where local identities, interests, and loyalties were still dominant, the political importance of the 'local notable' remained great, though Congress had looked to notables rather different from those who had aided the British *raj*. This process began long before independence, in the relations of Congress with Indian businessmen and the more prosperous peasant farmers enfranchised between the wars, who were welcomed into the party's discussions and institutions. After 1947 it did not hesitate to welcome the support of prominent rural figures who had once been at home in British *durbars*, and now paid court to the new *raj*: particularly when such landlords or former princes could fund the party or pay for their own election campaigns. But it also had to attract broader and deeper swathes of the population into the party or at least into the polling booths as its supporters. Rarely had it made truly populist appeals before, and the legacy of its past ambivalence towards the demands of the poorest suggested that it was ill-equipped for the task, now made more difficult by the social and economic problems it had inherited and which it was now responsible for solving. Furthermore, its public commitment to equality, freedom from want and exploitation, to a rising standard of living and universal education, and to a creative role for the state, helped to generate rising expectations and to set a new standard by which its performance would be judged.

Just a there was continuity in the problems facing imperial and independent governments in the 1940s there was similarity and continuity in the resources of government—in terms of institutions, personnel, and even ideas. Remarkably little changed after 1947 because the British had relied so heavily on Indians to man their *raj* and devolved so much power before they left, creating structures and traditions which endured because they worked, however fiercely Congress had originally decried them. The main changes occurred at the top of the governmental pyramid with the removal of the Viceroy and Secretary of State, signifying the end of the authority of the British crown and parliament, and India's transformation after a short phase as a Dominion with a Governor-General into an Independent republic freely associately with the Commonwealth.

The institutions of consultation, decision-making and legislation were laid down in the 1950 constitution drawn up by the Constituent Assembly, which after 1947 became a provisional Parliament.[50] It drew very heavily on the 1935 Government of India Act, taking from it about 250 articles virtually unchanged. Consequently the institutions already operating at provincial level in British India remained. Former provinces became states within the federal union of India. State governmental structure changed little, and is a miniature version of the Union government, each state having its legislative assembly (eight states also have second chambers). Each state has its Chief Minister appointed by the state Governor because he can form a stable ministry and run a government responsible to the legislature. The Governor is appointed by Delhi—by the President in consultation with the ministry in power in the state. At the centre the formal head of state is the President, chosen by a special electoral college representing elected members of state and central legislatures. He in turn appoints the Prime Minister who is normally the leader of the majority in the lower house of Parliament. Parliament consists of the Lok Sabha (lower house) and the Rajya Sabha (upper house), members of the former being elected at least every five years, members of the smaller upper house being Presidential nominees or men elected by the states.

Much of this structure was drawn form India's previous experience under the British, and beyond that from the British tradition of a parliamentary democracy with a head of state exercising a significant but limited constitutional role beside his symbolic and ritual functions. As at Westminster real power rests in the hands of the Prime Minister who must have parliamentary support. India's constitution also lays down the powers of the centre and the states, and the topics shared between them[51]—as had the two previous acts of constitutional reform. Residual power remains with the Union, not the states. By various devices, including the allocation of tax resources, the supreme power of the centre is maintained, though the centre simultaneously needs the states' co-operation in the implementation of policies. (In practice much depends at any time on whether the same party is in power at centre and state level, on the Prime Minister of the day, on the issue at stake, and on the extent to which states co-operate together against the centre.) Both the interplay between different level of government, and the strong centre, were remarkably reminiscent of the days of the *raj*. Those who had argued for a weak centre, and for decentralization on Gandhian lines were disappointed. Gandhi had never come to terms with the nature and potential of the state in the modern world; and disliking what he saw, he increasingly took fight from the practicalities of politics and so provided no genuine counter focus to those who argued for strong, centralized government. Congress was itself responsible for this fundamental continuity in the institutions of government and consultation—not just by its stance in the Constituent assembly, but because of its pre-independence role. By co-operating in the provincial institutions through which the British devolved power, by mobilizing men unversed in the politics appropriate such areas and encouraging and educating a widening social range of supporters of value them, it lowered foreign imports on to an indigenous social structure. By helping the reformed structures to strike deep social roots and ensuring that they responded to the need of local people it made them effective and durable.

Superficial consideration suggests that whatever institutional continuity remained through the decade and beyond, 1947 marked a sharp break in the ideological resources of government. Certainly the primary commitment of the new state to creating a freer, more equal and prosperous society is in strong contrast to the pragmatism of the nineteenth-century *raj* in its heyday, with its implicit rationale of supporting British world-wide interests. Although a belief in the 'white man's burden', his duty to reform the manners and morals of his Asian subjects, was interwoven with material interests in British imperial ideology, lack of men and money accompanied by fear of social upheaval prevented the government from considering radical social and economic reform. However, in the later years of the *raj* the interests it upheld had shifted markedly and far less was at stake for the metropolitan country. Furthermore, as constitutional reforms were instituted so Indian opinion increasingly determined policies, even if the British were nominally still masters. Tariffs and defence expenditure were examples. In some areas of public life Indian legislators also began deliberate reforms; as in the provision of primary education and the partial lifting of some disabilities, such as the ban on temple entry, form Untouchables, by provincial governments using the power devolved on them by the 1935 Act.

The great change in government's perception of its role occurred during the Second World War. The deep and painful impact of the war on the economy and the need to maximize India's contribution to the war effort forced government into unprecedented intervention and planning. It imposed an Excess Profiles Tax to reduce purchasing power, in order to control inflation. It regulated the issue of industrial shares, preventing the production of non-essential goods. Ultimately it had to control prices, organize rationing, and involve itself in production, procurement, and distribution of essential items such as food and cloth. It also began to hammer out a coherent plan for post-war reconstruction, which was published in 1944. It stated explicitly the 'need for planning for the whole of India and the exercise of far more initiative by the State than hitherto in matters of social reform and economic development'. Another but independent stream of thought favouring government planning and intervention joined the official one flowing from government necessity. Congress had committed itself to planning from 1938, and a planning committee had worked under Nehru, incorporating such leading businessmen as Purshotamdas Thakurdas, Ambalal Sarabhai and Walchand Hirachand. During the war, though Congress leaders were in jail, many representatives of Indian business continued to work along these lines and in 1944 published what became known as the Bombay Plan for the development of India's economy and the increasing prosperity of her people. It envisaged raising output in agriculture by 130 per cent, in industry by 500 per cent and in the service sector by 200 per cent within about fifteen years. Not surprisingly the new government after independence drew on both these ideological developments and committed itself to planned economic expansion and social change. In 1950 it established a Planning Commission to advise government on priorities and the most effect use of the country's resources. But the breakthrough to government visualizing but its as a creative and directive one had occurred not at independence but early in the decade, when the British themselves discarded their old assumptions and threw themselves into a role inconceivable in the 1930s.[52]

A further element of continuity in the ideas behind governmental practice before and after independence needs stressing if one is to understand a dimension of India's democratic experience which was most powerfully demonstrated in Mrs Gandhi's 'Emergency Rule' thirty years after independence. Although Congress in opposition had bitterly opposed government's ability to rule with emergency powers, yet as the party of government intent on welding a new state it incorporated into the constitution very significant provisions for just such the rule after 1947. It permitted the President to suspend the right to freedom and to constitutional remedies in situations of national emergency, and also provided for preventive detention of those thought likely to injure society. The family likeness to the *raj*'s coercive powers was even greater when in the early 1960s a

Defence of India Act provided for the detention of anyone thought likely to prejudice the defence of India. The old emergency powers of Viceroy and provincial governors reappeared in those given to the state's governors and the Presidents: both, like their British predecessors, have power to promulgate ordinances. Furthermore, the President can in certain circumstances suspend a state government and bring the state under Union control—so-called 'President's Rule'. Here is potential for coercion and authoritarian rule as stern as anything the British had produced.[53]

Even more strikingly than in ideology and institutions, the continuity in the resources available for governing India is apparent in actual people. Not only were many of the politicians who came to power at independence already experienced in government—at provincial level like UP's Pandit Pant, or in Delhi itself as in Nehru's case. Those who were paid servants and instruments of government rather than its elected members were initially employed and trained by the British and remained to serve new masters without radical re-training or ideological 'reformation'. The vast bulk of ordinary government officials, the police and the army, had been Indian throughout the British *raj*. Inheriting such a resource of trained, experienced servants was a valuable legacy in the face of threatened administrative chaos in the north; though a certain number of Muslims in all the services left for service in Pakistan. At partition about 230,000 soldiers were allotted to India: and the number in India's bureaucracy at independence was probably about three million. At the highest levels in the army, police, and civil service there were still a certain number of senior British officials. Half the army officers were British, but a far smaller proportion of the ICS, following deliberate Indianization of the service over the previous decades and the difficulties of European recruitment. At independence there were about ninety more Indians than British in the ICS. Few British people stayed on in the services for long after 1947 and for a short phase there had to be rapid promotion to the higher ranks and emergency recruitment to the lower levels to replace those whose careers suddenly blossomed at the departure of the British. (One Bombay ICS man recruited in 1927 became a Cabinet Secretary to the Government of India in 1946—a staggeringly swift escalation of the promotion ladder!)

However, even with the influx of new army officers and members of the Indian Administrative Service (IAS as the ICS became after independence), traditions and patterns of action in the services created over decades changed little. The traditions bred at Sandhrust among Indians commissioned and trained under the *raj* flourished as the surviving military elite moulded their successors at the Indian Military Academy at Dehra Dun, and by practical example in parade grounds and Officers' Messes in the old British cantonments up and down the country. English remained the medium of recruitment and training, military life-style and social conventions remained; as did a tradition of elegant professionalism and career orientation, and non-involvement in political matters. Indeed such has been the strength of the old ways in the officer corps that it has been the butt of parliamentary criticism as 'un-Indian'. Yet the legacy of an apolitical army has been of great significance in India's very existence as a democracy, in sharp contrast to the experience of newly independent territories in other continents, or in neighbouring Pakistan. More ambiguous for India's political future was the continuity in its police during the transition from colonialism to independence—given the manifest weakness of the police force, its corruption, and its record as an instrument of coercion lacking the trust of the people.

Similarly, the ICS tradition continues in the IAS. It remains an elite and highly paid administrative body, drawn by competitive examination from a small social range, its recruits being sons of professional men, many of them in government service, who could afford an English medium education for their children. New recruits are further shaped by their professional training and apprenticeship in the districts under established officers many of whom were produced by a similar process at the hands of British ICS men. The last officer recruited under the British only retired on 1980. The service maintained not only their tradition of 'general competence' rather than technical expertise, but he cumbersome and often paper-laden procedural rules of their predecessors. It is still the 'steel frame' of Indian governance, despite Nehru's insistence before 1947 that no new order could be built in India while the ICS spirit remained. However, Patel as Home Minister in the Interim Government was well aware that in the turbulent days of 1946-47 the ICS, whatever its previous image in the eyes of Congressmen, was bastion against chaos and the disintegration of government. He was partly instrumental in persuading other Congressmen that continuity in administration must be maintained. Clearly the service was a source of stability. But its capacity to serve a country where radical change was desired or essential was an open question.[54]

In retrospect the decade seems less the start of a new era or great divide in the experience of India's people, than a time of continuity or at least of changes shaped by existing trends. India's new rulers had no clean slate on which to draw a new world, and no new instruments with which to create new designs. They bore a paradoxical inheritance—from their imperial predecessors and from their own past as both party of provincial government and leaders of lossely co-ordinated movement of opposition to the raj in the name of a nation, the composition of which was unclear. The context of a stable society, a poor economy, and continuity in the problems and resources of government does much to explain the strengths and weakness of India's democracy in operation—both its deep roots and durability, yet its failures to respond to the country's most urgent needs.

NOTES

1. 14 August 1947, speech by Jawaharlal Nehru, B.N. Pandey (ed.), The *Indian Nationalist movement, 1885-1947* (London, 1979). P. 219.
2. Chronological accounts and details can be found in such general works as Spear, *India. A Modern History*, or H.V. Hodson, *The Great Divide. Britain-India-Pakistan* (London, 1969). For Wavell's Viceroyalty, 1943-7, a most illuminating and readable primary source is P. Moon (ed.) *Wavell. The Viceroy's Journal* (London, 1973).
3. For India's contribution to the war and the disruptions to her economy because of the war, see Tomlison, *IESHR*, vol. xiii, no. 3 (July-Sept. 1976), pp. 338-41; Tomlison, *The Political Economy of the Raj*, pp. 92-103; J.M. Brown's entry on India in I. Dear and M.R.D. Foot (eds.), *Companion to the Second World War* (Oxford, forthcoming).
4. Note appended to letter from Wavell to Pethick-Lawrence, 13 July 1946, N. Mansergh (ed.), *The Transfer of Power* 1942-7, vol. xiii (London, 1979). Pp. 50-2. See also Tomlison's analysis in the works cited in fn. 3. A useful general book on the international

and domestic contexts of Britain's decolonization is J. Darwin, *Britain and Decolonisation. The Retreat from Empire in the Post-War World* (Basingstoke and London, 1988), particularly chapters 1-3.

5. Voigt, 'Co-operation or confrontation? War and Congress politics 1939-42', Low (ed.), *Congress And The Raj*, pp. 349-74; J.H. Voigt, *India in the Second World War* (New Delhi, 1987); Brown, *Gandhi. Prisoner of Hope*, chapter 9; Tomlinson, The *Indian National Congress and the* Raj, chapter 5.

6. There is no single good study of the 'Quit India movement'. A summary of events from an all-India perspective is F.G. Hutchins, *India's Revolution. Gandhi and the Quit India Movement* (Cambridge, Mass., 1973), chapter 9. Analysis of why popular upheavals occurred in particular regions are Epstein. *The Earthy Soil*. Chapter 4; M. Harcourt, 'Kisan Populism and Revolution in Rural India: The 1942 Disturbances in Bihar and East United Provinces', Low (ed.), *Congress And The Raj*, pp. 315-48; S. Henningham. 'Quit India in Bihar and the Easter United Provinces: the Dual Revolt', Guha (ed.), *Subaltern Studies II*, pp. 130-79; Dadmodaran, *Broken Promises*, chapter 4.

   On the experience of one Indian ICS officer in UP during 'Quit India' and the collapse of administration in Ballia district, see N.B. Bonarjee, *Under Two Masters* (Calcutta, 1970), pp. 186-204; see also Hunt and Harrison, The *District Officer in India* 1930-1947, pp. 200-5.

7. Wavell to Amery, 25 February 1944, Amery to Linlithgow, 28 June 1943, N. Mansergh (ed.), *The Transfer Of Power 1942-7*, vol. iv (London, 1973), pp. 760-1, 36.

8. Sir T. Stewart to Linlithgow, 22 August 1942, N. Mansergh (ed.). *The Transfer of Power 1942-7*, vol. ii (London, 1971), pp. 789-91. See also evidence cited in Harcourt, 'Kisan Populism and Revolution in Rural India', Low (ed.), *Congress And the Raj*, pp., 342-3; Damodaran, *op. cit*., pp. 235-6.

9. Entry for 31 December 1946, Moon (ed.), Wavell. *The Viceroy's Journal*, p. 402; Wavell's 'Breakdown Plan', September 1946, Mansergh (ed.), *The Transfer Of Power* 1942-7, vol. viii, p. 456; D. Arnold, 'The Armed Police and Colonial Rule in South India. 1914-1947', *MAS*, vol. 11 part 1 (Feb. 1977), p. 124; and D. Arnold, 'Police power and the demise of British rule in India, 1930-47', D.M. Anderson and D. Killingray (eds.). *Policing and Decolonisation, Politics, Nationalism, and the police*, 1917-63 (Manchester and New York), pp. 42-61.

10. Note enclosed in letter from Sir H. Twynam to Linlithgow, 26 July 1943; Wavel to Amery, 24 November 1943; Mansergh (ed.), *The Transfer Of Power 1942-7*, vol. iv, pp. 123, 493. See also 'The Impact of War', Hunt and 'Harrison, op. cit, chapter 11.
11. On the loyalties of Indian members of the ICS, see Potter, *MAS*, vol. 7 part 1 (Jan. 1973), pp. 67-71 and *India's Political Administrators*, chapter 3; M and T. Zinkin, 'Impressions, 1938-47', Philips and Wainwright (eds.). *The Partition of India*, p. 547; Minutes of India and Burma Committee of the Cabinet, 11 December 1946, N. Mansergh (ed.). *The Transfer Of Power 1942-7*, vol. ix (London, 1980), p. 334.
12. Wavell's 'Breakdown Plan', September 1946, Mansergh (ed.), *The Transfer Of Power* 1942-7, vol. viii, p. 455; Moon (ed.) Wavell. The *Viceroy's Journal*, pp. 368, 402. The decreasing efficiency of administration in the provinces is confirmed in Bonarjee, *Under Two Masters*, chapter 12.
13. On the Cripps Mission see R.J. Moore, *Churchill, Cripps, And India*, 1939-1945 (Oxford, 1979), particularly chapters 3-5; R.J. Moore, 'The Mystery of the Cripps Mission', *Journal of Commonwealth Political Studies*, vol. xi. No. 3 (1973), pp. 195-212; E. Stokes, Cripps in India' (Review Article), *Historical Journal*, vol. 14, no. 2 (June 1971), pp. 427-34.
14. R.J. Moore, 'The Problem of Freedom with Unity: London's India Policy, 1917-47', Low (ed.), *Congress And The Raj*, pp. 391-6.
15. Entry for 12 August 1946, Moon (ed.) *Wavell. The Viceroy's Journal*, p. 333. See also Wavell's appreciation of the political situation, December 1945, ibid, pp. 196-7; Zinkin, 'Impressions, 1938-47', Philips and Wainwright (eds.), *The Partition Of India*, pp. 546-53; Potter, *India's Political Administrators*, pp. 135-7.
16. Linlithgow to Amery, 15 April 1943, Amery to Linlithgow, 31 March 1943, N. Mansergh (ed.), *The Transfer Of Power* 1942-7, vol. iii (London, 1971), pp. 889-90, 820-1.
17. British politicians constantly referred to the need to placate American opinion over India. One of the most forthright expressions of this came in a minute by the (Australian) Governor of Bengal, 'I don't think it is an exaggeration to say that we have to weigh in the balance good Anglo-American relations—or a neat and tidy Indian settlement. If we are obliged to remain in India for another 10 years, ill-disposed Americans will use this as a very heavy stick to beat us with—and this will poison Anglo-Americans relations—which is the most important matter in respect in the post-war world. Personally, I would rather get out

of India tomorrow than risk the damage to Anglo-American relations that would inevitably be entailed by any long drawn out negotiations for a settlement of the Indian problem.' Minute by R.G. Casey, 17 August 1944, ibid, vol. iv, p. 1208.

18. Undated notes by Attlee, early November 1946, Pethick-Lawrence to Wavell, 25 November 1946, ibid, vol. ix, pp. 68, 174. A detailed account of the Attlee government's policy towards India is R.J. Moore, *Escape From Empire. The Attlee government and the Indian Problem* (Oxford, 1983).

19. Jinnah to Pethick-Lawrence with enclosure, 12 May 1946, N Mansergh (ed.), *The Transfer Of Power 1942-7*, vol. viii (London, 1977), pp. 516-17; note on Muslim League meetings, 24-26 April 1943, ibid, vol. iii. P. 922; note by H.V. Hodson on his tour of Madras, Orissa, Assam, Bengal and Bihar, 8 November–7 December 1941. N. Mansergh (ed.), *The Transfer Of Power 1942-7*, vol. I (London, 1970), p. 66.

20. Extracts from Jinnah's presidential speech and the Pakistan Resolution, Muslim League meeting, Lahore, 22-4 March 1940, Philips and Pandey (ed.), *The Evolution Of India And Pakistan* 1858 to 1947, pp. 353-5. Jinnah's January (1940) article is quoted in G. Rizvi, *Linlithgow And India. A Study of British Policy and the Political impasse in India*, 1936-43 (London, 1978), p. 116.

    For the radical reassessment of Jinnah's politics now possible as a result of the availability to scholars of the Jinnah and Muslim League papers, see Jalal, *The Sole Spokesman:* and review article by A. Roy, 'The High Politics of India's Partition: The Revisionist Perspective', *MAS*, vol. 24, part 2 (1990), pp. 385-415.

21. 'I do not attach too much importance to Jinnah's demand . . . I would judge myself that his attitude at the moment id that, as the Congress are putting forward a preposterous claim which they know is incapable of acceptance, the equally will put forward just as extreme a claim.' Linlithgow to Zetland, 25 March 1940, quoted in Moore, 'British Policy and the Indian Problem, 1936-40', Philips and Wainwright (eds.), *The Partition Of India*, p. 93.

22. Extracts of 8 August 1940 and Cripps' 1942 offers, Philips and Pandey (eds.), op. cit., pp. 370-3.

23. Entry for 11 July 1944, Moon (ed.), Wavell, The Viceroy's Journal, p. 79.

24. Minutes of final meeting of Simla Conference, 14 July 1945, N. Mansergh (ed.), *The Transfer Of Power 1942-7*, vol. v (London, 1974), p. 1245, text of Wavell's broadcast announcing Simla Conference and its aims, 14 June 1945, ibid, pp. 1122-4.

25. Two resolutions of Muslim League Council, Bombay, 29 July 1946, ibid, vol. viii, pp. 135-9. Volumes vii and viii of *The Transfer of Power* documents contain the record of the complex details of the schemes proposed and the various objections and accusations made. See chronological appendix to this chapter, pp. 361-2, for an outline of the Cabinet Mission Plan.

26. Note by H.V. Hodson on his tour of Madras, Orissa, Assam, Bengal, and Bihar, 8 November-7 December 1941, Mansergh (ed.), *The Transfer Of Power* 1942-7, vol. i, p. 66

27. Governor of UP to Wavell, 29 August 1946, ibid. vol. viii, pp. 342-3; Zaidi, 'Aspects of the Development of Muslim League Policy, 1937-47', Philips and Wainwright (eds.), *The partition Of India*, particularly, pp. 267-71.

28. See I. Talbot, *Provincial Politics and the Pakistan Movement. The Growth of the Muslim League in North-West and North-East India* 1937-47', (Karachi, 1988); D.A. Low (ed.), *The Political Inheritance of Pakistan* (Basingstoke and London, 1991). On Sind see *Ansari, Sufi Saints and State Power*, pp. 118-28. On the Punjab see I. A. Talbot, 'The 1946 Punjab Elections', *MAS*, vol. 14, part 1 (Feb. 1980), pp. 65-91; D. Gilmartin, 'Religious Leadership and the Pakistan Movement in the Punjab', MAS, vol. 13 part 3 (July 1979). Pp. 485-517.

29. Governor of Bengal to Wavell, 22 August 1946, Mansergh (ed.), *The Transfer Of Power 1942-7*, vol. viii, pp. 293-303.

30. I.H. Qureshi, 'A Case Study of the Social Relations Between the Muslims and the Hindus, 1935-47', Philips and Wainwright (eds.), *The Partition Of India*, pp. 360-8; M.D. Wainwright, 'Keeping the Peace in India, 1946-7: the Role of Lieut-General Sir Francis Tuker in Eastern Command', ibid. pp. 127-47; Hodson. The *Great Divide*, Eye-witness accounts of the violence are F. Tuker, *While Memory Serves* (London, 1950): P. Moon, *Divide and Quit* (Berkeley and Los Angeles, 1962).

    Recent attempts to analyse the mechanics of violent outbreaks are Das. *Communal Riots in Bengal* 1905-1947; Damodaran, *Brokern Promises*, chapter 6; S. Bose, *Agrarian Bengal. Economy, Social Structure and Politics*, 1919-1947 (Cambridge, 1986), pp. 223-32.

31. Attlee's statement in Parliament on the transfer of power, 20 February 1947; 3 June 1947 plan for the immediate transfer of power; Philips and Pandey (eds.), *The Evolution Of India And Pakistan* 1858 to 1947, pp. 391-3, 397-402.

32. See Roy's review article, *MAS*, vol. 24, part 2 (1990), pp. 385-415; also the complete version of A.K. Azad, *India Wins Freedom* (London, 1988).

33. See K. Singh, *A History Of the Sikhs. Volume* 2:1839-1964; B.R. Nayar, 'Sikh Separatism in the Punjab', D.E. Smith (ed.), *South Asian Politics And Religion,* pp. 150-75; S. Oren, 'The Sikhs, Congress, and the Unionists in British Punjab, 1937-1945', MAS, vol. 8, part 3 (July 1974), pp. 397-418.
34. Sir E. Jenkins to Wavell, 27 May 1946, Mansergh (ed.), *The Transfer Of Power 1942-7,* vol. vii, p. 712.
35. The record of Sikh delegates' discussions with the Cabinet Mission and Wavell, 5 April 1946, ibid. pp. 138-43. Resolution of the Akali Dal, 22 March 1946, *Tribune,* 23 March 1946, quoted in Singh, op. cit., vol. 2, p. 259, fn. 5.
36. Baldev Singh to Pethick-Lawrence, 4 June 1946, Mangsergh (ed.), op. cit., vol. vii, pp. 797-8; see also Tara Singh to Pethick-Lawrence, 25 May 1946, ibid. pp. 696-7, and Resolution of Sikh Panthic Conference, 10 June 1946, ibid. pp. 858-9.
37. Diary of A. Campbell-Johnson, 23 September 1947, A. Campbell-Johnson, *Mission With Mountbatten* (London, 1951), pp, 204-5; Tara Singh's statements, February 1948, quoted in Nayar, 'Sikh Separatism in the Punjab', D.E. Smith (ed.), *South Asian Politics and Religion,* p. 153.
38. M. Windmiller, 'Linguistic Regionalism in India', *Pacific Affairs,* vol. xxvii, no. 4 (Dec. 1954), pp. 291-318.
39. See J. Manor, 'The Demise of the Princely Order. A Reassessment', W.L. Richer, 'Traditional Rulers in Post-Traditional Societies: The Princes of India and Pakistan', Jeffery (ed.), *People, Princes and Paramount Power,* pp. 306-28, 329-54; V.P. Menon, *The Story of the Integration of the Indian States* (Madras, 1961 edn.); C. Corfield, *The Princely India I Knew. From Reading to Mountbatten* (Madras, 1975); C. Corfield, 'Some Thoughts on British Policy and the Indian States, 1935-47', E.W.R. Lumby, 'British Policy Towards the Indian States, 1940-7', Philips and Wainwright (eds.), *The Partition Of India,* pp. 527-34, 95-103.
40. Minutes of meeting of Burma Committee of Cabinet, 11 September 1945, at which Wavell was present, N. Mansergh (ed.), *The Transfer Of Power* 1942-7, vol. vi (London, 1976), p. 253.
41. Cabinet Mission Memorandum on States' Treaties and Paramountcy, 12 May 1946, ibid vol. vii, pp. 522-4.
42. See, for example, the creation of Rajasthan in western India out of the former Rajputana States, which was completed in 1949. R. Sisson, *The Congress Party In Rajasthan. Political Integration and Institution-Building in an Indian State* (Berkeley, Los Angeles and London, 1972), particularly pp. 104-11.

43. Ibid. See also J. Manor, *Political Change In An Indian State. Mysore* 1917-1955 (New Delhi, 1977).

44. Statement by President of Hindu Mahasabha, January 1945, Philips and Pandey (eds.), *The Evolution Of India And Pakistan 1858 to 1947*, p. 369. Golwalker's book is quoted at length in J.A. Curran, *Militan Hinduism In Indian Politics. A Study of the RSS* (New York, 1951).

45. See D.G. Dalton, 'Gandhi During Partition: a Case Study in the Nature of Satyagraha', Philips and Wainwright (eds.), *The Partition Of India*, pp. 222-44. On the last months of Gandhi's life see Brown, *Gandhi, Prisoner of Hope*, chapter 10.

46. *Movement of Prices*, 1939-44

(August 1939 = 100)

Dec. (Year)	*Rice*	*Wheat*	*Cotton manufactures*	*Kerosene*
1941	172	212	196	140
1942	218	232	414	194
1943	951	330	501	201
1944	333	381	285	175

Quoted in Tomilson, *The Political Economy of the the Raj*, p. 94. Inflation resulted from expansion of the money supply to pay for the war effort when cash could not be shipped to India from Britain to pay for her contribution to defence expenditure, combined with a diminishing supply of consumer good to civilians as imports fell and Indian products were syphoned off to meet military needs.

The fragility of life on the subcontinent was devastatingly displayed in the Bengal famine of 1943-4: see P.R. Greenough, *Prosperity And Misery in Modern Bengal. The Famine of 1943-1944* (New York and Oxford, 1982).

47. For the impact of the war on India's economy see Tomilson, *The Political Economy Of* The Raj, pp. 92-103.

48. W. Malenbaum, *Modern India's Economy. Two Decades of Planned Growth* (Columbus, 1971), particularly chapter 2, 'The Economy At Independence.

49. Table showing distribution of land ownership in 1953, Maddison, *Class Structure and Economic Growth*, p. 106

50. A good introduction to the Constitution and the political structure is R.L. Hardgrave, *India. Government and Politics in a Developing Nation* (3rd edn., New York, 1980), pp. 47-86, 101-4. Detailed analysis of constituent Assembly and the constitution is in G. Austin, *The Indian Constitution: Cornerstone Of A Nation* (New York, 1966).

51. The centre has exclusive authority over such obviously national affairs as defence, foreign relations, currency, and income tax. It shares with the states law social and economic planning. States control public order, police, welfare, health, education, local government, industry, agriculture, and land revenue. In any conflict Union law prevails. The centre can also create new states, alter state boundaries, and even abolish a state.
52. On the official unofficial commitments to government intervention and planning see Tomilson, *The Political Economy Of The Raj*, pp. 97-100; K.N. Chaudhuri, 'Economic Problems and Indian Independence', Philips and Wainwright (eds.), *The Partition Of India*, pp. 310-12; C. Baker, 'Colonial Rule and the Internal Economy in Twentieth-Century Madras', Baker, Johnson and Seal (eds.), *Power, Profit and Politics*, particularly pp. 590-8 (this is a local examination of government involvement in a provincial economy).
53. This area of continuity is explored by R.E. Frykenberg, 'The Last Emergency of the Raj' in H.C. Hart (ed.), *Indira Gandhi's India. A Political System Reappraised* (Boulder, Colorado, 1976), pp. 37-66.
54. On the structure of the public services see Hardgrave, *India*, pp. 69-76; Potter, *India's Political Administrators*: see pp. 146-9 for Patel's role in securing the service's position.

3

The Political Theory of India's Struggle for Freedom

An Apology

It is rather presumptuous to pretend to weave a theory on a long and disjointed process which is what India's struggle for liberation was. It is a matter still unsettled among scholars of both historical and political persuasions, whether there was any 'theory' in political science in India at all, as compared to, say, Greece or Rome and later the Medieval Europe. India never had an Aristotle nor a Hobbes or any of the various political theorists of Europe who wrote on politics. Such of the political writings as have been handed down to us, are so interwoven into 'legal-ethical-religious' texture that informed all intellectual work in ancient and medieval India, (the latter's contribution in this regard being utterly negligible) that it is difficult to separate the political strand from them. According to the Hindu way of thinking, even scientific study of History was fruitless venture and thus legend and mythology so hopelessly coloured the few traces of history that one does not know where history begins and mythology ends. It is only after the Muslim conquest of India, that we have the beginnings of a chronologically, though at time with lot of bias[1], recorded list of events, which go by the name of history.

Ibn Khaldun's prodigious effort, the 'Universal History' has had no parallel in India. And where India excelled was in the speculative nature of their intellectual effort in which ethical and legal aspects formed an inseparable component. As a sort of obiter dicta, *Sukra Nithi*, or *Shanti Parva* may give a few guidelines as to what political ethics should be; but they are far from political theoretical treatises. One may mention *Artha Sastra* as a deviant case, rather unique from the general Indian tradition, that discusses political-cum-economic questions with a refreshing air of independence from the influence of ethics and myths. Perhaps '*Kamasutra*' is another in its field which, to some extent, takes an amoral stand, howsoever absurd and unscientific certain observations might be. On the basis of one Artha Sastra which is generally compared to Machiavelli's "Prince", (why one should seek solace and pride under such comparisons with things Western is rather unintelligible) to claim that India's political theoretical heritage is rich, would be rather unwarranted. If India did not have political theorists, well, she did not have them. She had other compensations. Why should Indian scholars labour hard to prove that the Indian political system was democratically informed as if democracy is the best form of government and any country that did not have it in its past is thereby condemned to be a backward country? Democracy is a value judgement and one needn't attach such importance to is especially when reading a country's history.[2]

Hence it is, that if there was no political theoretical heritage that is indigenous to India, there is no question of its continuity when India's struggle for independence began. The very beginnings of this struggle itself cannot be correctly assessed, though some Indian historians have characterised the Indian Mutiny of 1857 as struggle for independence.[3] Whether or not it was fought on the basis of any patriotism and nationalism is a matter of doubt, though two things were certain—

(1) That the people in those days were loyal to their Kings and Kings' battles were theirs and this loyalty also changed as easily when the Kings changed. Hence if the native rulers like Rani of Jhansi or Tantia Tope or Bahadur Shah Zafar revolted, their armies and their subjects were equally involved.

(2) There was a general dislike of the beef and pork eating while the *Feringhi* ruling over the Indians coming from a far away country had no such feelings. In a rather unarticulated form patriotic sentiment was expressed in

this dislike, though earlier the rise of Rajputs and Maharattas against the Mughuls was more distinct and articulate patriotic expressions. Even these risings were to establish the Hindu *dharma*.

Thus in the sense that Rousseau's 'Social Contract' and Voltaire's prodigious writings formed the ideological base for the French Revolution of 1789 or the writings of Locke formed the base for American War of Independence or Marx and Engels' writings led to further elaboration of Lenin's writings which formed the bases for the Russian Revolution, there was nothing that could be though as the basis for the Indian struggle for independence. The theoretical base for India's struggle was almost coeval with the birth pangs of the struggle for Indians' national identity and striving for liberty.

Another peculiar feature of India's struggle is the very nature of the struggle itself which qualitatively differed from similar struggles in other enslaved countries, though one must hasten to add here that many of these independence struggles all over the world gave Indians an inspiration and a moral strength. Thus the American War of Independence, the Sinn-Finn movement in Ireland, and the Russian Revolution did have their impact on the Indian patriots with different degrees of intensity at different times. Yet in the main, the struggle assumed a form where violent individual acts of terrorism, violent mass agitations, peaceful mass acts of protest and constitutionalism became components of a peculiar amalgum each one becoming a prominent feature at different stages in the whole movement. In America it was the same stock of people mainly, who revolted against the mother country on a rather constitutional issue that there should be no taxation without representation—a typical 'shop-keeper's' attitude. In the case of both French and Russian Revolutions again, it was the same people revolting against their ruling classes. All these are not strictly patriotic struggles, though they are struggles for democratic rights to start with. The Irish struggle was in a way a struggle of one country against another though even in this case, England felt that Ireland was an integral part of Great Britain and representation in the British Parliament was given to the Irish even as the Scotts and Welsh had it. But for the fact that there was a differences in the denomination of religions, Ireland might have got integrated with Britain even as Scotland and Wales did.

That way after the defeat of Napoleon and the Congress of Vienna in 1815, the movement for self-determination of nations began to be recognised all over West though struggles for national identification had to be waged much later. The whole concept of nationalism was getting crystallised in a gradual process, wherein people speaking the same language and professing similar culture divided into different empires began to feel a sense of solidarity breaking the boundaries and barriers set by empires. In this process, unification as evidenced in Italy under the inspiration and leadership of Mazzini, Garibaldi and Cavour, and Germany under Bistmarck's policy of 'blood and iron', and consolidation as in the case of Sweden under Gustuvus Adolfus, and reshuffling of boundaries to satisfy the Serbs, Croatians and Bosnians at a much later date, were all the different components. This process perhaps did not end with any finality as the reordering of boundaries in Europe again after the Second World War evidenced. As Bertrand de Jouvenal said, boundaries are the most perishable commodities in the world. All these examples are cited only to show that the struggle for independence in different countries took different forms, they went through the painful process of violent upheavals, wars, foreign interventions etc., for their ultimate resolution. Though President Wilson of the United States championed the cause of national self-determination to all nations, to the Western mind this principle was applicable only to the Western peoples. Be that as it may.

In India, there was no sentiment of nationalism, as such, in the beginnings though it is undeniable that Indians from Kashmir to Cape Camorin felt as one whole for ages in spite of there being certain measure of truth in the oft-repeated saying that India is a geographical expression. As in Europe, religion generally never interfered with politics as such in India. This needs a slight clarification. Except for giving advice to the Rajah or the Sultan, the *purohit* or the *mullah*, as the case may be, never interfered in purely temporal matters as the Church did in medieval Europe. There was no organised Church which sought to indoctrinate people and interpret the Ruler's actions in terms of Christian theology and pass verdicts of condemnation or commendation.

All these facts have to be mentioned in order to show the historical fact that there was no traditional roots for any national movements in India that could immediately appeal to the people and recruit them to the movement. Such of the movements as India had were purely religious movements or cults like Buddhism or *Vaishnavism* which were completely free from political overtones and were not movements of revolt or rebellion in the political sense. Later on, the various movements of revolt by the Hindus against Muslim Rulers were more due to the religious frictions than for organised capture of political power. As along as the Muslim Rulers left the people alone in their religious worship, the people by and large acknowledged their sovereignty (even to the extent prescribed in Autinian jurisprudence) and never demanded any secular rights. Even the neighbouring Rajput princes waged only defensive wars when their territory was attacked. Thus the concepts of patriotism and struggle for liberation etc. were unknown to the people in general who were as indifferent to an alien rule as they were to an indigenous rule. Hence the task of communicating the imperative need for struggle for liberty is rather stupendous. The process of introducing the concept not only among the intellectual elite but also among the general masses of Indians is not a mean task since, as argued earlier, there were no such traditions in the country. Secondly, by the time this new consciousness got generated, the different groups and communities began to seek their identification and in the process their mutual interests were running counter to each other. It is against this back-ground that any theory of national struggle had to be developed and not by going into the roots of traditions as found in Sanskrit texts and *Dharma Sastras*. This is not to disparage the most scholarly attempts by P.V. Kane or B.K. Sarker or Nilakanta Sastri etc., to dig into the post in pursuit of finding the line of continuity in the Indian political culture but only to demonstrate that whatever be the reality of the so-called continuing tradition, its influence on the political struggle was rather negligible. On the contrary, the influence of Western though was much more relevant. What was needed was a proper formula for adopting the Western concepts and fitting them with suitable Indian idiom and charging them with the sentiments of indigenous tradition.

The Early Political Theories

It is not the intention here to go through the historical development but only to see if those who were motivated of patriotism had any theoretical understanding for their acts of disobedience to a foreign ruler. From the battle for Plassey in 1757, there have been many uprisings throughout India against the British finally culminating in the Mutiny of 1857.[4] As Tara Chand rightly pointed out, "I was not inspired by any positive creative idea; it did not entertain either the vision of a higher social order or of a higher political system. As it as an almost spontaneous episodic outburst, there was no stable well-ordered organisation behind the movement as a whole. It lacked plan, programme and funds. The only thing which united the rebels was the desire to eliminate foreign rule. . . . It was dimly perceived that Hindu-Muslim co-operation was necessary, but it was not realized that the nation was an organic unity, that no mere temporary co-operation of independent units was enough, and that a fusion of communities into a higher political organism alone could guarantee success against a modern power.[5]

Thus excepting vague notion among the feudal elements that a foreign rule which had deprived them of their privileges should be ended, there was no political understanding as such and even the concept of an Indian nation was not known. The ancient Hindu division of India into fifty-six nations had of course undergone a change, but among the masses of the people loyalty was more to the sovereign than to the nation. Even in Europe, it may be argued, that nationalism as a concept came into vogue after the French Revolution and the Napoleonic wars. But it is to be noted, for example, that the British considered themselves as one people and continued to resist Norman rule. The Scotts rebelled against the English, the Dutch fought the French and so on, long before the Napoleonic wars. The ancient Athenians as people had resisted the Persians with a feeling of pride in their citizenship of City State. In Indian even the vagueness about political unity and national identity was non-existent though from time immemorial culturally, which included religion as well, India was deemed to be a 'Bharata Varsha'. But this unity and resilience is the most important dimension of our national character.

The British rule with it superior organisation, its scientific temper, its historical perspective and traditions of liberal thought indirectly helped to build in India a force that was to ultimately undermine the British rule itself. This is neither a great astounding truth nor is admission of this fact a point against Indian national self-respect, because the self same imperialist rule in other developing countries in Africa and South East Asia, for instance, did not produce any national consciousness till almost the Russian Revolution of 1917. Long before these people were awakened to national consciousness, India had developed a movement a number of political philosophical thinkers. It is in this sense that India's freedom became the harbinger of national liberation struggles all over the world.

After the unsuccessful bid for driving out a 'White-Foreigner', the responsibility of directing the political fervent begins to fall not on the forces that fought the British in 1857 and earlier, but on a new class of intellectual elite that formed the bridge between the rulers and the ruled. The British supremacy was accepted and the uniform administration it brought about throughout the length and breadth of the country enabled a free exchange of ideas among these intellectual elites and later on facilitated a co-ordinated mass action which was lacking in the Sepoy Mutiny, as noted earlier.

The political revolt was followed by a political lull and the self-feudal elements who led the revolt against the British later on became their most trusted vassals and vassals and in that sense have become irrelevant to the development of a positive political process in the country. Hence the political role had to be performed by others who were intellectually equipped for the task. The first impact of modernisation that the British administration wrought and the results that flowed from Macaulay's famous minute on education was on the Hindu middle classes since both the Hindu aristocracy and the general masses of Muslim kept themselves aloof from it[6]—the latter almost viewed English with contempt. The masses in general were also completely neglected in the scheme of education Macaulay contemplated. While critical of the mythological content that informed most of the works in the classical languages of Indian 'which would move laughter in girls at an English boarding school', he was oblivious to many 'historical' incidents in the in the Bible that would move a country yokel in India to peels of laughter, though even the most scientifically advanced Westerner to this day believes in them it is not to deny the role modern education played in shaping the Indian nationhood in the subsequent period. But because of the 'filtration theory advocated by the Anglicists[7] the process of modernisation did not permeate into the nooks and corners of the land and thus paved the way for the ever-widening chasm between the elites and the masses in the country. It is in this light that the insistence at later date by Gandhi for vernacularising education has to be viewed.

The impact of the new knowledge served to throw ample light on the dark crevices of the Indian society on the one hand and served to introduce a greater spirit of reverence to the profound thought content in the classical philosophies of India which was far superior to the superficial theology of the ruling classes. At purely philosophical level freed from the mythological references, they were comparable to the great non-Christian-theological philosophies of the West.

In the words of Swami Vivekananda, 'when the Oriental wants to learn about machine-making, he should sit at the feet of the Occidental and learn from him. When the Occident wants to learn about.... The meaning and mystery of this Universe, he must sit at the feet of Orient to learn.[7]

We are now here concerned with the first aspect of it viz., the exposure of the disabilities in the society to scientific scrutiny as a result of the refreshing light that English education threw on them it is here that Raja Ram Mohan Roy occupies a place of preeminence among modern Indian political thinkers-we use the term political thinkers quite advisedly because his quest for social reform was pregnant with political content. His depth of knowledge of both the modern and ancient learning enabled him to reinterpret the texts and show that so-called new thoughts were not altogether unknown to the ancients. He struck at the root of social evils not by quoting English texts but by quoting the ancient texts. Tilak later on did a similar thing by reinterpreting the *Bhagawad Gita* and imbuing a political meaning to its message which was relevant to the contemporary period.

Raja Ram Mohan Roy's struggle for the freedom of the press, his championing the cause of peasants against the *Zemindars*, his plea for the appointment of Indian Collectors, in the place of expensive European collectors, his petition against the July Act of 1827 which denied a place of honour to the Indians, his advocacy of Indianisation of the army, separation of the jury from the executive, etc., were all the precursors of the new political philosophy that was to shape the liberation movement in India. This spirit of intertwining social reform with liberation movement is one of the fundamental contributions to political theory in India starting from Raja Ram Mohan Roy and continuing up to Pandit Nehru's time. Leader after leader saw in the social disabilities a monstrous impediment to political and economic progress and when they not involved in a direct action against the British Raj, they all turned their might and mien to remove them. In various regions, especially Bengal, Maharashtra, Punjab and Andhra, there was a greater accent on social reform movements to integrate the Hindu society, remove untouchability. Liberate women from bondage, infuse rational and scientific spirit etc., and the medium of vernacular languages proved effective. An out-and-out religious reformer like Swami Vivekananda wrote in Bengali language exhorting Indians to be proud of being Indians and to declare that the 'ignorant Indian, the poor and destitute Indian, the Brahmen Indian, the Pariah Indian is my brother.

The Liberalist Philosophies of Nationalism

Along with this social reform movement and the plea for 'Western' out-look came a sort of a militant revolt against the West which almost verged on xenophobia. Though the Mutiny and the subsequent revolts against the Whiteman's rule were characterized by an intense hatred of the foreigner—his colour, his religion, his habits and his arrogance, political articulation for freedom started with Ram Mohan Roy, who understood the British system and played the game according to their rules. Thus he is generally believed to be the forerunner of the constitutional struggle waged by the Liberals subsequently. Together with this, but rejecting the rules of the British game, came the extremist thinking which with all the hatred for the British that was characteristic of earlier revolts was based on a more scientific and clear understanding of the political process. It took inspiration from these sporadic and disorganised movements for all the acts of courage and love the land they exhibited, but built its theory on a study of patriotic movements from the West. In their attempt to socialise the messes and involve them they searched out methods which were more indigenous and hence more appealing than the rules of the constitutional game. The "filtration theory" of which spoke earlier failed to penetrate deeper than the skin.

The Liberals for all their sympathy for the Indian masses failed to reach them and understand them. Since in the evolution of national struggle, the Liberal thinking came first, we shall examine the reason for this and then analyse their philosophy of political action. Then we shall proceed to examine how along with these liberal or moderate forces were, born the extremists who advocated violent and forceful methods to eliminate the foreign rule. Coeval with this or perhaps even pre-dating it were the forces of minority separatism based on the suspicion of the majority if the ;neutral; foreign rule were to be eliminated and democracy were to be established. We may ay that the forces of minority separatism began even during the agitation of the liberals because if as liberals argued, great political participation were to be permitted to the natives, naturally by sheer number the majority of the Hindus would clam more power.

Generally whenever an enslaved nation fights or emancipation it does not resort to constitutionalisms alone. It is at once a compliment to the nature of the British rule as well as the adaptability of the intellectuals of India to the new situation, that the struggle for independence in India took a constitutional form. It is also because the struggle was headed by the middle class intellectuals who took to English education and served in the British Government as their clerks, administrators and brokers, they understood the nature of English ruling class and contrived to speak the language the rulers understood. Secondly it is an undeniable fact that the British administration brought about a measure of stability and peace, which was rather unknown during the earlier princely rule whether it be Hindu or Muslim. For the first time the impersonal rule of law with all its concomitant factors like predictability, and equality was enforced and medieval arbitrariness was completely eliminated. In fact, as is well known, the seeds of national movement were sown by liberal Britishers themselves. Going back to the original rule of the Indian princes with all its tyranny and cruelty was completely out of the question, and hence even the most ardent patriot in Indian felt that British supremacy should continue while at the same time greater participation in the national affairs be provided for the Indians. It is also an important factor that quite a number of Englishmen themselves were in the beginning sympathetic to these moderate aspirations of the Indian leader. The writings and speeches by Surendranath Banerji or Dadabhai Naoroji or even Gokhale are replete with sentiments of loyalty to the British Crown and in the name of British justice they appealed for greater freedom to the Indian masses. In all the thinking of the liberals, the Indian masses in general were not taken into serious consideration even though they make reference to them to demonstrate the nature of foreign rule and its exploitative character. Moreover, being intellectuals and having studied the liberal though of the West, they devoted themselves to a great deal of introspection—to examine the Indian society and see that the inherent defects in the society were eliminated before they craved for freedom. A country cannot be free with all the social disabilities prevailing in it. Most of these moderate leaders were scholars both in English as well as the Indian classical languages. While they observed lives they were as Macaulay wanted—'English in taste, in opinion, morals and in intellect.

The introduction of English language about a fruitful dialogue and unity of action among all the intellectual Indians who were hitherto separated by linguistic, regional and sub-cultural and even religious barriers. This brought about a new political culture leading to the birth of a new political consciousness. The liberals, taking their origin from Raja Ram Mohan Roy began assiduously to reform Hindu society and attacked all attempts at revivalism Hindu religion. Mahadev Govinda Ranade challenging the revivalists' argument asks what in Hinduism is to be revived—the twelve forms of sons and eight forms of marriages, the *niyog* system, the debauchery of the *rishis* and their wives, the *Shakti* worship with all its sacrifices including human sacrifice, polyandry and polygamy and so on.... "Besides, it seem to be forgotten that in a living organism as any society is, no revival is possible. The dead are buried or burnt once for all, and the dead past cannot therefore be revived except by a reformation of the old materials into new organised beings.[10]

Together with this new spirit that was born among the Indian intellectuals to reform their society, pursue the policy of constitutional reformation as a result of the windows being throw open to the Western though, new ears and suspicious were generated among Muslim minority that they might lose in the competition with the more out-going Hindus. When English education was introduced and the process of reconciliation to the British rule was taking place, the Muslims, like Achilles were sulking in their tents, being too proud to accept the superiority of the Britisher and his language while at the same time too wounded to rise in militant revolt against the usupers of their dominance. The burden of historical memory was pulling them back from joining the mainstream of politics in which they saw the hitherto servile Hindus were participating in full vigour. This burden of historical memory has been haunting both the communities and still persists and influences not only the relationship between Pakistan and India adversely but also the feelings between Hindus and Muslims in India. The loyalty of the Muslim in India is always suspect in the eyes of the Hindu and the Hindu's political dominance in a democratic system by virtue of his majority has remained and irritation the Muslim.[11] All talk of secularism by the Hindus sounds ambivalent to the Muslim. All that the Muslim could concede, is that India is a *darual aman*[12] and hence he need not be opposed to it or disloyal to its. Thus, from the very initial stages of independence struggle, the role of the Muslims—their fears, suspicions, aloofness, was a major factor to be reckoned with. It is an over-simplification to brush aside the whole thing as creation of the British administration whose dictum was 'divide et impera'.

Though by and large an influential section of the Muslims kept themselves aloof from the main stream of independence movement, it had also to be borne in mind that quite a large number of Muslims did join not only national liberal movement but also the extremist terrorist and later on the socialist and communist movements. Side by side with the new liberal spirit of the Hindus, Muslim also gradually realised the importance of new education as is evidenced by the institution of Aligarh Muslim University under the stewardship of Sir Syed Ahmed Khan. Apart form Sir Syed, Muhammad Iqbal, the poet, bought to bear a vigour in Muslim exclusiveness by rationalising the precepts of Islam to harmonise with scientific with scientific thinking. It is not be intention in this paper to go into the details of this deviant trend in the political theory of national struggle but only to point out how this factor influenced political thinking to a great extent, sometimes frustrating attempts at secularising and unitedly articulating the national aspiration.

Extremists

Extremism in India is result of the smug attitude adopted by the British government towards the aspirations of the Indians. The protection of the minority Muslims also became an alibi for the British government's lack of response to India's demands. Since extremists, in which category the terrorists may also be included , rejected at he stand of the liberals, they had to find a theoretical basis in the indigenous traditions of the country and to interpret them in the light of contemporary situation. Going back to the traditional sources for theorising the patriotic struggle naturally meant interpreting the religious texts. As argued earlier, Indians, in particular the Hindus, had no political treatises as such nor did they have a sense of history. Such of religious texts as would be suitable for political action were very few. *Gita* was perhaps the only book which provided the suitable source since it had the battlefield as its background and it sought to inspire the dis-spirited Arjuna into militant action to wipe out *adharma* from the land. In the divine scheme of things, man had to do his duty in furtherance of the divine will viz., fighting injustice, tyranny and wickedness. At least the Muslims who rebelled against the British dominance could find not only a historical justification but also invoke the teachings of Islam in which political theory if closely inter-woven with religious doctrine. It should be borne in mind that in the rise of Islam not merely religious conversion but also political action played a great role. Islam has a clear cut division of state into *Dural Islam, Darul Aman* and *Darul Harb* and people living in these states has definite duties towards the state. The so-called *Wahabi* movement which started prior to the Indian Mutiny and even inspired it, and continued till, 1914 had declared British India as a Darul Harb against which a Mussalman was enjoined to fight.[13] Some of the Muslim religious scholars of the Deoband School advocated joining hands with the Hindus in the task of driving out the British. What is contended here is that the Hindu masses did not have the benefit of such clear-cut political philosophy on which they could base their call for struggle. Hence it is, that some of the revolutionary leaders had to create a theory using only some symbols that would inspire the people. They had also to take recourse to philosophies of revolt propounded in the Western countries. Thus the theories in the literature on French Revolution, writings of Mazzini etc., were intermixed with the Hindu religious texts. Not only the *Gita* but other symbols that would infuse courage and militancy like the "Shakti" were sought to be invoked. The writings of Aurobindo for instance in *Indu Prakash* are replete with militant exhortations to the Indians to awake and in the name of Motherland and God fight for deliverance. Rejecting the plea of the Moderate elements in the Congress as an attempt at flattery to gain the goodwill of the foreign rulers instead of relying on the inherent strength of the nation, he said that the work of national emancipation was a great and holy *'Yagna'*.[14] The partition of Bengal and the subsequent eruption of Bengali extremism gave rise to a veritable crop of revolutionary theorising. Writers like Bankim Chandra Chatterjee urged Bengalies to 'disanglicise' themselves. His *Ananda Math* became one of the first political novels inspiring the spirit of nationalism among the Hindus. The various terroristic activities were emotional outbursts displaying tremendous courage and self-sacrifice. To inspire such an abandon, a very powerful and passionate appeal was necessary and hence the religious or semi-religious appeals were made. But it was left to Tilak to base his revolutionary theory not on mere motive appeal but on terse logic of the Hindu classics. Tilak can be called the dozen of Indian extremists. He reinterpreted the message of *Gita* and organised political agitation by using the popular Hindu symbols and *Ganapathi* festivals.[15] He was one of the most colourful personalities that the Indian Freedom movement witnessed. He brought to bear his tremendous classical learning on his own philosophy of political action. He was rightly the 'Father of Indian Unrest' as the imprudent British Journalist

Sir Valentine Chirol called him. Using his knowledge of the ancient classics and comprehending the weaknesses and strength of both the British administration and the Indian people he propounded the theory of boycott as a political weapon. To him *Gita's* message was a political message. He very clearly visualised that no empire was dissolved by free grant of concession by the rulers to the ruled. Power must be wrested from the unwilling hands of the rulers.

Both the Bengalis and Maharashtra extremists in their militancy advocated the policy of 'disanglicising' and usage of vernacular as powerful medium for mass education in their respective regions. This should not be mistaken for any attempt at sub-national identity, but has to be understood as the only alternative left for them in the absence of any other national language to communicate with the masses, once English was rejected as one of the symbols of India's bandage.

Certain political scientists have observed that the theories of the extremists, for all their anti-British tone, tended to become communal and anti-Muslim. Their invocation of the ancient texts, their usage of symbols, their fierce nationalism drove the Muslims away from them and made even the Congress movement suspect in their eyes. Tilak, especially, has been subjected to this criticism. Most of the other extremists like Lala Lajpat Rai and terrorists like Chandra Sakhar Azad etc., have all been termed Hindu militants. In such characterisations, one has to go deeper than what just meets they eye. These men were dealing with large masses of ignorant people who were unaware of elementary patriotic obligations. They had taken the British dominance for granted and in accordance with the law of destiny suffered their grinding poverty and humiliation with a sense of abject resignation. Though the Muslims were also economically down-trodden. in many places much more acutely than the Hindus, they had one thing in which they were superior—their unity and identity as a community in general and a memory of their supremacy in the sub-continent. The majority of the Hindus had neither modern knowledge nor pride in the past. It is to such people that the message of freedom had to be carried and unless the leaders speak the idiom of the common people and use the symbols that they venerate it would be well nigh impossible to establish any communication between them and the elites. For mass mobilization proper techniques of mass-communication are essential and Tilak was the first to realize that unless there was mobilization of the people leading to their participation in the political struggle, nothing would come out of the few intellectual exercises that were indulged in by the Congress leaders. To do this Tilak exploited the memories of the glorious past, the memories of their common struggles and sufferings. It is in this light that his Ganapathi festivals become positively meaningful. He did not start them but he exploited these festivals where people congregated, to give them a political turn. To Tilak political action was the enjoined religious duty as *Gita* taught.[16] Thus Tilak was the first Indian political leader who had formulated a political theory based on teachings of Gita interpreted to suit the times with an indigenous strategy for political action. He destroyed the intellectual notion that constitutional methods should be adopted to bring about political change but argued in favour of even forceful overthrow of a government whose moral foundation and legitimacy he had rejected. To minimise the distance between the masses and the intellectuals and unite all the people in programme of action by a realistic understanding of the existing conditions in the country and not by quoting Mill or Bentham without any relevance to the Indian situation, he undertook to write extensively in both his English and Maharathi journals, *'Maratta'* and *'Kesari'*. Thus Tilak was not only the father of Indian unrest but also the father of Indian theory of political struggle which in its essentials was to be continued by Gandhi.

Tilak's fearless upholding of violence when necessary was in conformity with the philosophy Gita. Non-violence is after all not a Hindu creed and Tilak advocated boycott only as an alternative to violence since an unorganised people cannot defend themselves against a powerful enemy.

Gandhism

It may be rightfully said that it was Gandhi who for the first time sought to evolve a political theory for national struggle in India. The uniqueness in Gandhian theory of national struggle, if we may call it so, is in its originality, indigenous character and its ethical content. It is a positive synthesis of the economic and social reform visualised by the Liberals in their purely legislative activities with the dynamic action programme for mass mobilization attempted by the extremists. Unlike the Machiavellian way of thinking of politics as amoral or trying to rationalise many an unscrupulous act as apart of the *realpolitik*, and hence not to be condemned severely, which is what contemporary political scientists heavily influenced by the American political theorists are trying to do, it sought to give a positive moral and economic direction to political activity.

The influence of this American political models on Indian thinker forms a distinct subject in itself that deserves to be very carefully examined. It is not the purpose of this paper to go into this aspect.

The way Selig Harrison's book *'India, The Dangerous Decades'* was given an undue and disproportionate prominence by the Western thinkers and their Indian counterparts bears a clear testimony to the possibility of arriving at very misleading and sometimes dangerous conclusions, if a mechanical application of political models and methodology relevant in the American context is made in India. It would be too obvious a statement to say that Indian political development must be interpreted through the usage of concepts that are indigenous and certain courage and self-confidence are the essential requisites or this liberation. This liberation need not necessarily mean putting the clock back when political scientists were preoccupied only with constitutionalism and historians with listing of chronological events, it calls, for coming to grips with the real problems facing the country and entering into meaningful debate as to what political scientists should do in order to help political policy making and socio-economy planning.

The importance that was previously accorded to Tilak and his thoughts arises out of the fact that he was the first in a way to think of political action with a refreshing originality free from the Mill-Bentham jargon but relevant to the context of the times and the peoples. It is in this tradition that the role of Gandhi has to be viewed—a tradition with deep roots in the country absorbing the rich thoughts from the Western nations and synthesising them to suit the challenges of the Indian society which was essentially traditionalistic at its core. Tilak and after him Gandhi understood very clearly that to mobilise the people to action Indian philosophical tradition, Indian national character and the folk symbols have to be properly used and in so using them they also had taken into consideration the regional variations. Tialk used the Marathi medium for speaking to the people and Gandhi also used Gujarati language to communicate to the Gujarati masses. Thus the efficacy of using the vernacular language to communicate with the masses was realised by them.

Gandhi as is well known derived his inspiration from Tolstoy, Ruskin and Waldo whose teaching he blended with his own understanding of the philosophy of *Gita*, his knowledge of the India's national psyche, so to say, and evolved out of this a course of action wherein the means adopted to achieve his goal were to be as noble as the goal itself. He was thus trying to synthesise in the in his political philosophy the rich heritage of his own country's ethical and spiritual values with the philosophy of rightful protest as preached by the Western minds. This is very important because in India there has been no indigenous tradition of fighting for civil rights and carrying out a revolution or revolt against constituted authority, howsoever tyrannical it might be. The semi-political *obiter dicta* that are found in the epics of the Hindus deal with how a good prince should behave and uphold *Dharma* and certainly not how a prince should somehow try to maintain his authority by whatever means available as Machiavelli was advocating. Hence it is that Kautily's Arthasastra is peculiarly untypical of Hindu political thinking. There is not even the Hobbesian justification of absoluteness of the ruler or the state, though in effect what was obtaining in the country till the British established the rule of law was more or less Hobbesian tempered by the soothing all-pervasive influence of *Dharma* or the *Shariat* as the case may be. Gandhi was operating in a country where the bulk of the population did not know their rights to self-rule and such of those as knew it were Western educated elites who either followed the more convenient path of constitutionalism and bargaining or the hazardous and doubtful path of extremism. Both of these in a way did not count with the masses and the importance of mobilising them for action while simultaneously educating them about their own inherent right to breathe the air of freedom had to be stressed. Many terrorists by their reckless courage had sacrificed their lives to liberate the country but that had no effect on the masses as such most of whom did not even perhaps understand that it was all about. They kept themselves aloof as admiring on-lookers at best and indifferent cynics at worst. The Liberals confined their activities only among the urban people and that too among the intellectual elites. As mentioned earlier it was Tilak who tried to approach the masses and even he did not reach the mass of people who lived in rural areas. The unique nature of Gandhian struggle is the drawing into the vortex of struggle the peasantry in villages and the workers in both factories and even plantations Champaran *Satyagraha* led by him was by the plantation workers. In this respect Gandhi was like Lenin who devised new techniques of struggle.

Even in adopting and devising these techniques of struggle Gandhi borrowed from indegenous ways of resisting the government, though he did acknowledge his debt to Thoreau's article on 'civil disobediene'. These techniques which Gandhi adopted were said to have had their origin in the methods prevalent in Saurashtra from where he hailed. The people of Saurashtra whenever they were aggrieved by the ruler's misconduct adopted three methods:

(1) *Traga* was self imposition of pain to express righteous indignation.

(2) *Dharma* was bringing of moral pressure on the oppressor by squatting before the oppressor's house and fasting, and

(3) *Baharvatiya* was a method according to which the rebel outlaws himself and attacks the officials in order to make the people realize that the King's writ does not run.

One can easily see in the various struggles that Gandhi launched, traces of these traditional methods of resistance to authority which had ceased to have a moral sanction and hence in the Gandhian spirit legal sanctity. But in all these the central theme was non-violence and truth which to him were creeds and not mere tactics. This is where he differs with Lenin to whom tactics were different from creeds and to attain the latter there was always room for change in tactics. If ends justify the means, Gandhi would say ends are means since both are moral.

Only when people are moral, truthful and non-violent can they attain *Swaraj* and *Ram Raj* which to him was almost synonymous with socialism—Gandhi styled himself a socialist. If morality informs all actions and struggles, there is no defeat because even in physical defeat the Satyagrahi is the moral victor since immorality can gain only a momentary victory over morality and such a victory is no victory. If the government is moral, there can be no contradiction between the ruler and the ruled. No foreign government howsoever good it might pretend to be, is not morally justifiable and hence in the final analysis immoral and illegal. A good government is no sustibtute for self-government, as Gandhi maintained. If the struggle is itself informed by morality then all actions after victory, is won will have to be moral. One who follows the path of the morality which in quintessence is truthfulness and nonviolence, there is no place for the two evils of cowardice and hatred to exist.

Gandhi viewed political action not in its isolation but as an important part of the whole gamut of activities in the economic, social and cultural fields. To him winning of independence was linked up with Harijan uplift, Hindu-Muslim unity, vernacularisation, removal of social disabilities, cleanliness, Panchayat Raj, village uplift, uplift of women, economic self-sufficiency, upholding the cultural values and heritage of the country, etc. for the first time a political theory views all these aspects as components of an organic whole and all of them were woven by the thread of truth and nonviolence. As a result of this style of his politics he converted the Congress Party into a movement and not a party in the strict sense. That is to say, he opposed polarisation of issues by calling himself a socialist among socialists, a sanatan Hindu among Hindus, a unifier of Hindus and Muslims, iconoclast who demolished caste system, untouchability and such other traditional disabilities which he considered to be in the way of his struggle. This style did give the Congress Party an eclectic colour at best and an ambivalence at worst which still persists. The dread of cowardice was almost an obsession with him and he felt it was a part of the Hindu psyche. All his actions and preachings were aimed at the removal of cowardice. A person who upholds truth has no fear of fear. The 'Charkha' became the overall spinning symbol of this progress of a backward colonial and timid people towards a new transformation into an independent, self-reliant, fearless, truthful and virile nation.

It is not the purpose of this paper to go into the details of Gandhian philosophy and economics but only to indicate the fact for the first time a comprehensive political theory was propounded which is at bottom in consonance with India's indigenous tradition and culture but has assimilated in itself the theories of the West. It was a sort of a compromise between tradition and modernity, both of which Gandhi in a peculiar way championed. The same fusion of seeming opposites characterise many of his actions. While not being a four-anna member of the Congress, he was still its centre. While upholding democracy, he demanded absolute discipline and unity of action among the diverse elements that composed the leadership of the various parts of the country voicing divergent view points. It was perhaps the amazing elusive quality of his personality that baffled both the British and Jinnah but endeared him to the masses as the 'Mahatma'.

There are so many competent writings on ;the various facets of Gandhism that this exercise would be only superfluous and shallow. That there was equally competent and rich criticisms of Gandhian theory does not alter the fact of the strength of his theory and the fact of its influence to a very great extent upon the struggle of Indian for independence. Just as every post-Marxian theory of economics makes Marxism a point of reference so also every political theoretician in India as well as abroad, makes Gandhism a reference point and from there on goes to uphold it or criticise it or partly uphold and partly criticise it. From Communists and Royalists to communalists and traditionalists everyone had to contend with the force of Gandhian 'unlogic'.

The various sections of Socialists, Communists and others had all rallied round Gandhi agreeing with him on the main objectives of winning independence by defying the British, mobilising the masses for action, awakening them to the economic and social exploitation to which they were subjected, though they had their own concrete differences with him on various other counts. Even his own successor, Pandit Nehru, differed with him though Gandhi maintained that Nehru would speak his language after his death. His theory of trusteeship, his uncompromising stand on non-violence which went to the extent of his condemning the activities of terrorists, the militant stand of Subhas Chandra Bose, the R.I.N. Ratings' strike, his opposition to legitimate strikes by industrial workers in various places are all of questionable validity even if judged according to his own principles. In international affairs though he kept himself aloof he was not insensitive to the fact that the world was shrinking and international interdependence would be inevitable in the emerging new age. Even there he felt that political action should have morals and principles. Hence it is that he supported the cause of democracy against Nazism and Fascism though he was himself struggling with the British, who were on the camp of democracy. If democracy should triumphs as a principle, as a way of life, the British government also should give up its imperialist ambitions and grant independence to Indian so as to permit her as a free and democratic nation to participate in the war against fascism with the full support of her people. To this end he was prepared to negotiate with the British. Thus at the conference tables as well as in the streets, factories and fields he carried the struggle with a disarming freedom from hatred but with the relentlessness of a hard-boiled revolutionary.

His theory of democracy extends to the last unit of community life since to him democracy was a way of life and was quite indigenous to India's rural life as exemplified in the ancient village panchayats or the rural republics as he called them. He visualised a democracy which is not vitiated by uncompromising opposition but enlivened by active and positive participation of all people in the community. Out of a few houses a representative and out of those, a representative body for the village, out of a few villages a representative for a district and so on upto the national level was the sort of a structure he visualised for the country. This would prevent the community from being torn apart by parties, factions, castes and religions. Thus the Sarvodaya theory was developed. Jayaprakash Narayan's idea of Communitarian society is a further extension of Gandhi's seminal ideas on decentralised society. All these may be very idealistic visionary and out of tune with the times.

Pandit Nehru who spanned both the pre-independence struggle era and the post-independence developmental era tried to synthesise Gandhism and socialism; tried to bridge the gap between heavy industrialisation and rural small-scale industrialisation, tried to link representative big democracy with decentralised grass-root democracy, and in the field of international relations compromise rightful use of force with peaceful coexistence and settlement of disputes. M.N. Roy starting as a Marxist and a trenchant critic of Gandhi travelled for towards the last days of his life and arrived at humanism. Though he rejected the traditionalism of Gandhi, the religious outlook on life which stagnated Indian society and the advocated rationalism, basically his approach to social problems were near Gandhian inasmuch as he too advocated decentralisation of power and organised democracy and establishment of a moral order. "Any effort for reorganisation of society must begin from the unit of society - from the root, so to say".[17] But Roy's thought remained unrelated to the main-stream of India's politics.

Contemporaneous with Gandhi and Gandhian political thinkers mention must be made of the socialist and communist political theorists, though from the point of originality and applicability of theory to the political culture of the country, so to say, their contribution has not been significant. For a long time both the groups, socialists and communists, worked together and tried to apply the Marxian theory to the Indian situation. They were incapable of assimilating the Marxian thought and properly interpreting it to suit the Indian situation. This needed a deeper understanding of the culture of the Indian society which they seem to have lacked. Either they ended as camp followers of Gandhian leaders or became totally alienated from the people as most communists became. They lacked the original thinking and an understanding of the people of India to link those ideas meaningfully by a theory. This is precisely what Mao Tse-tung did in China. Though he was essentially a Marxist-Leninist he could propound an original theory of struggle most suited to the objective conditions obtaining in his country. Even G. Adhikari, the most outstanding theoritician that the communists could boast of, come out with a poor version of the theory of nationalities after unsuccessfully trying to support the demand for Pakistan and Sikhistan. Originally, misguided by their over-enthusiasm to support and win the minorities, the communists supported Jinnah and also the Sikh separatists. Punjab, said Adhikari, was the homeland of Sikhs. After a time this was sought to be replaced by a "new" theory of sixteen nationalities in India. This was nothing but giving the linguistic provinces a grand name of nationalists *a la* Soviet Union. But all these pseudo-theories did not produce any mass action and whatever mass mobilisation that the communists could accomplish was in their leading the working classes and the peasantry in their economic struggles. Even these were in the conventional communist fashion rather than according to any original theory. They failed to accomplish the task of politicalising the economic struggles except in small isolated pockets.

There has been no dearth of theoreticians in the pre-independence India but most of their thoughts have been systematically and coherently argued out. True it is, that most of them were not political philosophers mainly but men of action leading agitations and speaking to people. Only when in gaol, men like Nehru wrote anything, if at all and even then Nehru tried to run away from it all either to have glimpse of World history or to discover India. Even such an excellent and analytical mind like that of Rajaji's also did not produce any coherent treatise on politics, except for occasional articles. One has only to gleam through the various writings in different journals or papers by some of the intellectuals among the Indian leaders to churn out a political theory.

After independence, there has been a significant growth in intellectual activity and political theory came to be more meaningfully linked with socio-economic development. With the ushering in of planning a grasp of the proper linkages between the different systems within the country, social, political, economic, cultural, etc. as well as international, has been attempted. There has also arisen a great danger from pernicious and shallow theory-building mostly undertaken by some American political scientists and their Indian imitators who paint a distorted and fragmented picture of India's basic unity and resilience. They reject the historical context of the whole Indian nationhood and indulge in superficial theorisation based upon a pseudo-scientific interpretation of soft behavioural data acquired through means of doubtful validity. We are told, for instance, that these are dangerous decades, that our caste system is asserting itself as result of the participatory democracy and that the country awaits to be fragmented by the struggle for regional and linguistic identity. These theories need not be taken into serious consideration though they may serve to point out certain tendencies at the micro-level.

There is now need for thinking in terms of political theories that would take the socio-economic goals set before the nation into consideration and link them up with appropriate political structures and methods so as to achieve national goals of social change, national consolidation and national self-reliance both economic and military. The impact of administration and the need for a new outlook in the face of new challenges facing the country, the compulsions of international relations, the absorption and adoption of scientific and technological knowledge are all germane to the new thinking. It is a very idle exercise to go on discussing about parliamentary democracy or costitutionalism in the present context; as they perhaps were even during the context of our struggle for freedom. This does not mean doing away with democracy. On the contrary to a great extent, economists in the country have exhibited a great awareness of the national need for performance. This paper is an attempt to place this need for a proper political theory in the historic perspective.

NOTES

1. It should also be noted that some historians like Khaflkhan, for instance, wrote with an amazing sense of historical impartility.
2. Eminent scholars like K.P. Jaiswal, Beni Prasad and K.S. Aiyangar tend to import some of the Western political categories into the ancient Hindu political systems. May be some type of democracy and some varieties of republics existed, but they are not of the same type as those contemplated according to the Western norms.
3. Only V.D. Savarkar characterised it as war of independence and wrote rather passionately than historical accurately about it. This was of-course done with a purpose.
4. For details see Tara Chand. "History of the Freedom Movement in India"—Vol. II. Publications Division, Government of India, 1967. pp. 1-107.
5. *Ibid*, pp. 106-107

6. See R.C. Majumdar, *et al*: 'An Advanced History of India', London 1958, p. 816-821.
7. It is a well known fact that at the time, i.e., in the first quarter of the 19th century the thinkers in both India and Europe were divided into two groups—Orientalists and Anglicists. Raja Ram Mohan Roy was opposed to Orientalists because he felt that oriental education would keep the people in darkness. The Anglicists admitted that English education would not reach all the people but would spread through the medium of the English-educated elite to the people at large. This was called the 'filtration theory'.
8. Complete Works of Swami Vivekanada, Vol. IV, Almora, p. 151.
9. *Ibid*, p. 413.
10. See Chintamani "Indian Social Reform" Part II, Madras, pp. 89, 90.
11. See, Sir Syed Ahmed Khan "Akhari Maßamin" and other tracts.
12. According to Islamic jurisprudence Darul Islam is a country which is governed by Koranic injunctions and no Muslim can rebel against it. Darul Aman is a country which is not governed by Koranic injunctions but they are respected. A Muslim living in it is enjoined to be loyal. But Darul Harb is anti-Islamic state against which the Muslim has to fight.
13. It is a matter of doubt whether Wahabi movement could be termed as a national movement since it was aimed at re-establishment of Muslim rule in India. But in the sense that the Muslims were the rulers in India before the British occupied it, the re-establishment of the Indian rule albeit exclusively and dominantly Muslim rule has to be considered national in that, historical context. See Qahmed *The Wahabi Movement in India*, Calcutta, 1966.
14. See Aurobindo, 'Speeches' Calcutta, Arya Publishing House, 1948 and also Karan Singh, "Prophet of Indian Nationalism", London, George Allen & Unwin, 1963.
15. There are quite a large number of books on Tilak including some by Westerners who were fascinated by his political personality. I.M. Keisner and N.M. Golaberg, (Eds) *Tilak and the Struggle for Freedom*, New Delhi, 1966, T.L. Shay, *The Legacy of Lokmanya*, S.A. Wolpent, *Tilak and Gokhale; Revolution and Reform in the Making of Modern India* Berkeley, 1962.
16. See G.D. Parik 'Bal Gangadhar Tilak, Humanist Review, July-Sept. 1970 for an excellent exposition of Tilak's ideas regarding the minorities religious reform etc.
17. *See his New Humanism: A Manifesto, Calcutta*, 1947 for details.

4

Prospects for Indian Democracy

From the preceding chapters, it is clear that the record of the Indian Cabinet, both during and after Nehru's time, has been on the whole creditable. No one, of course, claims that the Cabinet has always done the right thing at the right time and in the right manner. But when we consider the vast size of the country and the nature of its diverse and difficult problems, the achievements of the Indian Cabinet should be regarded as praiseworthy. It has preserved the unity of the country, built up traditions of parliamentary democracy, maintained the rule of law, and tried to develop the economy through peaceful means. India's record is particularly commendable when compared with that of other Asian countries. In many of them democracy has disappeared and given way to dictatorship. Indeed, in the post-war world, few countries can boast of such a long and continuous period of political stability and democratic rule as India.

The question now arises how rapidly India will be able to progress in the coming years without impairing her democratic set-up. The great problems confronting the country at present relate to national integration, development of the economy, and improvement of administration. These issues are, of course, relaset-up. The great problems confronting the country at present not only on the efficient working of the Cabinet but on the extent to which it is able to enlist the support and co-operation of the Opposition.

How Strong Is The Union?

There is, of course, no immediate danger to Indian unity, but this feeling of oneness seems largely artificial, created by the Chinese aggression and the danger from Pakistan. The

Constitution of India, moreover, has been amended with a view to making the demand for secession illegal. But one has only to recall the conditions prior to the Chinese invasion in October 1962 to realize the dangerous extent to which fissiparous forces had strongly entrenched themselves in strategic parts of the Indian Union. The reorganization of States on a linguistic basis had created fierce rivalries and jealousies, and in the South, the movement for secession was gathering rapid momentum.

'It has been most distressing to us,' said the States' Reorganization Commission in its report in 1956, 'to witness a kind of border warfare in certain areas in which old comrades-in-arms in the battle for freedom have been pitted against one another in acrimonious controversy, showing little appreciation of the fact that the States are but the limbs of the same body politic and that territorial readjustments between them should not assume the form of disputes between alien powers.'

The States even defied the Centre, and some Chief Ministers negotiated directly with foreign countries for getting financial and technical aid without reference to the Government of India or the Planning Commission. This unconstitutional practice was stopped only when Nehru issued a circular to Chief Ministers early in 1962, strongly deprecating such a procedure. Attempts to develop the economy through the Five-Year Plan failed to evoke popular enthusiasm. The situation became so serious that the Prime Minister had to call a National Integration Conference in New Delhi in June 1961 and set up a number of influential committees to suggest measures for preserving the unity and independence of the country. But these Committees suspended their work when, soon after the Chinese invasion, the nation displayed a strong sense of solidarity.

Apart from the external danger, the personality of Nehru had been the most powerful unifying factor. Even his fierce critics freely acknowledged his remarkable capacity to weld together the various parts an serve as an effective symbol of a united nation, K.M. Munshi, a former Minister in the Union Cabinet and now a leader of the Swatantra Party, hardly exaggerated when, in his speech at the National Integration Conference in New Delhi in June 1961, he said, turning to Nehru who was in the Chair: 'This linguistic chauvinism can be crushed only in your lifetime. I say this, despite my political differences with you, and you know that I have never paid you an idle compliment.' But Nehru failed to strengthen the centripetal forces and place the country's unity beyond challenge.

The formation of linguistic States is now generally admitted to be a serious blunder, and the decision to make both Hindi and English as official languages at the Centre is likely, in the long run, to do great harm to Indian unity. Bilingualism may be all right as a temporary solution and it may perhaps work well even as a permanent arrangement. But in the present conditions this is unlikely. The reason is that both Hindi and English are not given the same status. Hindi is the principal language and English only an associate language. Moreover, an influential section of leadership is vehemently opposed, for sentimental reasons, to the continuation of English in any form. At the same time, public opinion in the South and in West Bengal is determined not to permit Hindi to be the sole official language. Meanwhile, the excessive importance attached to regional languages even in higher education will intensify provincial feelings and weaken national integration.

Communalism and casteism are two other obstracles to the development of democracy. Communalism, of course, is not as widespread and acute today as in the British period. Nevertheless it continues to exist to various degrees of strength in different parts of the country. Casteism too is a powerful factor in Indian politics. A study conducted by the Indian Institute of Public Administration in 1964 revealed that although caste stratifications had undergone subtle changes under the impact of socio-economic and political forces since independence, it was still a force to be reckoned with in Indian society and politics. The study pointed out that modern industrial forces, while helping to break down the barriers of caste in regard to eating, drinking and other forms of contact, had tended to bring members of the same caste together to capture the benefits of social and economic progress, Casteism, the study added, 'has a vested interest in backwardness', since it enables the people concerned to demand special treatment in terms of expenditure and reservations.

Thus the unity of India rests on insecure foundations and this fact may imperil the future of democracy. Indian history clearly shows that the country stood united in the past only when there was strong king or emperor; and when he was succeeded by weak rulers, the provincial chiefs began to assert their independence; and disintegration set in, often followed by foreign invasion. This was what happened after the death of Asoka, Harsha and Akbar; and it may happen again, now that Nehru is gone, unless the unifying forces are effectively strengthened. It was but appropriate therefore that in his first broadcast to the nation as Prime Minister, Shastri made a fervent appeal to the people to stand united in all circumstances. He said: 'Let people in different parts of the country, however strong their feelings might be on particular issues, never forget that they are Indians first and that all differences must be resolved within the unalterable framework of one nation and one country. Let us make every endeavour to foster this feeling of oneness and to carry forward the work of national integration started with the National Integration Conference in 1961.'

Stagnant Economy—Threat to Democracy

The failure of the Indian economy to develop rapidly is another major threat to the future of democracy. We have seen that the Five-Year Plans have not so far succeeded in improving the economic condition of the vast majority of the people. Consequently, the difference between the living standards of the people of India and those of other countries, great as it is already, is becoming more glaring. The *per capita* annual income in India in 1963 was only Rs. 303 as compared to Rs. 12,128 in the USA, Rs. 6,030 in the UK Rs. 6,025 in West Germany and Rs. 2,428 in Japan. A comparison of national income statistics of different countries has many limitations. But even so, it is obvious that the rate of our progress has been disappointingly slow. So unless the economic policies are suitably adjusted and the scourge of poverty and unemployment is tackled boldly, the unity and freedom of India will be gravely imperiled. Shastri therefore, gave high priority to the war against poverty. In his broadcast referred to above, he said: 'Of all the problems facing us, none is more distressing than that of the dire poverty in which millions of our countrymen continue to live. How I wish that *i* would be able to lighten the burden of poverty on our people. I cannot forget particularly the claims of the most backward sections like the Scheduled Castes and Scheduled Tribes, who had suffered neglect and had endured disabilities for many centuries. It would be my proud privilege to work for the establishment of a more just social order.'

But the outlook for economic development does not appear to be quite encouraging. The success of the Fourth Plan will depend largely on how efficiently and closely the public sector and the private sector work together in the interests of the country. But unfortunately the two sectors still seem to be engaged in a sort of cold war. The Government is determined to increase the sphere of the public sector steadily and even spectacularly. But the record of the public sector undertakings in terms of financial results has been disappointing. On a total investment of Rs. 1,026 crores as at the end of 1963-4 the net profit of public sector enterprises (other than departmental undertakings) was only Rs. 11.75 crores or 2.85 per cent. It is true that, individually, a few government enterprises have been able to show profit. But considering the public sector as a whole the performance has not been satisfactory. At the same time, the private sector is not being permitted, on ideological grounds, to expand vigorously. Excessive taxation, controls of prices, production and profits, and increasing regimentation of the economy are hampering the freedom initiative and enterprise of the private sector. At the annual meeting of the Federation of Indian Chambers of Commerce and Industry held in New Delhi in March 1965, Lal Bahadur Shastri complained that the private sector had withheld its co-operation from the Government in tackling the difficult food problem. Asoka Mehta, Deputy Chairman of the Planning Commission, who addressed the meeting, expressed his surprise at the fact that India's industrial parliament (that is, the Federation) had expressed with one voice its disapproval of the size and scope of the Fourth Five-Year plan. He advised them 'to cost off their tattered garments of pessimism and gloom and don the armour of optimism.' But the fact remains that on the eve of the inauguration of Fourth Five-Year Plan the gulf between government and industry remains as wide as ever. This is not conducive to rapid economic growth.

How to Modernize Administration

How fast the economy will grow will depend largely not only on the adoption of right policies but on the improvement of the administrative machinery. In this respect Nehru was not able to achieve much success. Although the first, second and third five-year plans laid great emphasis on the importance of administration, and a number of influential committees examined the problem form time to time, the administrative machinery, far from showing signs of improvement, is becoming less efficient. Year after year, the Federation of Indian Chambers of Commerce and Industry, at its annual meeting, draws pointed attention to the abnormal delays in carrying out schemes of industrial development because of the failure of the administration to cope with its growing responsibilities. At its annual meeting in March 1963, for instance, a resolution was adopted, deploring the fact that there was 'hardly any decision which the industry and trade can take without getting the approval of the authorities.' The resolution added:

> 'The administrative delays in the disposal of applications have been not a little responsible for procrastination and confusion. The Federation cannot help pointing out that Governmental policy seems to be influenced by considerations other than economic in disposal of applications for expansion of existing units and establishment of new ones. . . . The Federation also appeals for an impartial consideration of the root causes, which will reveal the connection between multiplicity of legislative measures, rules and regulations and administrative inefficiency, and unproductive time-consuming work all round, as also between indecisiveness and slackness in administrative machinery and the proliferation of governmental agencies.'

India's civil service, on the whole, has adjusted itself to the changing situation, and it is surely more efficient than its counterpart in other Asian counties. But any failure to cope with its new responsibilities is due, firstly to the complications arising from an increasingly regimented economy and, secondly, to the wrong relationship between minister and civil servant. Socialism in India is considered to be synonymous with nationalization of the means of production and distribution. But since proper attention is not given to the improvement of administration, socialism gets discredited, the economy stagnates, corruption grows and the people suffer. As the Planning Commission says:

> 'As large burdens are thrown on the administrative structure it grows in size; as its size increases, it becomes slower in functioning. Delays occur and affect operations at every stage, and expected outputs are further deferred. New tasks become difficult to accomplish if the management of those in hand is open to just criticism.'

The relationship between the civil service and the ministers has not always been as perfect as it ought to be. Parliamentary democracy requires that ministers should concern themselves with policy matters, leaving their implementation to the services. Ministers of course, should ensure that the policies laid down by the Cabinet and approved by Parliament are promptly and faithfully carried out, but there should be no political interference with the services in the discharge of their duties. 'The relations between a minister and his secretary,' said Disraeli, 'are, or at least, should be, among the finest that can subsists between two individuals. Except the married state there is none in which so great a confidence is involved and in which more forbearance ought to be exercised or more sympathy ought to exist.'

In India, ministers generally do not seem to appreciate the right role of the civil service in a democracy and, consequently, the civil service has been unable to perform its task fearlessly. On critical occasions, the services are reluctant to take decisions because they are not sure that ministers will not let them down. Ministers also sometimes interface too much with administrative details. This, for instance, is what Brecher said of Nehru:

> 'The fact of the matter is that Nehru is an inept administrator. Decisions are concentrated in his hands to an incredible degree, not only because of objective pressures but also because of his all-consuming interest in the pettiest of details. He lacks both the talent and temperament to co-ordinate the work of various ministries. More important, he has never shown a capacity or inclination to delegate authority. The result has been the administrative jungle which he bemoans.'

The comments of C.S. Venkatachar, a retired member of the Indian Civil Service, and a former Secretary to the President of India, are also worth quoting. He says:

> 'What has actually happened in Independent India is this: the civil servants are comparatively well paid and work in decent material conditions. At the same time, they are distrusted at higher levels. At district level, they are supervised by partymen of dubious virtue. The expanding nature of the functions of Government has made the civil servants more valuable than ever as specialists and scapegoats. Partymen prefer the civil service in the latter role but ministers at the Centres are disposed to be more tolerant and understanding. As you descend down the escalator from the higher regions of the Prime Ministerial Government and touch the ground floor of the district administration, you see glaring maladjustment between the democratic apparatus and the administrative machinery, marked warping of both, less efficiency and more confusion.'

Shastri, soon after he took over as Prime Minister, pledged himself to reform the administrative machinery. He said:

> 'The administrative organisation and its methods and processes must be modernized if its is to become an affective instrument of economic change. I shall do my best to have systematic attention paid to these major problems and I shall apply myself closely to the problem of administrative reforms in its various aspects.'

Mrs Gandhi also has expressed her determination to tone up administrative efficiency. In her first broadcast, she said:

> 'In economic development, as in other fields of national activity, there is a disconcerting gap between intention and action. To bridge the gap we should boldly adopt whatever far-reaching changes in administration may be found necessary. We must introduce new organizational patterns and modern tools and techniques of management and administration. We shall instil into Government machinery greater efficiency and sense of urgency and make it more responsive to the needs of the people.'

But administrative reform is not going to be easy, particularly in view of the introduction of bilingualism in the Central Government.

Crusade Against Corruption

Slackness in administration has been an important factor leading to widespread corruption. Its elimination from public life is one of the toughest problems confronting Indian democracy. In other countries also, corruption continues to flourish in various degrees. But the problem in India is somewhat different. In countries like the UK and the USA, the democratic tradition is strong, public opinion is alert and vigorous, the living standards are high, and the gap between the rich and the poor is comparatively small.

India, on the other hand, is a young democracy and the three Five-Year Plans have not succeeded in improving the living standards of the vast majority of the people. At the same time, the growth of the press, a powerful organ of public opinion, if retarded by the severe shortage of newsprint. In the circumstances corruption on a large scale is bound to demoralize the administration.

The nature of the problem is such as to defy an easy solution. Kautilya, that shrewd observer of human affairs, shows in his *Arthasastra* how difficult it is to catch the corrupt official. He says:

> 'Just as it is impossible not to taste the honey or the poison that finds itself at the tip of the tongue, so it is impossible for a Government servant not to eat up, at least a bit, of the King's revenue. Just as with fish moving in water, it cannot possibly be discerned whether they are drinking water or not, so it is impossible to detect Government servants employed on official duties when helping themselves to money. It is possible to mark the movements of birds flying high up in the sky but it is not possible to ascertain the secret movements of Government servants.'

Kautilya refers to about forty ways of embezzlement: what is realized earlier is entered later; what is realized later is entered earlier, what ought to be realized is not realized; and so on.

Corruption was not a major problem in India until the outbreak of the second world war because the Government mainly confined itself to the maintenance of law and order. But the war radically changed the situation. In the anxiety to achieve victory at any cost, corruption was connived at. So the evil grew and became worse after the attainment of freedom.

The Government of independent India from the very beginning was keen to put down corruption. This will be clear from the adoption of such measures as the Prevention of Corruption Act in 1947, the appointment of a committee two years later to review the working of this Act, and another committee in 1953 to enquire into corruption in railways administration. The establishment of the Administrative Vigilance Division in 1955 and the appointment of the Vivian Bose Commission in 1956 to probe into the working of the Company Law were among the other important steps taken to check corruption. But the canker had entrenched itself deeply into every level of administration that piecemeal measures could not deal with it effectively. The general feeling in the country was that action was being taken only against officials at the lower level and that the top men were allowed to go scot-free. Moreover, against ministers at the Centre and in the States suspected of corruption, the Government was unwilling to adopt a firm policy. This was mainly because Nehru was so loyal to his friends that he overlooked their faults; and even when serious charges were levelled against some of them, he was most reluctant to take swift and strong action. As Brecher says, 'He never thinks ill of an old colleague and rarely believes allegations of corruption. His normal response is to dismiss these charges as gossip or to question the accused directly and accept his denial without further investigation.' In 1956 C.D. Deshmukh, a former Finance Minister, suggested the appointment of an independent tribunal to enquire into corruption in high places. He said he had documentary evidence but he would place it only before an independent tribunal. But Nehru declined to do so. Ultimately, in June 1962, a Committee was set up with K. Santhanam, a Member of Parliament, as chairman, to enquire into all aspects of corruption.

The Committee submitted its report in March 1964. It made a number of important recommendations. But we shall confine ourselves only to those relating to ministers. The Committee observed that integrity in administration and public life could be maintained only if ministers at the Centre and the States set the correct example. 'The problem is difficult and delicate,' said the Committee, and added:

> 'There is a widespread impression that failure of integrity is not uncommon among ministers and that some ministers who have held office during the last sixteen years have enriched themselves illegitimately, obtained good jobs for their sons and relations through nepotism, and have reaped other advantages inconsistent with any notion of purity in public life. The general belief about failure of integrity amongst ministers is as damaging as actual failure. That these ministers have held office in the name of the Indian National Congress, which had evolved the highest notions of personal integrity and service under the inspiration of Mahatma Gandhi, has given rise to an exaggerated view of their failure to maintain high standards of integrity. It is a pity that neither the Congress authorities nor the great leaders who took over the Government of India realized the importance of evolving a suitable machinery and procedure for preventing and dealing with such corruption. We are convinced that ensuring absolute integrity on the part of ministers at the Centre and the States is an indispensable condition for the establishment of a tradition of purity in public services.'

The main recommendation of the Committee was that specific allegations of corruption on the part of a minister at the Centre or a State should be promptly investigated by an agency whose findings would command respect. If a formal allegation was made by any ten members of Parliament or a Legislature in writing addressed to the Prime Minister or Chief Minister, through the Speaker or Chairman, the Prime Minister of Chief Minister should consider himself obliged by convention to refer the allegations for immediate investigation. For this purpose, the Committee suggested the appointment by the President of India of a National Panel from which an *ad hoc* committee might be selected to enquire into the charges.

The Government did not accept the Santhanam Committee's suggestion to constitute a National Panel. But in October 1964 the government drew up a Code of Conduct for Central and State Ministers. The Code is an interesting document. Briefly the Code lays down that a person, before taking office as a Minister, should disclose to the Prime Minister or the Chief Minister, as the case may be, the details of his assets and liabilities and of any business interests of himself and of his family. The prospective minister should also sever his connections with the conduct and management of any business in which he has been interested. Moreover, as long as he remains in office, he should furnish annually to the Prime Minister or the Chief Minister a declaration regarding his assets and liabilities. The Code also lays down instructions regarding the sale and purchase of immovable property, collection of funds for political, charitable or other purposes, acceptance of gifts, and accommodation while on official tour.

The Code, however, is unlikely to be a very effective instrument for the prevention of corruption among ministers. The authority for enforcing the Code is the Prime Minister in the case of Central Ministers, the Prime Minister and the Union Home Minister in the case of Chief Ministers, and the Union Home Minister and the Chief Minister concerned in the case of State Ministers. But, as in the Biren Mitra and Patnaik case, described in the preceding chapter, the Prime Minister and the Home Minister may not always act with firmness and speed because of their understandable anxiety not to do anything, as far as possible, that is likely to damage the reputation of the Congress.

It is also significant that up to the end of March 1965 seven States had not accepted the code. These were Assam, Madras, Mysore, Rajasthan, Jammu and Kashmir, Maharashtra, and Nagaland. One would have thought that on so important a matter like prevention of corruption, all States would promptly endorse the Code with a view to creating confidence among the public. Even at the Centre, no uniform procedure has been laid down for dealing with or determining any alleged breach of this Code. The procedure will depend on the facts and circumstances of each case. But whatever the procedure, it is extremely difficult in a parliamentary democracy like India's to devise a system that will help to eliminate completely corrupt practices on the part of Ministers. Jennings rightly remarks that 'the most elementary qualification demanded of a Minister is honesty and incorruptibility. It is, however, necessary that not only should he possess this qualification but also that he should appear to possess it.' In the final analysis, the only effective remedy lies in an enlightened electorate, an alert Press, and a strong and responsible Opposition.

Too Many Parties

An efficient party system is the sine qua non of a parliamentary democracy. There should be at least two parties, both of them effectively organized and sufficiently strong so as to be able to form the Government when called upon to do so. It is also essential that while the parties may differ from one another on many issues of national and international affairs, they should agree on fundamental principles, especially on the need to protect democracy, to uphold the Rule of Law, to safeguard the independence of the judiciary, and to maintain the liberty of the individual.

But in India the party system has not developed on proper lines. For practical purposes, there are only two parties—the Congress and the Communists. The other parties are hardly of importance so far as the Central Government is concerned. The Congress, of course, has been continuously in office at the Centre ever since the attainment of freedom, and also in all States except Kerala—where for a brief period of twenty-seven months the Communists held power. So long as Nehru lived, the Congress, with all its rivalry and groupism, was able to function as the largest and the most efficient party in the country. The manner in which the Congress tackled the problem of succession after the death of Nehru and Shastri has helped to enhance its reputation; and even if in the next few years its overwhelming majority in the Lok Sabha is reduced to some extent, it will continue to remain the largest political party for a long time to come.

It seems, however, odd and unfortunate indeed that the world's largest democracy has no effective Opposition. Although there are a number of political parties opposed to the Congress there is none which is sufficiently organised so as to be able to function as an alternative government. The Praja Socialist Party was wound up in June 1964 when about a thousand members, including Asoka Mehta, resigned and joined the Congress, while the rest of its members merged themselves with the Socialist Party. But the latter under Lohia's leadership has hardly any influence in all-India politics or even at the regional level. The Swatantra Party, which came into existence in 1960, seems to have created a good impression, but like the Congress, it suffers form a dearth of talent. C. Rajagopalachari, its founder, commands considerable respect throughout the country but, in view of his advancing age—he is now eighty-six—he will be unable to provide effective leadership. Other Swatantra leaders like M.R. Masani and N.G. Ranga are competent parliamentarians but they have yet to acquire all-India status. The Jan Sangh is powerful in certain areas like Rajasthan, but is most unlikely to grow as a responsible opposition because of its rather communal outlook.

The Communists perhaps could have emerged as a powerful Opposition party. But at present they are sharply split into two—the Right Wing and the Left Wing. The differences between the two arose after the Chinese aggression of India in 1962. While the right Communists disapproved of Chinese policy towards India, the Left Communist thought that it was India that had committed aggression against China! But both sections have no firm faith in parliamentary democracy. Both look upon the legislature merely as a convenient instrument with which to capture power, if possible, in course of time. Moreover, neither section fully identifies itself with the interests of India. The Right Communists look up to Moscow for inspiration and instruction and the Left Communists to Peking.

The Left Communist have been even accused of conspiring with China to overthrow the Government of India. Towards the close of 1964, several leading members of the Left Communist Party were arrested; and although some of them were elected to the Kerala Legislative Assembly in the mid-term elections in February 1965, the Government of India declined to release them. The Government's view was that these leader were detailed without trial because they constituted a grave risk to India's security. Nanda, the Union Home Minister, disclosed in the Lok

Sabha on March 12, 1965 that the Left Communists had been instructed by Peking to prepare for a violent revolution in India. The methods suggested included the creation of secret cells, arms dumps and training in guerilla warfare.

The Home Minister also stated that the Left Communists had received 'considerable financial resources' from China and used them for various purposes. Nanda defended their detention without trial on the ground that the country was passing through an Emergency and therefore it was not possible to resort to the normal legal procedure to deal with the Left Communists.

It is difficult to say at this stage how long the Communist Party will continue to remain divided as at present. Some observers point out that the differences between the two groups are not really of a serious nature and that at heart they are inspired by the same ideology. It is stated that the Right Communists fully supported the Left Communists in the elections to the Kerala Assembly in February 1965.[1]

It is thus clear that there is no prospect in the near future of the emergence of a united Opposition. But then is it really necessary for the successful working of democracy? The late K.M. Panikkar said that while a powerful Opposition, capable of providing an alternative government, was undoubtedly desirable in a democratic system, it was by no mans essential. 'What is necessary, he said, 'for a proper functioning of democracy is freedom of criticism, a strong and effective public opinion, a vigilant and independent Press, and a public alive to its rights.' Panikkar was right in saying so but then the Opposition parties tend to become obstructive when they know they have no chance of being entrusted with power.

How deeply the Opposition parties in the Indian Parliament are divided among themselves was illustrated clearly during the historic no-confidence resolution, the first ever brought forward against the Union Cabinet in August 1963. The motion was sponsored by seventy-two members of the Lok Sabha, but it was defeated: 346 members voting against it, sixty-four in favour and twenty-four abstaining. M.R. Masani claimed that although the Opposition did not succeed in getting the resolution passed, it did help to highlight the fact that the Congress did not enjoy as much confidence in the country as the voting seemed to indicate. He said, 'As Achraya Kripalani pointed out a year ago, only 44.72 percent of the electorate voted for the Congress Party in the last general election. It got 361 seats. I have calculated as accurately as I could, in respect of the members who stood up in support of this motion the other day, that the parties, groups, and elements they represent polled in all forty-five million—39 per cent of the electorate in this country. If we had a system of proportional representation such as is common in many democratic countries in the world, it would be not seventy two but 316 as opposed to your 361. Let us realize that nearly 40 per cent of the country is behind this vote of no-confidence and that the position has changed further in the last twelve months. The Chinese attack and our disastrous defeat, the gold control order, the last budget, and rising prices have further shifted public opinion as recent by-election have shown.'

Masani's mathematics may be correct but the fact remains that the Opposition parties themselves do not have much in common. The resolution merely expressed lack of confidence but it did not specifically mention a single reason because, as a commentator observed, 'to accommodate the seventy-two sponsors, seventy-two conflicting reasons would have had to be given.'

Quorum and Decorum

It is not surprising then that the Indian Parliament has not been able to conduct itself as effectively as, for example, the House of Commons. No doubt, as compared to the legislatures in other Asian countries, the record of the Indian Parliament has been commendable; and credit for enhancing its reputation should go largely to Nehru. Of Churchill it was said that 'he loved England with the passionate enthusiasm which Pericles felt for Athens and he trusted the House of Commons as no one else.' That could also be said of Nehru in relation to India and her Parliament.

Nehru was very regular in attending the session of Parliament, and he always treated it with great respect, and zealously tried to maintain and enhance its prestige. How Nehru conducted himself as a parliamentarian was thus described by Sardar Hukum Singh, Speaker of the Lok Sabha, in the course of his tribute to the Late Prime Minister, 'Personally,' said the

Speaker,

> 'it was a pleasure to see Nehru enter the Lok Sabha. Nehru would walk to his seat with elegance. He would give the utmost respect of the Chair. He was the first to rush to the House when the quorum or division bell was rung, provided he was in the precincts of Parliament. He used to follow the discussions carefully. His answers to questions were straight and full of information. He was always eager to give the fullest information and many a time supplemented the answers given by other ministers, if he thought the information was not adequate. He possessed detailed information about the administration and was never hesitant to share it with Parliament. Nehru kept certain standards and had left many wholesome traditions in democracy. It would be difficult to find a greater democrat than Jawaharlal. He could listen to criticism against him with patience and tolerance and could reply without rancour.'

But it is a fact that the Indian Parliament is not in a position to cope with the vast and complicated problems that confront the nation. Elections under adult suffrage have adversely affected the quality of membership.[2] In the Lok Sabha, consisting of about 500 members, there are hardly a dozen who are very well informed on economic matters, and can contribute usefully to the debates on vital issues. The quorum of the Lok Sabha is only fifty but it has always been a difficult task for the Speaker to get this minimum attendance.[3] Even when Nehru made important speeches, the attendance was not more than 200 to 300. The maintenance of discipline has been another delicate problem. Walk-outs on the slightest provocation and a tendency to defy the Chair have been too common. And the inability of a large number of members to understand either English or Hindi impedes seriously the efficient working of Parliament.

On the Prime Minister—A Heavy Responsibility

Indian democracy thus has many serious shortcomings such a inefficiency in administration, glaring economic inequalities, and the absence of an effective and responsible Opposition. But there is no cause for despair about the future of democracy, provided the Congress, as the most powerful organization, sets its house in order and gives the right leadership to the country.

If Congress concentrates its attention on having a clean and efficient administration and provides the people with their elementary necessities like food, clothing and shelter, it will have rendered the greatest service to democracy. The achievement of self-sufficiency in food is, after all, relatively a simple task—it is mainly a matter of effective co-ordination of the various agencies both in the Centre and in the States connected with the development of agriculture. The provision of adequate clothing should not be difficult, considering the fact that our cotton textile industry is the second largest in the world, next only to that of the United States. The problem of housing also is not hard to solve since most of the building materials are available within the country. What is required is that economic policies should be divorced from ideological bias, and they should be implemented with speed and vigour; and a sincere effort should be made to obtain the co-operation of private enterprise which hitherto has been kept at arm's length for political reasons.

The Prime Minister should ensure that the Cabinet works as a well-knit team and that ministers do not speak with different voices, particularly on major issues. The Prime Minister should also avoid the temptation to take important decisions without consulting Cabinet colleagues. Nehru sometimes did so but his position was different. As Byrum E. Carter points out, the practice of some Prime Ministers acting without Cabinet authorization is 'unusual and not without danger' because such action impairs Cabinet unity. He says, 'A Prime Minister who has such proclivities will do well to restrain them. Each incident further intensifies the strain on the thread which holds the Cabinet together, thus endangering its stability and the security of the Prime Minister in his place'. According to Attlee, a Prime Minister to be successful should function through a minister. He explained to his biographer, Francis Williams: 'A Prime Minister ought to keep his hand on the pulse and know how his ministers are doing, of course but he must not interfere and overrule a minister.' Such a policy enabled Attlee to function effectively and at the same time enjoy much leisure. As he said, 'I read the whole of Gibbon when I was Prime Minister just at week-ends or at Chequers. I saw more of my family when I was at Number 10 than ever before or after.'[4]

There should also be closer co-operation between the Cabinet and the Congress Parliamentary Party on the one hand and between the Prime Minister and the Congress President on the other. In recent months there is an increasing tendency on the part of some senior Congress leaders to attack the Government openly either in Parliament or outside. For example, Mrs. Pandit, sister of Nehru, in her maiden speech in the Lok Sabha in March 1965 strongly criticized the Government, and the Prime Minister in particular, for weakness and vacillation in dealing with domestic issues and foreign problems. She described the Prime Minister as 'a prisoner of indecision'. V.K. Krishna Menon also attacked the economic policy of the Government and described the Central budged of 1965-66 as 'a rich man's budget'. Shastri was hurt by these open attacks on his leadership. Addressing a meeting of the Congress Parliamentary Party on April 2, 1965, Shastri said, 'What is happening these days is very painful to me. If we do not realize our responsibilities, we cannot deal with the opposition. In Parliament, in future, we should be more careful. We are passing through critical times,' Shastri added, 'What is this propaganda about indecision? It hurts me. We should not harm the party. The party has been consulted often and we meet usually once a week.' The personal relationship of Shastri and Kamaraj, the Congress President, continued to be quite cordial and the two were able to work together in close co-operation.

The Cabinet system of government under Mrs. Gandhi and her successors may not work exactly as it did under Nehru and Shastri. Changes in the methods of working are bound to take place, depending largely on the personality of the Prime Minister. Even in England, the Cabinet system today works in a somewhat different manner as compared to few years ago. On account of vast changes in the economic and political situation in the post-war period, power has now passed from the House of Commons into the hands of the Prime Minister and the party. The House of Commons seems to have become 'merely a forum for debate between well-disciplined political parties.' As an example of the waning power of the House of commons, we may cite the appointment of Sir Alec Douglas-Home as Britain's Prime Minister. When in November 1963 Harold Macmillan was compelled to give up his Prime Ministership because of ill-health, he advised the Queen to send for Lord Home to form the Government. Lord Home accepted the Queen's invitation and relinquished the earldom. Thereby he ceased to be a member of the House of Lords and, at the same time, he was not a member of the House of Commons. Thus for the first time in history, Britain had for a few days a Prime Minister who was a member neither of the House of Lords nor of the House of Commons.

As R.H.S. Crossman says, in his introduction to Bagehot's *The English Constitution*:

> 'The post-war epoch has seen the transformation of the Cabinet government into Prime Ministerial government. Under this system, the hyphen which joins and the buckle which fastens, the legislative part to the executive part becomes one single man. . . . In so far as ministers feel themselves to be agents of the Premier, the British Cabinet has now come to resemble the American Cabinet.'

Crossman, however, adds that 'the old doctrine of collective Cabinet responsibility is scrupulously maintained and enforced, even though many of the decisions for which members must assume responsibility have been taken above their heads and without their knowledge.'

In India also, whatever changes may take place in the coming years in the Cabinet personnel and procedure, it is clear that it must function strictly on the basis of joint responsibility if the nation is to make any progress. There will be no unity or discipline in the country if the Cabinet remains divided and, worse, makes its dissensions widely known. But collective responsibility is not an easy system to operate, especially in a vast country like India where parliamentary democracy has yet to take firm root. As Jennings says, 'collective responsibility assumes the team spirit of rugby football, or a well-drilled dramatic cast.' Even so, it should not be difficult to work on this principle, provided the electorate chooses leaders of ability and integrity who will always conduct themselves in the best interests of the country.

NOTES

1. The pro-Peking Communists won forty out of the 133 seats in the Kerala Legislative Assembly.

2. In April 1964, H.V. Kamath moved a resolution in the Lok Sabha for prescribing a minimum gratification and an upper age limit for candidates to the Lower Houses of Parliament and State Legislatures. The resolution said that a candidate should not be above seventy-five years of age and should have in the case of the Lok Sabha passed at least a secondary education test and in the case of State Assemblies, a primary education test. The resolution, however, met with stout opposition and was rejected.
3. The Cabinet was put to great embarrassment on April 27, 1964, when the Constitution (Seventeenth Amendment) Bill failed to secure in the Lok Sabha the requisite number of votes at the introduction stage. The Bill sought to allow State Legislature to initiate measures of land reform where difficulty was being experienced as a result of judicial interpretation. Under the law, a constitutional amendment Bill has to be passed at all stages by a majority of the total membership of the Lok Sabha and not less than two-thirds of those present and voting. The Lok Sabha has 510 members and a minimum of 256 votes is required to pass every motion. But when the motion for consideration of the Constitutional (Seventeenth Amendment) Bill was put to the vote, there were only 206 in favour.

   Also consider the following report which appeared in the *Hindu* of June 24, 1964: 'In a speech in Madras on June 23rd, Professor M. Ruthnaswami, a member of the Rajya Sabha, called for a public agitation to ensure greater attendance of Members of Parliament and Ministers in the House. Ruthnaswami said not more than ten or fifteen members of about 200 in the Rajya Sabha were present in the House at a time, while in the Lok Sabha the number averaged thirty to forty out of about 500. He said that the members' lack of interest in the proceedings of the House was depressing.'
4. Consider, in this context, Shastri's remarks at a meeting in New Delhi on March 20, 1965. He said the he had read a large number of books on various subjects while in jail, but in recent years he had hardly any time for reading. Turning to a Member of Parliament who belonged to an Opposition party the Prime Minister said, 'perhaps I will find time for reading if his party comes into power.' The M.P. said, amidst laughter, 'I will then put you into jail.'

5

Quintessence of the Constitution

Before we study the working of the Cabinet, it will be worthwhile to analyse briefly the nature of the Indian Constitution and its main provisions. We have seen how parliamentary institutions came to be established in India after the advent of the British rule, and how Indian leaders enthusiastically adapted themselves to the new type of Government. It was therefore a relatively easy task for them to prepare a constitution for their own country. The Constituent Assembly completed this task in about three years and the Constitution came into force on January 26, 1950.[1] Some idea of the enormous labour that went into its making will be clear from the fact that it consisted of 251 pages, 395 Articles, twenty-two Chapters and eight Schedules. It is a cosmopolitan Constitution in the sense that it incorporates certain aspects from the Constitutions of almost all the important countries of the world particularly from Britain, the USA, Eire and the Dominions. Above all, it has drawn heavily from the Government of India Act, 1935.

The Preamble to the Constitution proclaims India to be a Sovereign Democratic Republic. It makes it clear that the power of the Government is derived solely from the people of India and it promises to secure for them social economic and political justice; liberty of thought, expression, belief, faith and worship; equality of status and of opportunity; and to promote fraternity, assuring the dignity of the individual and the unity of the nation.

The Constitution has enumerated in detail the Fundamental Rights of the citizens. There rights include equality before the law; prohibition of discrimination on grounds of religion, race, caste, sex or place of birth; equality of opportunity in public employment; abolition of untouchability; protection of certain rights regarding freedom of speech as well as of life and personal liberty; prohibition of traffic in human beings, forced labour and employment of children in factories; right to freedom of religion; cultural and educational rights; right to property; and right to constitutional remedies. The Fundamental Rights have been included in the Constitution to protect the citizen against arbitrary action and discriminatory treatment by Government. The rights are enforceable in the courts; and the law-making authorities at the Centre and in the States are forbidden to enact measures in violation of these rights. But during times of national emergency, the rights may be suspended under the Constitution.

'Directive Principles of State Policy' are a unique feature of the Indian Constitution. These are not enforceable by any court. Nevertheless, they are, in the words of the Constitution, 'fundamental in the governance of the country and it shall be the duty of the State to apply these principles in making laws.'

The Directive Principles enjoin the State to promote the people's welfare by securing for them adequate means of livelihood, by equitable distribution of the ownership and control of the material resources, by preventing concentration of wealth and means of production to the common detriment, and by ensuring equal pay for equal work for women and men. Special care is to be taken to protect the interests of the weaker sections of the population particularly those of the Scheduled castes and Scheduled tribes. Further, the State shall endeavour to raise the level of nutrition and the standard of living of its people, and to bring about prohibition of the consumption, except for medicinal purposes, of intoxicating drinks and of drugs injurious to health. Finally, the State is called upon to promote international peace and security, maintain just and honourable relations between nations, foster respect for international law and treaty organisations, and encourage settlement of international disputes by arbitration. The incorporation of these Directive Principles has been criticized as being superfluous, ineffective and theoretical because nobody can compel the Government to observe them. Although this criticism may seem valid to some extent, it must be admitted that these principles do serve a useful purpose by setting forth laudable ideals to which no responsible Government can afford to remain indifferent.

The Government of India is a federation although this term is not used in the Constitution. The Constituent Assembly preferred the name 'the Indian Union' so as to emphasize the fundamental unity of the country. The powers have been distributed in such a way as to provide for a strong Centre. The subjects assigned to the Centre are indicated in the Union List consisting of seventy-seven items, the more important of them being defence, foreign affairs, currency coinage, foreign trade, railways, posts and telegraphs, ports and airways, industries the control of which by the Union is declared by Parliament to be expedient in public interest, regulation of oil fields and mineral resources, organization of the Supreme Court and the High Courts and inter-State migration. The State List contains sixty-six items including public order, police, administration of justice, prisons, constitution and powers of municipal corporations, public health and sanitation, education, agriculture, land revenue, forests, fisheries and industries not controlled by the Centre. The concurrent list consists of forty-seven subjects including criminal law, preventive detention, marriage and divorce, civil procedure, economic and social planning, trade unions, social security, price control, factories, electricity, newspapers, books and printing presses. The Constitution also provides that, in the national international interest, a subject in the State List can transferred to the Union List for a period not exceeding one year provided the Rajya Sabha by a two-thirds majority approves of the proposal. A subject can also be shifted to the Concurrent List by a special procedure requiring the consent of legislatures of half the number of States. On subjects in the Concurrent List, both the Centre and States. Can legislate but the Central law can override that of the State in case of inconsistency. It will be thus seen that the Constitution has vested vast powers in the Centre, and the exigencies of planning in the last fifteen years have enormously strengthened it further.

The Indian Constitution is a flexible one. But being a written Constitution it is not as flexible as that of Britain. Nor has it the rigidity of the American Constitution. The flexibility of the Indian Constitution is seen in the fact that till now it has been amended nearly twenty times.[2] The procedure for amendment is rather simple. An amendment can be initiated by introducing a bill for the purpose in either House of Parliament, and the amendment becomes law I passed in each House by a majority of the total membership of that House and by a majority of not less than two-thirds of that House present and voting; and it becomes valid after receiving the President's assent. But the amendment requires ratification by the legislatures of States in certain cases as for instance. When changes are contemplated in the procedure for the election of the President or representation of States in Parliament. The Constitution is also flexible in another sense, namely, that in an emergency it can be converted almost into a unitary State with the President assuming extraordinary powers under Article 352.

The Union Executive

The executive power of the Indian Union is vested in the President and is exercised by him through the council of Ministers. Here is suffices to note that the Constitution provides for the parliamentary type of government chiefly on the model of Britain. The Council of Ministers consists of Ministers who are members of the Cabinet, Ministers of State who are not members of the Cabinet but hold Cabinet rank, the Deputy Ministers. The Council as such rarely meets. It is the Cabinet that meets frequently to decide policy matters.

The principal departments of the Government of India at present[3] are External Affairs, Home Affairs, Finance, Railways, Defence, Food and Agriculture, Steel and Mines, Education, Labour and Employment, Rehabilitation, Information and Broadcasting, Law, Petroleum and Chemicals, and Parliamentary Affairs and Communications. Each of these departments is under a Cabinet Minister assisted, in some cases, by a Minister of State and a Deputy Minister. Some subjects like commerce, Industry and Heavy Engineering, Health, and Irrigation and Power are in independent charge of Ministers of State. As regards Deputy Ministers, their main function is to assist the Ministers concerned both in Parliament and outside.[4] The Secretary is the administrative head of the Ministry. He is the chief adviser to the Minister. A Ministry has several divisions, branches and sections in charge of Deputy Secretaries, Under Secretaries and

Section Officers respectively. To ensure the smooth functioning of the administration, the Constitution empowers the President, on the advice of the Prime Minister, to make rules and to allocate the subjects among ministers.

Parliament

The Indian Parliament is bicameral, consisting of the Lok Sabha or the Lower House, and the Rajya Sabha or the Upper House. The Lok Sabha represents the people and the Rajya Sabha the States. In ordinary law-making, the two Houses enjoy coequal power and in cases of disagreement between them, the President of the Republic is empowered to call a joint meeting. The question on which there is disagreement will be decided by a majority of members present and voting.

The Lok Sabha is more important, more powerful and more popular than the Rajya Sabha. The Lok Sabha consists of not more than 500 members elected directly by adult suffrage, all citizens of twenty-one years and above being entitled to vote, provided they are not otherwise disqualified. Provision is made for the reservation of seats for the Scheduled castes and Scheduled tribes and for the nomination of two representatives of the Anglo-Indian community. A member of the Lok Sabha must be an Indian citizen and not below twenty-five years of age. The duration of the Lok Sabha is five years. It has the right to elect its chairman, called the Speakers, whose status and powers are more or less similar to those of the Speaker of the House of Commons.

The Lok Sabha is empowered to legislate on all subjects in the Union List as well as on those in the Concurrent List. It controls the executive by putting interpellation, by adjournment motions, by resolutions of no-confidence and, above all, by its power over the purse. All money bills originate only in the Lower House, a money bill being defined as one dealing with the imposition, abolition, remission, alteration or regulation of any tax; the regulation of the borrowing of money; the custody of the consolidated fund or the contingency fund and the appropriation of moneys out of such fund. And in case of a dispute as to whether a Bill is a Money Bill or not, the decision of the Speaker is final. After a money bill is passed by the Lok Sabha, it shall be transmitted to the Rajya Sabha. The latter shall return it with its recommendations within a fortnight, and the

Lok Sabha may or may not accept them. The bill is then presented to the President for his assent.

The Lok Sabha has a number of committees to facilitate its work such as the Public Accounts Committee, Estimates Committee, Select Committees, Committee on Privileges, Rules Committee and Committee on Government Assurances. The Public Accounts Committee scrutinizes the expenditure of the different department of the Government and reports to the House how far the public funds are utilized in accordance with the budgetary provisions. The Estimates Committee examines the working of the various ministries and suggests measures to ensure economy and improve efficiency. Select Committees are set up whenever the House feels that certain legislative measures need detailed study. The Committee on Privileges deals with case referred to it relating to breach of privilege. The Rules Committee ensures that the rules for the conduct of the business of the House work smoothly and suggests amendments to them if necessary, while the committee on Assurances takes steps to see that the promises made by ministers are carried out in a reasonable time.

The Rajya Sabha is the Upper House. It consists of not more than 250 members. Of these, twelve are nominated by the President from among those with special knowledge or of practical experience in literature, science art and social services. The rest are chosen by the elected members of the Legislative Assemblies of States in accordance with the system of proportional representation by means of the single transferable vote. The Vice-President of the Indian Republic who is the ex-officio Chairman of the Rajya Sabha, presides over its meetings and in his absence, the Deputy Chairman, elected by the members from among themselves, takes the Chair.

The Rajya Sabha is never dissolved but one-third of its members retire every two years. A candidate for membership should be a citizen of India above thirty-five years of age. The Rajya Sabha can also control the Cabinet by means of questions, adjournment motions, and critical speeches, but it cannot remove the ministers by a vote of censure. It can initiate any bill except a money bill, and its consent is essential for other bills to become law.

However, if the Rajya Sabha declines within six months to pass bill sent up by the Lok Sabha, it will become law as passed by the Lower House. The Rajya Sabha can also amend a money bill with the concurrence of the Lok Sabha. But if the Rajya Sabha does not give its assent to a money bill passed by the Lok Sabha within fourteen days of its reference to the Rajya Sabha, it will be deemed to have been passed in the it deemed to have been passed in the form in which it was adopted by the Lower House.

Finally, we should refer to another important power vested in the Indian Parliament. Unlike many other federations. Parliament in India is empowered, under Article 3 of the Constitution, to form a new State by separation of territory from any State or uniting two or more State or parts of States or by uniting any territory to a part of any State; increase or decrease the area of any State; alter the boundaries of any State; and alter the name of any State. In bringing about these changes, the legislatures concerned have the right only to an expression of view on the proposals.

State Governments

So far as State are concerned, there are at present sixteen of them namely, Andhra Pradesh, Assam, Bihar, Gujarat, Jammu and Kashmir, Kerala, Madhya, Pradesh, Madras, Maharashtra, Mysore, Nagaland, Orissa, Punjab, Rajasthan, Uttar Pradesh and West Bengal.[5] It is important to note that many States are far bigger in area and population than some independent countries of Europe. For example, the Uttar Pradesh has an area of 1,13,654 square miles and a population of fifty-four million, Madhya Pradesh has 1,71,217 square miles and a population of thirty-two million and Andhra Pradesh has 1,06,286 square miles and a population of thirty-six million. The States enjoy a good deal of autonomy in the spheres allotted to them by the Constitution but, as pointed out earlier, in practice their powers have been to some extent whittled down on account of the exigencies of defence and development.

The executive power in the State is vested in the Governor. Unlike the Unlike the USA where the State Governor is elected by the people, in India he is appointed by the President on the advice of the Union Cabinet. The governor shall be a citizen of

India, above thirty-five years and he shall not be a member of either House of Parliament or the State Legislature; nor shall he hold any other office of profit. He remains in office during the pleasure of the President and normally his tenure is five years.

The Governor is the Constitutional Head of the State. He is provide with a Council of Ministers, with the Chief Member at the head, to advise him in the exercise of his functions except where he is required by the Constitution to act in his discretion.[6] The leader of the majority party in the Lower House of the State Legislature is appointed as Chief Minister by the Governor, and the other ministers are appointed on the advice of the Chief Minister. The Chief Minister is enjoined to communicate to the Governor all decisions of the Council of Ministers relating to the administration of the affairs of the State and proposal of legislation; and to furnish such other information as the Governor may call for. The Governor may also submit for the consideration of the Cabinet any matter on which a decision has been taken by a Minister but which has not yet been considered by the Cabinet.

The Governor has certain legislature powers also. Laws passed by the Legislative become valid only after his assent. He is empowered to withhold his assent to a bill, to reserve it for the President's consideration or return the bill to the Legislature for reconsideration. The governor also can issue Ordinances when the Legislature is not in session and immediate action is called for. He may address the Legislature either separately or jointly. He may send messages to the Legislature whether in respect of a bill pending before it or otherwise.

As regards financial powers, the Constitution provides that the Governor shall in respect of every financial year cause to be laid before the Legislature a statement of the estimated receipts and expenditure of the State for that year. No demand for a grant shall be made except on his recommendation.

The judicial powers of the Governor consists of the right to grant pardons, reprieves, respites or remissions of punishment to any person convicted of any offence against any law relating to a matter under the jurisdiction of the State Government.

Every State is provided with Legislative Assembly. Some States have two Houses—the Legislative Assembly and

Legislative Council.[7] The Assembly is more popular and powerful. Members of the Assembly are chosen by direct election on the basis of adult suffrage, but a certain number of seats is reserved for Scheduled castes and Scheduled tribes as well as for Anglo Indians. Normally the duration of the Assembly is five years. The Assembly elects its own Speaker and Deputy Speaker. The strength of the Assembly shall not be more than 500 and not less than sixty.

The Legislative Council is a permanent body not subject to dissolution. One-third of its members retire every two years. The Constitution provides that the Council's strength shall not exceed one-fourth of the total number of members of the Legislative Assembly of the State, but in no case it shall be less than forty. Of the total number of members of the Council, (a) as nearly as one-third is elected by municipalities, district boards and such other local bodies; (b) one-twelfth is to be elected by those who have been for at least three years graduates of an Indian university or its equivalent; (c) one-twelfth by persons who have been at least for three years engaged in teaching in schools not below the secondary standard; (d) one-third to be elected by the Assembly from among persons who are not members of the Assembly; and (e) the rest will be nominated by the Governor from among persons with special knowledge or practical experience in literature, science, art, the co-operative movement and social service. Members are elected in accordance with the system of proportional representation with the single transferable vote.

The State Cabinets are collectively responsible to the Lower House of the Legislature. They remain in office so long as they enjoy its confidence. The Ministers are in charge of one or more departments and jointly they formulate the policy of the State Government. The Cabinet procedure in the States is more or less the same as at the Centre.[8] But the strength of the Cabinet varies form State to State.[9] In some States, in addition to Cabinet Ministers, there are Ministers of State and Deputy Ministers.

Zonal Councils

A number of States has been grouped together into zones under the States Reorganization Act of 1956. There are at present five zones—the Northern Zone with the Punjab, Rajasthan,

Jammu and Kashmir, Delhi and Himachal Pradesh; the Central Zone with Uttar Pradesh and Madhya Pradesh; the Eastern Zone with Bihar, Orissa, West Bengal, Assam, Manipur and Tripura; the Western zone with Gujarat, Maharashtra and Mysore, and the Southern Zone with Andhra Pradesh, Madras and Kerala.

The zonal council consists of a Minister of the Government of India nominated by the President, the Chief Minister of the State concerned and two ministers nominated by the State Governors. The Minister nominated by the President is the Chairman of the zonal council.

The zonal council have been formed to serve as forum to bring about closer co-operation among the States, to settle inter-States disputes and to formulate inter-State development schemes. The councils take decisions by majority vote, the Chairman having a casting vote. Sometimes, two or more zonal councils may hold join meetings. Each council has also a Secretariat to carry out its work.[10]

The Judiciary

The Indian Constitution provides for a Supreme Court with a Chief Justice and a number of other judges, all of who are appointed by the President. The Supreme Court has exclusive jurisdiction in disputes between the Government of India and the States and between the States themselves. The Court has appellate jurisdiction in civil and criminal cases and the power to sanction special leave to appeal from any judgement, decree or order passed by any court in the country. The Court also issues directives, orders or writs for the enforcement of Fundamental Rights. The law declared by the Supreme Court is binding on all courts in India. Besides, the Supreme court may advise the President on such questions of law or fact as may be referred to it by him. Above all, the Court has the power to nullify the acts of Parliament and State Legislations on the ground that such laws violate the Constitution. Thus the Supreme Court plays a crucial role in Indian democracy by acting as the guardian of the Constitution and protector of the people's fundamental rights.

The judiciary in the States consists of a High Court and other subordinate courts. The High Court has Chief Justice and other judges whose number is fixed form time to time by the President. The High Courts are the highest courts of appeal in civil and criminal matters in the States. The High courts in Bombay, Madras and Calcutta have both original and appellate jurisdiction.

These then are the main features of the Indian Constitution. How it has been working in the last sixteen years will be evident form the manner in which the Central Cabinet has been carrying on the administration of the country.

NOTES

1. The Constituent Assembly held its inaugural session on December 7, 1946 and completed its task on November 26, 1949. But the Assembly continued to function as Parliament until the first general election was held in 1952.
2. The Statesman of Calcutta, in an editorial in January 1965, observed: 'The Constitution has been amended on an average more than once a year; hardly an impressive record, especially when so many of the amendments have tended to deprive the ordinary citizen of existing rights and safeguards rather than, as in the American Constitution, to confer new rights.'
3. This was the position under Shastri's premiership. For the distribution of portfolios under Mrs. Gandhi see appendix.
4. A.K. Chanda writes in Indian Administration: 'Some Ministers make extensive use of Deputy Ministers, delegating most of the functions to them; others do not, allowing the Deputy Ministers merely to handle minor parliamentary work such as answering questions. Neither of these arrangements seems appropriate, and a *modus vivendi* has to be found, which will give the Deputy Ministers necessary experience without retarding government business or irritating the permanent officials.
5. In addition there are nine Union Territories, namely, Andaman and Nicobar Islands, Delhi, Himachal Pradesh, Laccadive Minicoy and Amindivi Islands, Manipur, Tripura, Dadra and Nagar Haveli, Goa, Daman and Diu and Pondicherry.
6. But only in Assam the Governor is empowered to act in his discretion in regard to the administration of frontier areas. In other States, the Governors do not have to act in their discretion.
7. The States with bicameral legislature are Bihar, Maharashtra, Madras, Punjab, Uttar Pradesh, West Bengal, Andhra Pradesh, Mysore, Madhya Pradesh, and Jammu and Kashmir.
8. This aspect has been dealt with in chapter IV.

9. This has been discussed in detail in chapter IX.
10. In practice, the activity of the zonal councils depends largely on the personality of the Union Home Minister. As the *Statesman* of Calcutta remarked in an editorial in January 1965, 'The zonal councils, heralded with some fanfare, are kept longer in mothballs than out, and even when they are convened., are mostly called upon to deal with relatively minor matters. Pandit Pant, when Home Minister, took the councils seriously, and had interesting ideas about them. But these died with him. To Mr Shastri's temperament the councils were a gift; but if he used them to evolve a consensus on many problems the country did not hear about it. Mr Nanda has yet to show what his intentions are. So if Mr Kamaraj wishes to put the zonal idea to work, he has many precedents to ignore.'

6

Basic Principles

If the division of power is the basis of civilised government, a constitution is the best device by which such division could be facilitated. Constitutionalism is an achievement of the modern world. But it is a comparatively recent achievement. As such, it has not become fully stabilised. Meanwhile, every constitution aims to build up a governmental structure based upon certain basic principles. And these principles are more or less well - established. Although some of these principles are common to most constitutions, there are other which vary from constitution to constitution. Such variations are the product of the varying conditions and circumstances that determine the principles of the constitution. The Constitution of India is not an exception to this rule and it has its own basic principles. We shall, therefore, begin by a study of the basic principles of the constitution, which form the foundations of democratic government in India.

A careful study of the Constitution will show that there are at least six basic principles which are embodied in it and which form the foundations of democracy in India. These are: (1) popular sovereignty, (2) fundamental rights, (3) directive principles of State policy, (4) judicial independence, (5) federalism and (6) cabinet government. We may examine briefly the scope of each of these principles.

Popular Sovereignty

The Constitution proclaims the sovereignty of the people in its opening words. The preamble begins with the words, "We the people of India, having solemnly resolved to constitute India into a sovereign democratic republic". The idea is reaffirmed in several places in the Constitution, particularly in the chapter dealing with elections. Article 326 declares that "the elections to the House of People and to the Legislative Assembly of every State shall by on the basis of adult suffrage". As a result, the Government at the Centre and in the State derive their authority from the people who choose their representatives for Parliament and the State Legislatures at regular intervals. Further, those who wield the executive power of the government are responsible to the legislature and through them to the people. Thus, in the affairs of the State, it is the will of the people that prevails ultimately and not the will of a few selfish individuals. This is the principle of popular sovereignty.

There have been kings, revolutions, constitutions and vast bureaucracies since time immemorial. But the idea of adult suffrage and the common man as elector are of very recent origin. To Aristotle the ideal from of democracy meant that the vital decisions affecting the community made by the assembly of the whole citizenry in the market place. Today, it means that every adult citizen—men and women alike-goes to the polling booth and casts his or her vote in favour of those who in his opinion are the best persons to represent him in the management of the affairs of his Government. Elections are not the only possible method for securing representatives. But they are considered the most democratic method. They are democratic because every adult citizen gets a chance at regular intervals to participate in the selection of those who will rule over him. It is impossible, therefore, to over-emphasise the importance of free popular elections to ensure a democratic government based upon the consent of the governed.

In spite of the ignorance and illiteracy of large sections of the Indian people, the Constituent Assembly adopted the principle of adult franchise with faith in the common man and the ultimate success of democratic rule. The Assembly was of the opinion that democratic Government on the basis of adult suffrage would alone "bring enlightenment and promote well-being, the standard of life, the comfort and decent living of the common man".

The principle of popular sovereignty has not been a mere ideal embodied in the Constitution but has been a living reality during the last decade during which the Constitution has been in operation. The two general elections the country has had so far (1951-52 and 1957) have demonstrated that the illiterate and presumably ignorant masses of India are not altogether incapable of independently exercising the right of franchise. In fact, this precious right in their hands, which ensures the democratic ideal of "one man, one vote, one value", irrespective of his wealth, education, social status and "importance", has, in fact, enhanced their self-respect as citizens of a democratic India. It has instilled in them the belief that they are no more "hewers of wood and drawers of water", but are important enough as members of a vast new human society engaged in the great cooperative enterprise of building up a new nation. The awareness that the strength of the State is the aggregate strength of its individual citizens is fast dawning upon them. They are also fast realising that suffrage is the link that binds, in a bond of mutual interest and responsibility, the fortunes of the citizens to the fortunes of the State. It is this realisation and its increasing impact in successive elections in the future that will prove the strongest and the most enduring base on which the super-structure of democratic government in India is to flourish.

Free elections, are, perhaps, the greatest forum of mass education. The dangers inherent in adult suffrage among an illiterate people can be mitigated only by the blessings of universal education. In a country like India, eighty percent of whose population is illiterate, the attainment of universal education is a goal still a long way off. But this need not necessarily mean that until a certain minimum standard of universal education is realised, the Indian masses are incapable of properly exercising their right of franchise. Illiteracy is not quite the same thing as ignorance. A free election, which ensures the free exchange of ideas and free canvassing by contending parties who stand for differing programmes of social organisation for the realisation of the common welfare, offers the best medium for the political education of the illiterate masses. It is this that the Constitution guarantees. The constitution-makers were not satisfied by merely providing for adult suffrage. They wanted to ensure free elections by creating an independent constitutional authority to be in charge of everything connected with elections. Free election is a reality in India. It ensures for the electors both freedom of choice and the secrecy of the ballot. The two general election have demonstrated that the ordinary man, in spite of his so-called ignorance, has been able to exercise his robust commosense in electing candidates of his choice. Neither money nor social status nor official position has been powerful enough to make him a convenient tool in the hands of self-seeking politicians. This perhaps is the surest and the most welcome guarantee that popular sovereignty will remain a living reality in India despite the fact that most of its people are steeped in ignorance, poverty and social backwardness.

Fundamental Rights

Discussing the implications of democracy in his, *Liberty* in the Modern State, Harold Laski says, that, first, it involves a frame of government in which men are given the chance of making the government under which they live, at stated intervals. We have seen above how this principle is safeguarded under the Constitution. Secondly, he says, it involves the securing to the citizens certain fundamental human rights and the maintenance of those rights by the separation of the judicial form the executive powers. Thirdly, it involves the bringing into existence of a Bill of Rights for safeguarding the fundamental human rights, such as freedom of speech, protection from arbitrary arrest and the like. According to Laski, the supremacy of the "rule of law" is essential for the working of a democracy. Only where the rule of law prevails, true democracy can function and the success or failure of a democracy depends largely on the extent to which civil liberties are enjoyed by the citizens in general.

Liberty, however, is not an easy word to define. "The world has never had a good definition of the word liberty." Said Abraham Lincoln on 18, Aril 1864, soon after the American civil war on the question of slavery, "and the American people just now, are much in want of one. We all declare for liberty; but in using the same word we do not all mean the same thing. With some the word liberty may mean for each man to do as he pleases with himself, and the product of his labour; while with others the same word may mean for some men to do as they please with other men, and the product of other men's labour. Here are two, not only different, but incompatible things, called by the same name, liberty. And it follows that each of the things is, by the respective parties, called by two different and incompatible names—liberty and tyranny."

Genuine democracy must forever guard against the temptation to transform itself into a system under which the ruling majority claims infallibility for itself. While democracy requires that the will of the people limit the freedom of the Government, it also requires that the freedom of the popular will be limited. A popular will not so limited becomes the tyranny of the majority which destroys the freedom of political competition and thus uses the powers of the government to entrench itself permanently in the seat of power and to prevent a new majority form forming. Further, it will tend to think and act as if it will provide the ultimate standard of thought and action and there is no higher law to limit its freedom. As Laski has put it, "If in any State there is a body of men who possess unlimited political power, those over whom they rule can never be free." The emergence of such a state of affairs will result in the disappearance of certain vital characteristics of democracy, the spirit of questioning and individual initiative. Their place will be taken up by unquestioned submissiveness and conformity, the most distinguishing characteristics of a totalitarian system. This is perhaps the most serious danger inherent in the dynamics of modern democracy which is to be strongly guarded against.

There are two possible alternative safeguards which a constitution can provide to remedy the situation. First, it can guarantee certain basic rights to the individual citizen against all encroachment by the State. Secondly, it may so divide the powers of the State and entrust them to separate agencies that no body of men possesses unlimited power. The Constitution of India has chosen the first alternative and tries to achieve the objective by embodying in it a set of fundamental rights and guaranteeing them through an independent judiciary. These rights impose limitations both on legislative and executive powers. On the one hand, the legislature is prohibited from passing certain laws which would curtail the individual's freedom. On the other, the executive is compelled to adhere to certain formalities and procedures when it deals with the citizens. Thus, in an attempt to secure fundamental freedoms, the Constitution delimits the respective spheres of activity of the State and the individual and erects a wall, as it were, between the government and the people.

The Constitution affirms the basic principle that every individual is entitled to enjoy certain rights as a human being and the enjoyment of such rights does not depend upon the will of any majority or minority. No majority has the right to abrogate such rights. In fact, the legitimacy of the majority to rule is derived form the existence of these rights. These rights include all the basic liberties such as freedom of speech, movement and association, equality before law and equal protection of laws, freedom of religious belief, and cultural and educational freedoms. The Constitution has classified these rights into seven categories and one of them is the right to constitutional remedies which entitles every aggrieved person to approach even the Supreme Court of India to restore to him any fundamental right that may have been violated.

It is, thus a basic affirmation of the Constitution that the political system that it establishes should provide conditions favourable for the maximum development of the individual's personality. The framers of the Constitution were conscious of the fact that in the absence of the enjoyment of the above-mentioned rights, such development of the personality was impossible and democracy would sound an empty word. Having spent most of their lives under a foreign rule and having fought relentlessly for the enjoyment of these rights by themselves, it was only natural that they should have wanted to embody them in the Constitution they framed for the establishment of a democratic political order. They hoped to build this political order on the firm foundation of the freedom of political competition. The prime importance of these rights if that while the will of the majority decides how these freedoms are to be implemented, the existence of the freedoms themselves is not subject to that will. On the contrary, these freedoms set the conditions under which the will of the majority is to be formed and exercised. They establish the framework of "democratic legitimacy" for the rule of the majority.

It must be stressed, however, that the fundamental freedoms guaranteed to the individual under the Constitution are not absolute. Individual rights, however basic they are, cannot override national security and general welfare. For, in the absence of national security and general welfare, individual rights themselves are not secure. Freedom of speech does not mean freedom to abuse another; freedom of movement does not mean freedom of physical attack on others. The Constitution has made express provisions dealing with such limitations of fundamental rights so that those who seek to enjoy the rights may also realise the obligations attending them.

Directive Principles

The wall of separation which the fundamental rights erect between the government and the people is indeed one of the greatest and surest safeguards of the life, liberty and the pursuit of happiness of the individual. But conditions of absolute and unhindered growth of private power, like absolute governmental power, are capable of destroying individual freedom. Concentration of private power, mainly in the form of economic controls, in the hands of a few individuals is equally destructive of the dynamic qualities of a democratic society as a dictatorial government could be. In a highly capitalist society, a few giants in the industrial and financial world, who concentrate in themselves the bulk of economic power, can easily subject the rest of the community to the travails of a new feudalistic order. After having provided against the emergence of a totalitarian system through the constitutional guarantees of fundamental rights, the framers turned their attention to deal with the possible future menace of a private capitalist concentration of economic power and to ensure the establishment and sustenance of a society which provided for the diffusion of economic power among the different sections of the people. The methods they sought to provide for the purpose are embodied in the chapter on Directive Principles of State Policy, which embodies another Basic Principle of the Constitution.

Writing about post-war constitutions which are estimated to number over fifty, a thoughtful critic has observed:

> "Liberty the constitutions could and did promise, but not bread and the modicum of economic security the little man yearns for. To him it is the plain and unadorned truth that the political decisions which are vital for the well-being of all no longer occur within the frame of the constitution. The social forces move and battle extra-constitutionally, because the constitutions did not even attempt the required solutions."

Critics of the Constitution of India cannot accuse the framers of any lack of awareness of this problem or of not attempting to provide solutions for it.

While many of the older constitutions including that of the United States adopted the second method, namely the separation of powers for avoiding the evil and largely failed in their attempt, the Constitution of India adopts a different method, following the example of the Constitution of the Irish Republic. According to this method, the State and every one of its agencies are commanded to follow certain fundamental principles while they frame their policies regarding the various fields of state activity. These principles, on the one hand, are assurances to the people as to what they can expect from the State and, on the other, are directives to the Government, Central and State, to establish and maintain a new "social order in which justice, social, economic and political, shall inform all the institutions of national life."

(a) that the citizens, men and women equally, have the right to an adequate means of livelihood;

(b) that the ownership and control of the material resources of the community are so distributed as best to subserve the common good;

(c) that the operation of the economic system does not result in the concentration of wealth and the means of production to the common detriment;

(d) that there is equal pay for equal work for both men and women;

(e) that the health and strength of workers, men and women, and the tender age of children are not abused and that citizens are not forced by economic necessity to enter avocations unsuited to their age or strength;

(f) that childhood and youth are protected against exploitation and against moral and material abandonment.

In short, these and other Directive Principles form a new Magna Carta, a charter of economic freedoms, to the under-privileged, ordinary man in Indian society.

Speaking about the value of their inclusion in the Constitution, Ambedkar said in the Constituent Assembly:

"The Draft Constitution as framed only provides a machinery for the government of the country. It is not a contrivance to install any particular party in power, as has been done in some countries. Who should be in power is left to be determined by the people, as it must be, if the system is to satisfy the tests of democracy. But whoever captures power will not be free to do what the likes with it. In the exercise of it, he will have to respect these instruments of instructions which are called Directive Principles. He cannot ignore them. He may not have to answer for their breach in a Court of Law. But he will certainly have to answer for them before the electorate at election time. What great value these directive principles possess will be realized better when the forces of right contrive to capture power."

Judicial independence

"Justice is the end of government," said *The Federalist*. "It ever has been and ever will be pursued until it be obtained, or until liberty is lost in the pursuit." No wonder, therefore, if justice has been often characterised as the primary, or even the only *ideal* purpose of government.

The judicial function is indeed a delicate and difficult one. It involves the process of deciding what is just in a controversy between two or more contending parties. If the parties have no confidence in the impartiality of the judiciary, justice becomes an empty word. Man's long struggle has been to live under a government of laws, not of men. Equal justice under law has for long been his cherished ideal a system under which the same law is applicable to all alike. Man has in all ages been striving to escape the regime that dispenses justice according to the political or religious ideology of the litigant or the whim or caprice of those who run the Government. As a consequence of this struggle, there was established a principle of abiding value, that no judiciary can be impartial unless it is independent. In fact, the judicial process ceases to be judicial the moment those who seek to judge cease to be independent of every form of external influence. Hence the importance of judicial independence.

As Lord Hewart has pointed out, the independence of the judiciary is essential because many of the significant victories for freedom and justice have been won in the law courts and the liberties of the citizen are closely bound up with complete independence of the judges. Obviously, the men who are to administer justice in the courts, the methods by which they are to be chosen, the way in which they are to perform their function, the terms upon which they shall hold power, these and their related problems become inseparably bound up with the ideal of judicial independence. Judicial independence acts as a safeguard, not merely against the manipulations of the law for political purposes at the behest of the government in power, but also against the corruption of judicial organs of the State by bribery and intimidation by powerful outside interests which threaten the impartial administration of justice from time to time.

The framers of Constitution were aware that democratic freedoms, were meaningless in the absence of an independent machinery to safeguard them. No subordinate or agent of the Government could be trusted to be just and impartial in judging the merits of a conflict in which the government itself was a party. Similarly, a judiciary subordinate either to the Centre or the States could not be trusted as an impartial arbiter of conflicts and controversies between the Centre and the States. These were the compelling reasons for the creation of an independent judiciary as an integral part of the Constitution and for the adoption of judicial independence as a basic principle of the Constitution.

In its bid to establish complete independence of the judiciary, the Constitution has first erected a wall of separation between the executive and the judiciary. After effecting such separation, it has created conditions that are conducive to making the judiciary independent. Thus, rigid qualifications are laid down for the appointment of judges and provision has been made for compulsory consultation of the Chief Justice of Indian in the appointment of every judge of the Supreme Court and the High courts. The Judges are appointed almost for life and their conditions of service cannot be altered to their disadvantage, once they are appointed. They are given high salaries and their conduct is made a subject beyond the scope of discussion in the legislature. They can be removed from office only for proved misbehaviour. For this purpose, both the Houses of Parliament will have to pass resolutions against a judge supported by a two-third majority of those who sit and vote and at least an absolute majority of the total membership of the House.

The judiciary in India, even under the British rule, was noted for its integrity and independence. Under the Constitution, its position has been made doubly secure so that it can become in reality the most impartial arbiter of the conflicts and controversies which fall within its jurisdiction. Anyone can approach it to secure the restoration of a fundamental right whenever it is violated. Even a casual analysis of the hundreds of decisions which the Supreme Court and the High Courts have giver so far will easily prove that the judiciary in India is working in a spirit of impartiality and in an atmosphere of independence.

Federation

Federalism is one of the most important aspects of modern constitutionalism. It is established all over the world perhaps, as the only form of political organisation suited to communities with a diversified pattern of objectives interests and traditions, who seek to join together in the pursuit of common objectives and interests and the cultivation of common tradition, the basic objective of federalism is thus unity in diversity, devolution in authority and decentralisation in administration. Its fundamental characteristic is the division of powers between two sets of government—a Central Government and Local or State Governments—each independent of the other in its own sphere of activity. The framers of the Constitution turned to federalism as a solution of a number of problems they confronted in their attempt to frame a constitution for a new, united India. Particularly, they wanted to preserve both the "infinite variety and the innate unity" that animated the length and breadth of India.

The choice of federalism as a constitutional form and as the basis of a national government in India was not a sudden development upon the transfer of power on 15th August, 1947. It was there for many years and, in a limited form it was already in operation in British India. For the solution of the constitutional problem of a multi-racial, multi-lingual and multi-communal country like India with a vast area and a huge population, federalism was only a natural choice. Nevertheless, the farmers were cautious to ensure that the unity they sought to establish through federalism was of an abiding nature, and in case of a future conflict between that unity and the diversity preserved under the Constitution, the former should prevail over the latter. In other words, it was their intention to crate an indestructible Union and the supremacy of the Union over the States in number of matters affecting the interests of the nation.

Cabinet Government

The most distinctive characteristic of a Cabinet System of Government is the complete and continuous responsibility of the executive to the legislature. The Cabinet is composed of the Prime Minister' who is the chief of the executive, and his senior colleagues who share the responsibility with him for the formulation and execution of the policies of the government. In contrast to a system of cheeks and balances as obtains under the Presidential system of the United States, the Cabinet System embodies the principle of concentrated authority under strict control. The Cabinet is the central shaft to which all the other agencies of government are geared. Individual members of the Cabinet are the heads of the different departments of the administration. Collectively, the Cabinet shapes the programme of legislation which is submitted to Parliament and from it emanate the broad and general policies. The Parliament also checks and controls the performance of the administration. Thus, the Cabinet system facilities, on the one hand, the intimate cooperation between the executive and the legislature and, on the other ensures the responsibility of the executive to the legislature, the representative of the people.

Under the Cabinet system, the Head of the State occupies a position of great dignity, but practically all authority, nominally vested in him, is exercised by the Cabinet or the Ministry which assumes full responsibility for acts performed in his name. The unity and collective responsibility of the Cabinet are achieved through the Prime Minister, who is the key-stone of the Cabinet arch. His colleagues in the Cabinet are appointed on his recommendation and they always go out of office along with him. He is thus central both to the formation and the dissolution of the Cabinet.

The real merit of a Cabinet system is that the executive being responsible to the legislature is always being watched. The moment it proves unequal to the task, or it goes off the track or flouts the will of the legislature, it can be removed from office by a successful vote of no-confidence. Under the modern party system, if the Party in office has a stable majority in the legislature, the Cabinet may wield overwhelming power, so long as the members of the Party are solidly behind it. Under such conditions, as Herman Finer put it, the Cabinet although a creature of Parliament becomes a creature which leads its creator. But under different conditions, Parliament will assert and no Cabinet will be able to dominate. If instability of Cabinet does not become chronic as was the case under the Fourth Republic of France, a Parliamentary executive is preferable to a Presidential executive whose main merit is the stability of the executive for a fixed period.

The Constitution of India has adopted as a basic principles the British Cabinet system almost tin its entirety. The only special feature of the Indian Constitution which deserves special mention in this context is the position of the Prime Minister. The Constitution expressly gives him a distinctly superior position by making him the head of the Council of Ministers. In Britain, although in practice the Prime Minister holds a superior position, he is, at least in theory, to be described as first among equals. In India, the Cabinet system of government under the Constitution is established not only at the Central level, but also in the States. In every State there is a Council of Ministers headed by a Chief Minister, just like the Prime Minister who heads the Central Cabinet.

7

Fundamental Rights: General Nature

The conflict between man and the State is as old as human history. Although attempts have been made for centuries to bring about a proper adjustment between the competing claims of the State and the individual, the solution seems to be still far off. This is primarily because of the dynamic nature of human society, where old values, ideas and forces constantly yield place to new ones. It is obvious that if individuals are allowed to have absolute freedom of speech and action, the result would be chaos, ruin and anarchy. On the other hand, if the State has absolute power to determine the extent of personal liberty, the result would be tyranny. Hence, the eternal problem that faced statesmen and political scientists was how to make a fitting adjustment between individual independence control, the need for protecting personal liberty against governmental power and that of limiting personal liberty by governmental power.

This problem assumes extreme difficulty only under a democratic system of government. For, the success or failure of a democracy depends largely on the extent to which civil liberties are enjoyed by the citizens in general. A democracy aims at the maximum development of the individual's personality; and the personality of the individual is inseparably bound with his liberty. Only a free society can ensure the all-round progress of its members which ultimately helps the advancement of human welfare. Therefore, every democracy pays special attention to securing this bare objective to the maximum extent without, at the same time, endangering the security of the state itself. A common device that is adopted by most them for this purpose is to incorporate a list of fundamental rights in their constitutions and guarantee them from violation by executive and legislative authorities.

The British Position

Almost every modern constitution has followed this pattern. The only exception to this almost universal rule is the case of the British Parliament as constitution-making body. This is why the written constitutions of British Dominions like Canada and Australia embody no fundamental rights. British politicians and constitutionalists are generally of the view that written rights are not of much practical value. Abstract declarations, according to them, are useless there exists the will and the means to make them effective. The real guarantee of liberty lies in an effective public opinion and the existence of a government that is amenable to such public opinion.

Fundamentally, this a is a sound position. It is true that in Great Britain today there is perhaps more individual freedom than in most of the countries in the world. Yet, the British attitude towards written rights is not unimpeachable. For, one might ask the simple question: "How long has it taken Britain to reach the present position? And at what price?" One can easily point out at least two revolutions in the process, one "bloody" and the other "bloodless". For establishing the liberties which the present generation of Englishmen enjoy, thousands of their ancestors paid a heavy price with their life, liberty and property. Further, no one can ignore the stupendous importance of documents like the Magna Carta, the Bill of Rights, the Petition of Rights etc., in establishing the basic rights which a citizen ought to enjoy both as a human being and as member of given political society, and safeguarding them against all encroachments by the executive authority of the State. The most striking feature of the fight of the British people for civil liberties was that it was always directed against the arbitrary power of the Executive but seldom against Legislature. This was because the despotic power of the king stood in the way of Parliament, the representative of the people. Hence, the British were always anxious to cut down the power of the executive and correspondingly increase that of the legislature. This is why the great charters like the Magna Carta speak only of limiting the powers of the King. The British never accepted the ideal that a legislature could also become a tyrannous body and that hence the individual's liberties are to be safeguarded against legislative majorities too. The doctrine of Parliamentary sovereignty is the product of such an attitude.

The American Position

In contrast, the framers of the American Constitution, although most of them were educated in the British tradition, were unwilling to accept the British position. They did not believe in the sovereignty of the legislature however popular that body might be. True, the original constitution had not included in it a Bill of Rights. But within two years of the inauguration of the Constitution, a series of amendments were enacted in order to constitute such a Bill of Rights. The task of enforcing and protecting these rights was entrusted to the judiciary, particularly to the Supreme Court of the United States. The American concept, as one can see from the nature of these rights as well as the manner in which they are safeguarded, is that fundamental rights are not matters to be drawn into the vortex of political controversy or to be placed at the mercy of legislative majorities. They are to be definitely recognised in the constitution and protected against any violation either by the authority of the executive or by the Legislature through an independent and impartial judiciary.

Why Guaranteed Rights

What is the purpose of guaranteed fundamental rights? Their very purpose is to withdraw certain subjects form the changing pattern of political controversy, to place them beyond the reach of a majority in legislature and officials in the government and to establish them as legal principles to be applied by the Courts. For, if the danger of personal rule by despotic rulers has more or less disappeared as result of representative institutions coming into their own, that from legislative interference has correspondingly increased because of the high-handed manner in which majorities might manage affairs in the legislature. A dominant group of legislators could pass any discriminatory or unjust legislation and prejudice the interests of considerable sections of the people. This meant in reality the substitution of one kind of tyranny by another, the replacement of the personal rule of the monarch by the tyranny of a legislative majority. One's right to life, liberty and property, to free speech and free expression, freedom of worship and assembly, and other fundamental rights are not subjects to be submitted to vote. They should not depend on the outcome of elections.

When legislatures were prohibited from encroaching upon certain rights through constitutional safeguards, the protection of these rights was achieved against the arbitrary conduct of both the executive and the legislature. When an independent judiciary was made the guardian of these rights by the constitution itself, the process of the protection of fundamental rights was complete and the enjoyment of these rights by all irrespective of wealth or social status, race or religious belief, was fully ensured. Herein lies the importance of fundamental rights. The United States has led many countries in this respect. Today, the idea of a list of written rights as an integral part of a new constitution has been generally accepted. Even the British do not seriously contest the wisdom of this arrangement and are prepared to concede its value at least to a limited extent.

The Indian Demand for Fundamental Rights

The idea of incorporating a list of fundamental rights in a new constitution of India had excited the imagination of almost all political thinkers and constitutionalists in India from the time the idea of the transfer of power from Britain to Indian hands had taken shape. The American Bill of Rights had a tremendous impact on Indian thinking of this subject. The Indian National Congress, the Liberals, moderates of all shades and the religious minorities like the Muslims, the Christians and the Sikhs, all considered it not only desirable but essential, both for the protection of the rights of minorities and for infusing confidence in the majority community. The British Government, however, never agreed with this idea and, therefore, none of the constitution Acts passed by the British Parliament contained any fundamental rights.

The absence of guaranteed fundamental rights showed how free the Government of India was to do whatever it liked however illegal it was. During the war years, civil liberties lost all their meaning in India and the Courts including the Federal Court of India found it impossible to safeguard them. A series of ordinances by the Governor-General replaced legislative enactments in this field. Special Courts were set up to try persons for all types of political activities. Such courts ignored even the provisions of the Code of Criminal Procedure. Their decisions were placed beyond any review by High Courts. When the Federal Court declared the Ordinance which established these Courts invalid, thereby rendering the imprisonment of thousands of persons illegal, the Governor-General promulgated another Ordinance in identical terms the very next day! Hundreds of cases were brought before the various High Courts seeking protection from wanton conduct on the part of the Executive, but the Courts could not help, for there was no constitutional guarantee under which they could act. A decade of the working of the Constitution Act of 1935 amply demonstrated the imperative necessity of incorporating a list of fundamental rights in the Constitution of independent India.

As a result, the British Cabinet Mission agreed upon the necessity of the incorporation of a separate chapter of fundamental rights in the future Constitution of India.

Attitude of the Constituent Assembly

When the Constituent Assembly met for the first time in 1946, no member opposed the ideal of a chapter of fundamental rights as an integral part of the constitution. In fact, it was unreservedly supported by all sections of opinion in the Assembly. Over the Special Committee appointed for the purpose, Sardar Patel presided and it included prominent members of the various minority communities. The Committee made a detailed study of the whole problem and recommended a number of measures. On the basis of this report, the Drafting Committee of the Constituent Assembly prepared the provisions on Fundamental Rights as embodied in the Draft Constitution.

Even a rapid glance over the two chapters of the Constitution—Fundamental Rights and Directive Principle—will satisfy any impassioned observer that the one desire that was dominant in the framers of the Constitution was for the rapid, modernisation of the country's political, social and economic institutions. That desire has found its expression in the chapter on Fundamental Rights along with that on Directive Principles.

In this regard, they were primarily guided by the ideals of the American and French Revolutions. Intellectually, the leaders of contemporary India are the children of the West, that region of the world where modernism had its birth and growth. Hence it was no wonder that in the constitution they framed, an important place was given to these rights with a view to modernising their political, social and economic institutions.

The rights which were thus fell broadly into two categories—public and private—but both had the same purpose in view, namely, to put an end to arbitrary rule. Among the public or political rights were the rights of men to choose their rulers, the right to hold them responsible for their conduct, the right to a share in law-making and the right to bear arms. Among the private rights were the right to personal freedom, the right to freedom of religious belief, the right to freedom of thought and expression, the right to equality and to the possession and use of property. Political thinkers of the age gave a philosophical explanation for these rights being regarded as fundamental. Assuming that happiness is the goal of human life, they pointed out, that man had, independently of his government, a right to the enjoyment of all those conditions which are essential for the pursuit of happiness. To such conditions, the term 'Rights' was applied and this meaning of Rights has, no the whole, come to stay although political thinkers of more recent times refer to the goal of human life as the development of personality. From their point of view, rights are those conditions which a person shout possess if he is to develop his personality and become the best that he is capable of becoming. The two views do not however make much of a difference so far as enunciation of fundamental rights is concerned. By about the beginning of the nineteenth century, philosophers as well as statesmen were able to evolve a formula of fundamental rights and those who framed new constitutions in the subsequent period had not much difficulty in selecting the rights to be safeguarded as fundamental for incorporation in the constitution.

The fathers of the Indian Constitution wee, therefore, is a happy position to examine the experience of a variety of constitutions form different parts of the world. Of these, the Bill of Rights of the American Constitution, the French Declaration of the Rights of Man and the Irish Constitution of 1935—all of the era preceding the Second World War—were the most important which influenced them among the post-war constitutions, those of Japan (which was American-inspired) and Burma (which had many problems similar to those of India) were the two which attracted them most. There was also the influence of the Universal Human Rights Charter which was almost at its final stage of adoption by the United Nations. It must be emphasised, however, that the Indian Constitution-makers were not content with merely borrowing from experience abroad. They were profoundly influenced in the selection of these rights by at least three other factors to the situation in India. First, there were the special disabilities form which they suffered during the British rule, the disabilities which were similar to those to which the peoples of the West were subject in the days of despotism, but with the added circumstance of alien domination. The second was the institution of caste which was the dominant feature of the Indian social system as consequence of which a large section of the people came to be treated as "Untouchables". The third was the existence of a number of religious, linguistic and racial minorities in the country whose cultural rights had to be safeguarded. Some of the rights included in the Constitution, therefore, owe their origin to one or other of these three factors.

The real problem that confronted the framers, however, was how to limit their selection of rights to certain categories only. What rights were fundamental and what were not, and why? It the rights to life, liberty and property were fundamental, what about right to employment and education? Has not the traditional concept of fundamental rights in its individualistic setting undergone a change in the modern era of the Welfare State? The framers had no doubt about the answers to these question. They were quite conscious of the change in the character of the modern State. They knew that the age of the American Bill of rights which believed in the "perfectibility of man and the malignancy of government" had gone for ever. And yet, it was task of utmost difficulty. This was because the State in India was not yet in a position to guarantee the right to employment or education. It was a matter of physical impossibility, not the lack of will. Hence, they divided these rights into two categories, justiciable and non-justiciable. Justiciable rights are those which can be enforced by a court of law. Part III of the Constitution which is entitled "Fundamental Rights" contains justiciable rights like the right of life, liberty and property. Part IV, "The Directive Principles of State Policy", contains non-justiciable rights such as right to employment and education. The citizen has no judicial remedy if he is denied the enjoyment of these rights.

We may now consider in detail the various provisions relating to Fundamental Rights.

General Provisions

Article 12 defined the term "States" as it applies to the provisions of this chapter. According to it, State includes the Government (Executive) and Parliament of India and Government and Legislature of each of the States and all local and other authorities within the territory of India or under the control of the Government of India. The definition is made so comprehensive that it includes every governmental authority, legislative or executive, Central, State or Local and the rights are guaranteed against violation by every one of those authorities.

Article 13 has two important aspects. On the one hand, it invalidates all laws which were in force at the commencement of the Constitution in so far as they were inconsistent with the Fundamental Rights and to the extent of their inconsistency with those rights. On the other, it imposes a prohibition upon the State not to make any law which takes away abridges the rights conferred by this provision, such law would be invalid to the extent of its inconsistency with any of the rights guaranteed. The importance of this provision is that it makes express provision for judicial review of legislative enactments as to their conformity with the Constitution.

In addition to Articles 12 and 13, Articles 33, 34 and 35 in the chapter on the Fundamental Rights also contain certain general provision. Article 33 gives the power to Parliament to suitably modify the Fundamental Rights so as to apply them to the Armed Forces with a view to ensuring the proper discharge of their duties and the maintenance of discipline among them. Article 34 deals with the restriction of Fundamental Rights while martial law is in force in any area. If the right to life and personal liberty cannot be violated except according to procedure established by law, the application of martial law might become impossible in the country and it would be impossible for the States to restore order quickly in an area which has become rebellious, riotous or in any other way violently disorderly. Therefore, it was thought necessary to make a special provision to permit any act proclaimed by the Commander-in-Chief of the area where martial law prevails, as an offence to be reckoned as an offence under the established law. Similarly, the procedure prescribed by him shall be procedure deemed to have been established by law. Further Parliament is empowered to indemnify any person in respect of any act done by him in connection with the restoration and maintenance of order in any area where martial law was in force. Thus, Article 34 makes the operation of martial law and the consequent restoration of peace possible.

Article 35 deals with legislation intended to give effect to some of the provisions dealing with Fundamental Rights. Under this, Parliament has been given exclusive power to make laws with respect to the following matters: Right to Constitutional remedies; prescribing residence qualifications required for public employment; Armed Forces and martial law. Parliament is given exclusive power also for prescribing punishment for those acts which are declared to be offences under the chapter on Fundamental Rights. The Constitution in express term prohibits the States from passing any law with respect to these items. The purpose of these provisions is clearly to establish uniform standards for the whole country as these are subjects which if handled by the States would create different standards which would be detrimental to the ideals of single citizenship and national unity which the Constitution aims to establish.

8

How the Cabinet Works

Practice in Britain

A description of the essential aspects of the cabinet system, as it has developed in England and from whose Constitution we have incorporated its main features, will be helpful to the proper understanding of the working of the Indian Cabinet. Writers on the British Constitution have used expressive phrases to emphasize the importance of the Cabinet. Bagehot, for instance, calls it 'the hyphen that joins, the buckle that fastens, the executive and legislative departments together.' Sir John Mariott refers to it as 'the pivot round which the whole political machinery revolves.' In the words of Ramsay Muir, the Cabinet is 'the steering wheel of the ship of State,' while Sir Ivor Jennings considers it as 'the core of the British Constitution.'

The chief characteristics of the British Cabinet are political homogeneity, responsibility to the House of Commons, joint responsibility, and the ascendancy of the Prime Minister.

Political homogeneity means that members of the Cabinet should belong to the same party. Their outlook should be more or less similar and their loyalty to persons and principles should, to a great extent, be common. In a coalition cabinet there will be members from more than one party but this does not affect the principle of homogeneity so long as they agree to work on the basis of collective responsibility.

The members of the Cabinet are responsible to the House of Commons for 'every policy that they embark upon and for every action that they take.' In the early stages of the development of the cabinet system in England, ministerial responsibility was an individual, not a collective, matter. Ministers were often impeached individually and removed from office when the Sovereign declined to dismiss them.

But by the end of the eighteenth century, joint responsibility had become a well established practice in the British Constitution. This principle means, according to Lord Morley.

> 'that every important piece of departmental policy is taken to commit the entire Cabinet and its members stand or fall together. The Chancellor of the Exchequer may be driven from office by a bad despatch from the Foreign Office and an excellent Home Secretary may suffer for the blunders of a stupid Minister of War. The Cabinet is a unit—a unit as regards the Sovereign and a unit as regards the legislature. It gives its advice as a single whole both in the royal closet and in the hereditary or representative chamber. . . . The first mark of the Cabinet, as that institution is now understood, is united and indivisible responsibility.'

Collective responsibility does not mean that a minister can misbehave with impunity. A minister can certainly be dismissed if he commits any act of official indiscretion. Or he may resign of his own accord when he knows that he has incurred the displeasure of the public and parliament, and that the latter will censure him.

The ascendancy of the Prime Minister is another fundamental feature of the Cabinet. For many years, the Prime Minister's position was not officially recognized. Walpole, Britain's first Prime Minister, was not only unwilling to be designated as such but denied any intention to assume supremacy in the Cabinet[1] and, strange as it may seem, it was only in 1937 that statutory recognition was given to this post. But the Prime Minister invariably has been holding a ministerial position, usually that of the first Lord of the Treasury. To what extent the Prime Minister is able to dominate the Cabinet depends largely on his own personality. As we have explained in a subsequent chapter, recent developments in the political and economic sphere have enormously enhanced the power and prestige of the office of the British Prime Minister.

The Cabinet is the chief executive body. In a parliamentary democracy, the executive consists broadly of two elements—the political and the bureaucratic. The political element is represented by ministers and the bureaucratic element by civil servants. Ministers remain in office so long as they enjoy the confidence of the legislature. Ministerial changes do not normally affect civil servants. The latter enjoy permanency of tenure. Civil servants are experts while ministers generally are amateurs. The success of democracy depends chiefly on how closely and efficiently the expert and the amateur work together in the interests of the country.

The main functions of the Cabinet are to lay down policies, to initiate legislation and to co-ordinate the work of the various departments of the Government. It is the Cabinet's responsibility to control, direct and instruct the administration and to see that the will of the nation as expressed in parliament is carried out.[2]

Procedure In India

Articles 74 and 75 of the Indian Constitution, quoted below, describe the functions of the Cabinet:

74 (1) There shall be a Council of Ministers with the Prime Minister at the head to aid the advice the President in the exercise of his functions.

(2) The question whether any and, if so, what advice was tendered by Ministers to the President shall not be enquired into any court.

75 (1) The Prime Minister shall be appointed by the President, and other ministers shall be appointed by the President on the advice of the Prime Minister.

(2) The Ministers shall hold office during the pleasure of the President.

(3) The Council of Ministers shall be collectively responsible to the House of people.

(4) Before a minister enters upon his office, the President shall administer to him the oaths of office and of secrecy according to the forms set out for the purpose in the Third Schedule.

(5) A minister who, for any period of six consecutive months, is not a member of either House of Parliament

shall, at the expiration of that period, cease to be a minister.

(6) The salaries and allowances of ministers shall be such as Parliament may from time to time determine and until Parliament so determines, shall be as specified in the Second Schedule.

The Indian Constitution does not use the word Cabinet but it does incorporate the essential features of the Cabinet system as it operates in Britain, such as the supremacy of the Prime Minister and collective responsibility. Although the Constitution says that the ministers shall hold office during the pleasure of the President, in practice they can do so only as long as they enjoy the confidence of the Prime Minister. However, there have been instances when a minister could not continue in office even when he had the confidence of the Prime Minister. The most conspicuous example was that of V.K. Krishna Menon who as Minister for Defence, was forced to resign in November, 1962 by pressure of public opinion although the Prime Minister was very anxious to retain him in the Cabinet.[3]

The Indian Cabinet generally meets once in a week. The meetings are held in New Delhi at Rashtrapati Bhawan where the office of the Cabinet Secretariat is also situated. Sometimes, particularly when Parliament is in session, more than one meeting in a week may be held, depending on the urgency and importance of the business to be transacted. The agenda and the connected papers are circulated to the members of the Cabinet a few days prior to the meeting. An item not on the agenda can be raised at the meeting with the permission of the Prime Minister, provided it is of great urgency. The duration of a Cabinet meeting depends on the nature of the agenda. The longest session ever held by the Cabinet was on October 14, 1964 when it sat for four hours at a stretch to consider the outline of the fourth Five-Year Plan.

Only Cabinet Ministers are entitled to attend the meetings. But Ministers of State are asked to attend when the subjects with which they deal come up for discussion or when the Cabinet Minister concerned is unable to be present. Chief Ministers are sometimes invited to the meetings when questions relating to their States are discussed and their presence is considered helpful. For example, P.C. Sen, Chief Minister of West Bengal and B. Patnaik, Chief Minister of Orissa, attended the Cabinet meeting on June 6, 1963 when the food problem in the Eastern region was causing concern. When issues of a technical nature—economic, scientific or military—are discussed, the expert concerned is invited to the meeting and explain personally. The Deputy Chairman and the members of the Planning Commission are also asked to attend when problems relating to their respective planning portfolios are on the agenda.

The Prime Minister presides over the Cabinet meetings. In his absence, the Deputy Prime Minister used to preside so long as Sardar Patel held that post. Thereafter, the practice has been for the senior-most minister to take the Chair when the Prime Minister is unable to preside. Among those who have presided over the Cabinet meetings at one time or the other are Maulana Azad, Govind Ballab Pant, Morarji Desai and Gulzarillal Nanda.

There is no quorum for Cabinet meetings. A vote is taken rarely, the decisions being arrived at on the basis of mutual discussions and understanding. Referring to the practice in the British Cabinet, Attlee told his biographer Francis Williams: 'You don't take a vote. No, never. You might take it on something like whether you meet at 6.30 or 7.30 but not on anything major. In the same way, you never take a vote at a Commonwealth meeting of Prime Ministers. The Prime Minister collects the voices.' Herbert Morrison says: 'No voting, for the holding up of hands or the calling of Aye and No would not only be regarded as a breach of Cabinet decorum but would also be felt to symbolize and demonstrate, nakedly and unashamedly, a lack of Cabinet unity and solidarity, which is always deprecated.' In this respect also the Indian Cabinet is following the same procedure as in England.

The decisions taken at the Cabinet meetings are forwarded to the ministers concerned. The records of Cabinet meetings are kept confidential and in matters of exceptional secrecy, the decisions are not put down in writing.[4]

There are no definite rules as regards the subjects to be brought up for the Cabinet's decision. Matters of a routine nature are disposed of by the relevant department. Only very important issues are referred to the Cabinet. Sometimes even major problems are decided by the minister concerned in consultation with the Prime Minister or they are referred to the committee of the Cabinet and later confirmed by the latter. In some cases, the Prime Minister may take the decision on his own responsibility and then inform the Cabinet. Whether a subject is to be placed before the Cabinet or not depends mainly on the nature of the problem and the discretion of the minister. It is no easy task for a minister to take a decision in this regard because as Sir Ivor Jennings says, 'a minister who refers too much is weak, he who refers too little is dangerous.'

Cabinet and Budget

A matter of great importance that the Cabinet does not discuss is the general budget. It may seem odd indeed that such a vital subject as the budget, which affects intimately every department of the Government, should be outside the purview of the Cabinet. The detailed taxation proposals, prepared by the Finance Minister, are shown only to the Prime Minister and perhaps to one or two senior ministers. This procedure may appear unsatisfactory. In fact, Asok Chanda, former Comptroller and Auditor General of India, does not seem to favour the present practice of preparing the Central budget. He recalls in his book *Indian Administration* that till 1935 the Viceroy's Executive Council used to meet at a special session to discuss the budget proposals.' But since 1935 this procedure was discontinued with a view to preserving secrecy. The Finance Member of the Council, in preparing the budget, consulted only the Secretary of State for India, the Governor-General and the provincial governments in respect of those proposals that affected the latter's revenue. The taxation measures were conveyed to the Executive Council at a special meeting on budget day. Chanda says that the adoption of this procedure by the interim government led to 'serious differences' over Liaquat Ali Khan's budget proposals of 1947-48. Chanda observes; 'Despite this experience, the responsibility for the budges remains with the Finance Minister who discusses his taxation proposals with the Prime Minister and obtains his approval. The Prime Minister may take one or more of his senior colleagues into his confidence or direct the Finance Minister to do so; but the proposals are divulged to the Cabinet only on the budget day in Parliament as before. So much for joint responsibility in a vital matter affecting directly the economic life of the country and indirectly its political orientations.'

C. Rajagopalachari also strongly criticized the budge procedure while commenting on the budget of 1963-64 which imposed additional taxation of about Rs. 275 crores in a single years..

Rajagopalachari said:

> 'The way in which the budgets are made and got ready for presentation leaves no room for the whole or a material section of the Cabinet to examine and advise upon it, or even to go through it. In order to safeguard secrecy, all consultation is avoided. The budget is hatched by the officials working under the nominal guidance of the Finance Minister. If both the Prime Minister and the Finance Minister happen to be persons blissfully ignorant of the business of budget making, when all the economy of the country comes under the direct or indirect influence of the budget, the consequences are, what we see now, disastrous.'

But Chanda and Rajagopalachari do not seem fully justified in their criticism. It is very unlikely that Liqaqut Ali Khan would have refrained from his drastic tax proposals if only members of the interim government had been made aware of the details before presenting the budget to the Central Legislature. Nor could Morarji Desai have avoided the heavy taxation in 1963-64 in view of the sharp and sudden increase in defence expenditure, following the Chinese invasion of India in October, 1962. It should be remembered that India is following in this respect the same practice in regard to the budget as prevails in England and other democratic countries. Lord Wooltan stated in his memoirs:

> 'The Chancellor is called upon to carry a responsibility much too heavy for any one man to carry. . . . Incidentally, other members of the Cabinet are placed in considerable difficulty by this problem, since they become politically committed to financial decisions with which they may not agree; the decision to resign, and so disturb all the other work of the Government, is a hard one to take unless some vital national principle is involved.'

In the view of Anthony Eden, 'A Chancellor of the Exchequer is wise if he shares his burdens to some extent with the Prime Minister; clearly, he cannot share them with the whole Cabinet.'

It should also be noted that though the Cabinet cannot discuss the budget before presentation, it can examine it afterwards, and it is always open to the Cabinet to modify the proposals before any mischief is done. Indeed, the Cabinet can even overthrow a budget altogether, in which case the Finance Minister will have to resign. The present procedure may not be perfect but so long as secrecy has to be maintained, there appears to be no alternative.[5]

Cabinet Committees

The Cabinet has a number of permanent committees to deal with important subjects like Foreign Affairs, Economic Affairs, Defence, Rehabilitation of Refugees, Parliamentary Affairs and so on. Sometimes committees are set up to consider special problems that may come up. Such committees are dissolved after their task is completed. For instance, in November, 1964 a special committee was constituted, consisting of the Home Minister, the Finance Minister, the Defence Minister, the Minister for Steel, the Law Minister, the Minister for External Affairs and the Education Minister to examine the charges of corruption levelled against the Chief Minister of Orissa and his colleagues. The duty of this committee was to recommend to the Prime Minister its views on the charges so as to enable him to decide whether a detailed enquiry was called for and if so, in what form it should be conducted. The committees may also set up sub-committees whenever necessary.

Referring to the role of Cabinet committees in England, J.P. Mackintosh says:

> 'No Government or Cabinet could operate nowadays without the shifting process and the preparatory work done by such committees. Sometimes committees set up to handle difficult and vital developments . . . take control of the major lines of policy and, for a period, become the effective centre of Government...Many issues are settled in these committees and never reach the Cabinet while some important questions go from the departments though the committees to the Prime

Minister, the Cabinet receiving a report after a decision has been taken.'

This is practically the same procedure adopted in India.

In view of the great importance of Cabinet committees, it is understandable that ministers feel aggrieved when they are left out of some committee or the other. Thus Ambedkar complained to the Prime Minister when he was excluded from the Economic Affairs Committee in spite of the fact that he was primarily a student of economics and finance. In October 1962, the Emergency Committee was set up soon after the Chinese invasion, consisting of six members, namely, Nehru, Krishna Menon, Morarji Desai, Krishnamachari, Lal Bahadur Shastri and Nanda. This committee assumed great importance and many issues were discussed and disposed of by it without reference to the Cabinet. The other twelve Cabinet Ministers felt hurt at their exclusion and three of them were reported to have protested to the prime Minister against their being kept out of this committee. Their protest, of course was unheeded because no Prime Minister in a democracy could be expected to consult all his Cabinet colleagues when the nation is confronted with a serious threat to its very existence, and vital decisions have to be arrived at quickly and implemented with speed and vigour. As Byrum E. Carter says, 'War requires that the Prime Minister exercise all his powers. It is not possible to rely upon brilliant colleagues, for decision will not wait for discussion nor will it wait for proposals to go through the regular channels.'

The formation of the Emergency Committee led to inactivity of most of the other Cabinet committees. The Economic Affairs Committee and the Foreign Affairs Committee, for instance, held no meetings at all throughout 1963. Early in 1964, an attempt was made to revive the regular Cabinet committees to enable ministers, who were not members of the Emergency Committee, to take part in decision-making.

The Cabinet Secretariat

In England the Cabinet had no separate secretariat until Lloyd George introduced it in 1916 during the first world war. Till then, no record was kept of Cabinet meetings, apart from the report that the Prime Minister submitted to the Sovereign. In such circumstances, there was obviously a good deal of uncertainty and confusion about the decisions reached at the Cabinet meetings. As Lord Curzon remarked, 'The Cabinet often had the very haziest notion of what its decisions were: cases frequently arose when the matter was left so much in doubt that a minister went away and acted upon what he thought was a decision which subsequently turned out to be no decision at all, or was repudiated by his colleagues.'

In India the secretarial work of the Executive Council was looked after by the Viceroy's Private Secretary. But until 1935 the Private Secretary was not allowed to attend the meetings of the Council. It was Lord Willingdon, Viceroy of India between 1931-36 who initiated the practice of taking his Private Secretary to the Council's meetings. Willingdon's successor continued this practice and the Private Secretary was also designated as the Secretary to the Executive Council. After the attainment of independence, the Cabinet replaced the Council, and the Council's Secretary was designated as the Cabinet Secretary.

Thus the Indian Cabinet from the very beginning has had the advantage of a separate secretariat. It consists of the main secretariat, Organization and Methods Division, Military Wing, Economic Wing and the Central Statistical Organization.

The functions of the main secretariat are to prepare the agenda for Cabinet meetings, in consultation with the Prime Minister; to circulate the agenda and the background papers to Cabinet Ministers and to record the proceedings of Cabinet meetings. The main secretariat also serves the Cabinet committees and sub-committees.

The Organization and Methods Division works directly under the Prime Minister and is responsible for constant and critical evolution of the administrative procedures with a view to improving efficiency. The Division has Director who is also the Joint Secretary of the Home Ministry, a Deputy Director, an Assistant Director and secretarial staff. There are units of the Division in every ministry and meetings are held frequently to exchange ideas and evolve better methods of official procedures.

The Military Wing looks after the secretarial work of the Cabinet Defence Committee and of such other committees set up under the auspices of the Ministry of Defence. The Economic

Wing serves the Economic Affairs Committee and other committees connected with problems of production and distribution.

The Central Statistical Organization set up in 1951 is responsible for co-ordinating the statistical work of the different ministries and for the publication of a number of periodicals such as the Annual Statistical Abstract, Monthly Abstract of Statistics, and the Weekly Bulletin of Statistics. The Central Statistical Organization works under the Honorary Statistical Adviser to the Cabinet.

We shall now consider the role of the Prime Minister in the Indian Cabinet.[6]

NOTES

1. Walpole said: 'I unequivocally deny that I am sole Prime Minister and that to my influence and discretion all the affairs of Government must be attributed.'
2. The functions of the British Cabinet were described in the Report of the Machinery of Government Committee of 1918 as follows:
   (1) The final determination of the policy to be submitted to Parliament;
   (2) The supreme control of the national executive in accordance with the policy prescribed by Parliament;
   (3) The continuous co-ordination and delimitation of the activities of the several departments of State.

   But the above description does not fully and clearly bring out the important role of the British Cabinet of the present day. As Byrum E. Carter points out, 'one would not realize from the statement that the Cabinet actually exercises effective control over the Parliament and that nearly every measure of major importance is of Cabinet origin. . . . The theory of parliamentary control of the Cabinet is only an illusion behind which is hidden the reality of Cabinet control of the Parliament.' (*The Office of Prime Minister by Byrum E. Carter.*)
3. This is described in detail in chapter VI.
4. Despite their confidential nature, Cabinet decisions sometimes leak out to the Press. For instance, Inder Malhotra, Political Correspondent of the Statesman, *wrote* in his paper on December 25, 1964: 'During seventeen years of freedom, the Cabinet has found time to devote thought to external publicity precisely twice: first in 1948 and then exactly ten years later in 1958.'

5. We may refer in this context to the embarrassing position in which the Minister for Industry found himself on February 29, 1964. In the forenoon of that day Nityananda Kanungo, Minister for Industry, told a member of the Lok Sabha, in reply to a question, that there was no proposal on the part of the Government of India to appoint a Commission to enquire into monopolies and concentration of wealth. But on the same day in the afternoon T.T. Krishnamachari, Finance Minister, while introducing his budget for 1964-65, announced the government's intention to set up a Commission to enquire into monopolies and concentration of wealth. A few days later when members of the Lok Sabha pointed out the contradiction in the statements, the Minister for Industry apologized to the House for the answer he had given on February 29, and explained that what was being considered by the Finance Minister would not be known to the members of the Cabinet, Kanungo added: 'At the time I gave the answer, the position stated by me was, as then known to me, correct and I have no hesitation in admitting this position.'
6. Lal Bahadur Shastri, after he became Prime Minister in June 1964, introduced some changes in the cabinet procedure. These are described in chapter X. Cabinet procedure under Mrs. Gandhi continues to be the same as it was under Shastri.

9

Keystone of Cabinet Arch

It was Lord Morley who described the Prime Minister as 'the keystone of the Cabinet arch.' He said:

> 'Although the Cabinet members stand on an equal footing, speak with an equal voice and, on rare occasions when a vote is taken, are counted on the principle of one man, one vote, yet the head of the Cabinet is *primus inter pares* and occupies a position of peculiar and exceptional authority.'

He added that the Prime Minister could assume powers not inferior to those of a dictator so long as he enjoyed the confidence of the House of Commons.[1]

The powers and functions of the Prime Ministers of England and India are to a great extent similar due to the fact that both countries have the parliamentary type of democracy. The Indian Prime Minister, like his counterpart in England, is the leader of the majority party in the Lower House of the Parliament. The Prime Ministers are formally appointed by the constitutional head of the state, namely, the Queen in England and the President of the Republic in India. The Prime Ministers remain in office so long as they enjoy the confidence of the Lower House. Their Cabinets are collectively responsible to its. In both countries the Prime Ministers select the ministers, allocate portfolios, co-ordinate work, settle difference, and help to impart harmony and homogeneity to the Cabinet. The Prime Ministers can compel recalcitrant colleagues to quit the Cabinet. In both countries, the Prime Ministers have vast powers of patronage. But in India these are greater because the Prime Minister also appoints, subject to the formal approval of the President, the Governors of sixteen states. Moreover, by virtue of the unique position of the Congress Party, the Prime Minister has a major voice in the selection of Chief Ministers of states and their Cabinets.

In some important respects, however, the office of the British Prime Minister differs form that of the Indian Prime Minister. The British Prime Minister's powers and functions are based largely on constitutional conventions. In India, on the other hand, the role of Prime Minister is described in the Constitution itself. The Prime Minister in Britain must be a member of the House of Commons, and he cannot take part in the discussions in the House of Lords. The Indian Constitution does not specifically prevent a member of the Rajya Sabha or the Upper House from becoming the Prime Minister; but by convention he will have to be an elected member of the Lok Sabha or the Lower House, since it is the more popular and representative chamber. But he can take part in the proceedings of the Rajya Sabha as well.[2] The British Prime Minister does not hold charge of any particular department; he confines himself to general supervision and overall control of the ministry. But in India, until recently, the Prime Minister, in addition to his duties of co-ordination and supervision, was in charge of the Ministry of Foreign Affairs. In both countries the office carries tremendous prestige. It calls for tact and talent of a high order, and it was fortunate that India chose as her first Prime Minister a leader of the ability and integrity of Jawaharlal Nehru.

Nehru became Prime Minister at fifty-eight, the average age at which many Prime Ministers of England assumed office in the present century. Asquith and Baldwin were both fifty-six, Salisbury fifty-five, Loyd George fifty-three, Balfour fifty-four and Eden fifty-seven when they formed their first administration. But two of the famous Prime Ministers—Churchill and Attlee—could occupy to Downing Street, only when they were sixty-six and sixty-eight respectively.

Most Prime Ministers of England had acquired vast parliamentary or ministerial experience before they held this high office. For example, Henry Campbell-Bennerman has been a member of the House of Commons for thirty-eight years, Balfour for twenty-eight years. Asquith for twenty-two years. Lloyd George for twenty-six years. Baldwin for fifteen years., Mac-

Donald for eighteen years, Churchill for forty years and Attlee for twenty years, prior to their first appointment as Prime Minister. But Nehru had no such experience. His father Motilal Nehru had won great renown for his debating skill in the Legislative Council of the United Provinces[3] and in the Indian Legislative Assembly where he was the leader of the Congress Party for many years. But Jawaharlal Nehru had no occasion to enter the legislature either at the Centre or in his State during the British regime.[4]

However, Nehru had other qualities and qualifications for being chosen as India's first Prime Minister. Educated at Harrow and Cambridge, he had travelled extensively in most parts of the world and acquired an intimate knowledge of international relations. He had achieved fame as the author of some best-selling books and his views on national and foreign problems were generally considered progressive. Although a student of science, he had taken from an early age, a lively interest in economic and political problems. He recalls in his autobiography how while studying at Harrow, he surprised his teacher by reeling off the names of all the members of the Cabinet of Henry Campbell Bannerman who became Britain's Prime Minister in 1905, and he was the only student of his class who could do so. Moreover, by his sacrifice and suffering—he had spent a total of nine years in jail—he had endeared himself to millions of his countrymen especially the youth, who looked up to him for inspiration and guidance.

There were other leaders like Sardar Patel, Rajagopalachari and Rajendra Prasad who had also achieved all-India fame for their heroic part in the struggle for freedom and who, therefore, enjoyed in a considerable measure the affection and esteem of the masses. But the nation's choice fell on Nehru because, apart from his other qualifications, he was much younger than his colleagues; he was better known both in India and abroad than any other leader except Gandhi, and above all, he was preferred by the Father of the Nation for holding the most important office in independent India.

There were five Cabinets under Nehru's leadership. He formed his first Cabinet on August 15, 1947 and the second on January 26, 1950 when India proclaimed herself a Republic. The third, fourth and fifth Cabinets were formed on May 13, 1952 April 17, 1957 and May 12, 1962: after the first, second, and third general elections respectively. There were during the seventeen years of Nehru's rule many ministerial resignations and reshuffling of portfolios, but the Cabinet as whole maintained a remarkable stability and continuity mainly due to his personality and the overwhelming majority of the Congress Party in parliament.

Nehru's career as Prime Minister can be divided broadly into three phases: the first, from August 15, 1947 till December 1950; the second from January 1951 till August 1963; and the third from September 1963 till his death in May 1964.

Phase I: During the first phase, Nehru's authority as Prime Minister was severely limited due to the fact that the Cabinet consisted of several powerful colleagues who did not see eye to eye with him on major problems. There were veteran leaders who had not only not belonged to the Congress but who had been its staunch opponents. There was, for instance, Ambedkar, for many years a vehement critic of Gandhi and the Congress, especially in respect of their policy towards the untouchables. There was Shyama Prosad Mookherjee who was closely connected with a communal organization like the Hindu Mahasabha. There was Shanmukhm Chetty who had been a pillar of the Justice Party which fiercely but unsuccessfully fought the Congress in South India. The Congress, nevertheless, included these leaders in the first Cabinet because of its understandable anxiety to make it as broad-based as possible and to create an impression among the masses that the Congress, though it had a huge majority in Parliament, did not want to monopolize power. It was eager to share it even with those who had opposed it all along during the British regime.

But it was not the presence of these men which really limited Nehru's supremacy in the Cabinet. It was Sardar Patel's powerful personality that prevented Nehru from having that amount of freedom in the Cabinet which he came to have after 1950. Although Sardar Patel throughout his career had been a staunch Congressman and a close follower of Gandhi, he and Nehru differed widely on many major issues.

Patel was conservative in his views on political, economic and social problems. He never favoured a policy of appeasing the Muslims. He was, of course, eager to do justice to the Muslims but he was not, unlike Gandhi and Nehru, prepared to show them generosity at the cost of Hindus. He wanted to follow a tough policy towards Pakistan because he believed that any sign of weakness would expose India to attack and also lead to the oppression of the Hindu minority in that country.

In the economic sphere Patel wanted the country to achieve quick progress by enlisting the full co-operation and enthusiastic support of the business community. Consequently he did not approve of controls or other drastic measures like indiscriminate nationalization which would cripple private initiative and enterprise. The acute shortage of capital and technical skill was another factor that influenced Patel's policy. On land reforms, Patel's outlook was progressive but cautions. He insisted, as in the case of the Princes, that *zamindars* and *jagirdars* should be fairly compensated if their property was to be taken over by the Government.

Nehru, a firm believer in socialism, wanted the State to participate actively in the industrial development of the country. Although he acknowledged the importance of private enterprise, he would not give it the same amount of freedom that Patel favoured. Nehru was anxious to go ahead with sweeping agrarian reforms and he was impatient with legislative and judicial procedures that slowed down progress.

As Deputy Prime Minister and Minister for Home Affairs, State, and Information and Broadcasting, Patel, fourteen years senior to Nehru in age, held effective control over the administration including police and propaganda; and his authority over the party organization also was very considerable. The administrative services appeared to have more confidence in Patel than in Nehru. The Indian Civil Service, which had produced some very able and patriotic officers, entertained genuine fears about their future on the eve of the transfer of power. They were afraid that their high salaries and privileges would be slashed and their security of tenure affected.[5] It was Patel who effectively dispelled their fears and inspired confidence in them by his assurance of fair treatment so long as they discharged their duties efficiently.

In view of Patel's strategic position, Nehru could not dominate the Cabinet in the same way as he could at a later stage. Although Nehru had a free hand in shaping foreign policy, in internal matters no major decision was, or could be, taken without the assent of Patel. There were occasions when Nehru and Patel were unable to agree on fundamental issues like the treatment of Muslims in India and the policy towards Pakistan. The details of their differences, which have been admirably described by Brecher in his biography of Nehru, need not concern us here. What is important to note is that at one stage the split became so serious that Nehru even considered dismissing Patel from the Cabinet while Patel, too, manoeuvred to get rid of Nehru. Fortunately, the intervention of Gandhi saved the situation. Gandhi declared straight out that the Prime Minister had a right to select his own colleagues and could ask Patel to quit if his attitude to Muslims violated Cabinet policy. Nehru and Patel also came to realize, particularly after the assassination of Gandhi, that they could not any longer afford to carry their differences too far and that unless they worked together, there could be no unity, peace or progress in India.

From the country's point of view, it was certainly a great advantage that Nehru and Patel jointly guided the destinies of the nation in the period immediately after the attainment of freedom. Those were years of great anxiety and strain, and any false step would have seriously affected India's integrity and independence. Nehru and Patel acted as check on each other, and their combined wisdom helped India to tide over a most critical phase in his history. As V.P. Menon, who played a crucial role in the transfer of power and in the integration of the States, says:

> 'It was, indeed, India's good fortune that during the initial stage of freedom, the destinies of the country were jointly entrusted to Pandit Nehru and Sardar Patel. One provided ideology while the other furnished realism. Both wielded equal hold on the Congress; as such, in every act of theirs, both Nehru and Patel were compelled to turn their searchlight inwards and think of the possible reaction to the other. This avoided the two extremes; and in politics, the middle course is always the safest. It is, in my opinion, the greatest tragedy

that this combination should have lasted only for forty months after the transfer of power.'

Phase II: Patel died in December 1950, and thereafter Nehru came to enjoy far greater power in the Cabinet than before. There was no one now with the same towering personality who could act as a check on him. There were indeed very competent and experienced leaders like Pandit Govind Ballabh Pant, Maulana Azad, Rafi Ahmed Kidwai, Gopalaswami Iyengar and, at a later state, Lal Bahadur Shastri, Morarji Desai and S.K. Patil. But none of them could fill the void left by the indomitable Sardar. The designation of Deputy Prime Minister was specially created for him, and it is significant that till now this post has not been revived.

How then did Nehru utilize this tremendous power and responsibility? This question can be examined with reference to the choice of colleagues, allocation of portfolios and co-ordination of work.

Although in theory the Prime Minister in a democracy is free to choose his colleagues, in practice his freedom is greatly restricted by political and practical considerations. The Prime Minister must give due importance to leaders who have distinguished themselves by their patriotism and party work. A shrewd Prime Minister will always see that he gathers around himself colleagues who are not only able but whose exclusion may be a source of embarrassment.

As we have seen, in the early stages Nehru had to take into the Cabinet persons who had even fought against the Congress. His first Cabinet consisted of five non-Congressmen, namely, Shanmukham Chetty, John Mathai, C.H. Bhabha, S.P. Mukherjee and Ambedkar. But gradually the number of non-Congressmen was reduced, and by 1958 all the senior posts were held by Congressmen. In the choice of his colleagues Nehru had to take into account not only regional but also communal factors. Although all the States could not be given representation in the Cabinet, important ones like Uttar Pradesh, Maharashtra, Gujarat, Madras, the Punjab and West Bengal could not be un-represented at any time. But Nehru gave too much weight to his own native State of Uttar Pradesh, which at one time had as many as four representatives in the Cabinet, including himself. Apart from regional claims, important communities like the Muslims and Sikhs must always be properly represented in the Cabinet. One unfortunate result of the influence of regional and communal factors was that the size of the Cabinet became big and unwieldy—an undesirable trend both form the point of view of efficiency and economy.

So far as the distribution of portfolios is concerned, although this is mainly the responsibility of the Prime Minister, here, too, his freedom is limited by practical considerations. As Ivor Jennings rightly remarks, some members of the Cabinet choose themselves and they have much to say about their assignments. Consequently, the Prime Minister's free choice generally applies to less important offices.

In India, Sardar Patel was very keen in having the portfolios of Home and States. T.T. Krishnamchari declined to rejoin the Cabinet after the general election in April 1962 unless he was given Finance,[6] which he had held earlier. Manubhai Shah refused to take the oath as Minister of State for International Trade in April 1962 unless he was made a Cabinet minister. This was the first occasion when a minister refused to take the oath after his appointment had been announced by the President. But a few days later he agreed to work as Minister of State. Another example to show the Prime Minister's limitation in the choice of portfolios is provided by S.K. Patil's resistance to Nehru's attempt to shift his portfolio form Food to Railways in July 1963. Patil declared publicly that he would quit the Cabinet rather than change his portfolio and he submitted his resignation. Patil's objection was that a shift in his assignment, at a time when the Government was being strongly criticized for its failure to increase food production, would be tantamount to a reflection on his work. Nehru, therefore, dropped the proposal and allowed Patil to handle Food.[7]

Apart from limitations caused by personal factors, the distribution of portfolios in the Cabinet during the period under review was not done on a rational and realistic basis. Thus the Minister in charge of Food and Agriculture—a subject of great importance in view of the persistent food shortage—had no control over irrigation, on which depends largely the prosperity of agriculture, while the Ministry of Community Development, whose main task was to increase agricultural production, was handled by a separate ministry.

The Ministry of Commerce and Industry, another key portfolio, was split in the most haphazard way. This Ministry at one time was a compact one, controlling practically all the important industries and main aspects of industrial policy. But gradually many major industries like coal, fuel, oil, steel and heavy engineering were taken away from it and entrusted to separate Cabinet Ministers while International Trade was given to a Minister of State.

Defence, always a vital subject, became more so after the Chinese aggression in October 1962. Yet surprisingly there was considerable confusion even in this sphere. In 1962-63 there were two Cabinet Ministers dealing with defence—Chavan, the Defence Minister and Krishnamachari, the Minister for Economic and Defence Co-ordination. Besides Biju Patnaik, the Chief Minister of Orissa, was also consulted defence problems. In fact, Patnaik was given a room in the Ministry of External Affairs while he continued to be the Chief Minister of Orissa, until his resignation in August 1963 under the Kamaraj Plan.

There is perhaps nothing very wrong in allocating portfolios in the above manner, provided the Cabinet as whole worked like a team and the Prime Minister effectively co-ordinated the work of his colleagues. But this was not done. On the other hand, the various departments pulled in different directions, ministers openly criticized one another, and no serious attempt was made to weld the Cabinet into a cohesive unit. And nowhere was this lack of co-ordination seen more glaringly than in handling the food problem.

Although under the Constitution agriculture is a State subject, the Central Government, too, has a great responsibility. It is the Centre's duty to regulate imports, to ensure adequate and timely supply of fertilizers, to sanctions sufficient funds for agricultural schemes, and to arrange the smooth movement of food-grains among the different parts of the country. But the Centre has failed to play its role properly. Brave declarations made by the Prime Minister from time to time to achieve self-sufficiency came to nothing, and even now, after over a decade of planning, agricultural production continues to be a gamble in rains and about Rs. 100/- to Rs. 150/- crores are spent annually on importing foodgrains form abroad. The way in which the Centre has handled the food problem provides an illuminating commentary on the working of the Cabinet system.

Ajit Prasad Jain, who was Minister of Food and Agriculture from December 1954 to August 1959, told the Lok Sabha after his resignation that important decisions on food policy were taken not by the Food Ministry or the Cabinet but by other agencies like the Planning Commission, the National Development Council and the Congress High Command and, regrettably, these decisions were often taken without a proper study of their implications. Referring, for instance, to the decision of the National Development Council to introduce State Trading in foodgrains and to increase the target for food production in the second plan from fifteen per cent to forty per cent, Jain said: 'On both the occasions, the decision descended meteor-like from the sky. Neither specially nor by implication was either of the items mentioned. No studies were made by the Ministry of Food and Agriculture which was responsible for implementing the decision. No notes were prepared and put up before the Council. No State Minister knew that he would be called upon to give his views until the proposals burst upon the Council.'

Jain also pointed out that complaints against the Food Ministry should be directed against other ministries—the Ministry of Irrigation and Power which was responsible for providing water for cultivators; the Ministry of Community Development for growing more food; the Ministry of Commerce and Industry for the supply of fertilizers; the Ministry of Health for checking the rise in population; the Ministry of Railways for movement of food-grains, and lastly, the State Governments for the actual implementation of the various policies relating to agriculture.

S.K. Patil who succeeded Jain as Food Minister[8] also had to encounter serious difficulties on account of the lack of co-operation from other departments and *from* the Planning Commission. In fact, there were even open clashes between him and Nanda, the Planning Minister, on food policy. For instance, at the meeting of the All-India Congress Committee held in New Delhi in April 1963 Patil said that Planning Commission had fixed unrealistic targets. He complained of lack of co-operation among the ministries and observed that his department had no control over irrigation, Co-operation and Community Development. Nanda said that Patil's speech created the impression that the Ministry of Agriculture had nothing to do with agriculture but everybody else had! He called for clear ideas on the subject and said: 'Let not our own party man go on undermining our institutions.' Nanda confessed that many of the difficulties arose out of the fact that the administration was subordinated to politics and that one section of the Congress worked against another even a ministerial level. 'If things were to improve,' he declared, 'there should be someone to enforce discipline'.

The lack of co-ordination was also seen in handling defence. We have stated earlier that after October 1962, defence problems were looked after by two Cabinet Ministers and State Chief Minister. There is no doubt that the association of Patnaik with the work of defence was clearly unconstitutional and politically improper.

Patnaik was a young and daring politician—he was only forty-eight when he became Chief Minister of Orissa in 1962—and he had shown remarkable powers of organization in achieving the victory of the Congress Party in the elections of 1962. He took a keen interest in aviation and created a sensation when the flew the Indonesian Premier Sutan Shahriar during the Indonesian freedom fight against the Dutch. He was the first Indian pilot to land in Srinagar after Pakistan's invasion of Kashmir in 1947. He had also won his laurels as successful industrialist. These achievements seemed to have impressed Nehru who described Patnaik as a man with 'unusual experience'.

But Patnaik soon proved himself tactless by the statements he made in the USA, which caused considerable embarrassment to the Prime Minister, the Defence Minister and Parliament. In March 1963 the Prime Minister sent him to the USA, with the approval of the Emergency Committee of the Cabinet, to have exploratory talks with the American government on certain aspects of defence. Ordinarily, either Chavan, the Defence Minister, or Krishnmachari, the Minister for Economic and Defence Co-ordination, should have been assigned to this job. But to the surprise of many, Patnaik was chosen; and in his talks with the US newsmen, he gave several details of India's military preparations and her requirements of radar, communication facilities, planes and other essential equipment.

Patnaik's disclosure caused indignation in India. Members of the Lok Sabha angrily asked the Prime Minister how Patnaik, the Chief Minister of a State, who was not a member of Parliament, could disclose vital facts about defence, which had been deliberately withheld form the House on ground of security. Nehru admitted that he himself was 'surprised and distressed' but he sought to justify Patnaik's action by saying that the latter was adopting the practice followed in the USA where the authorities gave the public many particulars about military preparations. The Lok Sabha was however unconvinced and the Speaker deplored the fact that Patnaik had given out information that had been denied to the House.

The role of Krishnamachari as Minister of Economic and Defence Co-ordination created considerable uncertainty and embarrassment to his colleagues for some time. He rejoined the Cabinet in June 1962 as Minister without Portfolio but was designated Minister for Economic and Defence Co-ordination in November 1962. The main departments of this Ministry were the Department of Supply, the Department of Technical Development and the Department of Economic Co-ordination. None of these departments was new. The Supply Department was a part of the original Works, Housing, Supply and Rehabilitation Ministry. The Technical wing was part of the Commerce and Industry Ministry, while there was already a cell in the Cabinet Secretariat dealing with the problem of Cabinet co-ordination. All these departments were now brought under one ministry.

But neither Parliament nor Krishnamachari himself was quite clear about the exact nature of his duties.[9] During the debate in Parliament on the budget in April 1963, members from all parties persistently questioned the Minister about his assignment and complained that, far form effecting co-ordination, the Ministry was creating complications.[10] Thereupon Kirshnamachari explained that his Ministry's functions were similar to those of the Ministry of War Production in the Untied Kingdom, which was created in February 1942 and assigned to Lord Beaverbrook.

The latter however resigned owing to ill-health and Oliver Lyttleton (later Lord Chandos) took it over. Krishnamachari read out the following passage from a speech delivered by Lyttleton in the House of Commons in March 1942:

'I think it is the wish of the House that I should deal with the powers that have been conferred upon me. I would like to make it clear that they are the powers or which I ask, and that as far as I have been able to see during a short study of the problem, they are both adequate and precise. They have not been incorporated in a White Paper and I am sure the House will agree upon two things. The first is that to work upon a charter over such an extremely wide and varied field would be extremely difficult and would involve a very long document of almost legal precision when something more flexible is required. Secondly, I think that the actual control over certain vital supplies and services will count much more than any paper mandate.'

Krishnamachari added, 'That fits in with the broad picture of the duties that the Prime Minister has assigned to me.'

The division of responsibility for defence between the two ministers caused friction and misunderstanding. As the Parliamentary Correspondent or the Statesman pointed out in a despatch form New Delhi in April 1963,

'There is no evidence yet, there is much to the contrary, that the two ministers directly concerned with security are working together as a war-time team, each informed by a sense of crisis and each giving the other all the co-operation it can. In either of them one can hear loud complaints against the other, much of it backed by facts and figures, and each insists that greater efficiency is possible only if more powers are transferred to it.'

The lack of co-ordination was bad enough. What however was more unfortunate was that even senior ministers publicly criticized one another, sparing neither the Prime Minister nor the Government as whole. We have already referred to the open quarrel between G.L. Nanda and S.K. Patil. Another example is that of Kirshnamachari who, in his address to the thirty-fifth annual meeting of the Central Board of Irrigation and Power on February 25, 1963, criticized the Planning Commission (of which

Nehru was the Chairman) for unrealistic planning, the Government departments for being too slow, the States for being too parochial, and his own Ministry of Economic and Defence Co-ordination for lacking the composite picture of production plans which it should have. He also deplored the tendency to talk about the achievements of the various ministries through the Press and the radio, while what was more important was to realize the nature and extent of the work to be done.

Manubhai Shah, Minister of International Trade, wrote a personal letter to the Prime Minister in April 1963, strongly criticizing the working of the Ministry of Commerce and Industry, particularly its industrial licensing policy. He pointed out that the licensing policy was responsible for frustrating the socialistic objective of avoiding concentration of the means of production in fewer hands. The policy was also not helpful for promoting export. He reiterated his views that his charge had been given a subordinate status in spite of the fact that it handled foreign trade; and he complained that a number of subjects relating to international trade did not come within his jurisdiction. For instance, light industries, certain heavy industries and free trade zones, which were intimately connected with the foreign trade programme, had been spread over three different ministries, as a result of which his initiative was considerably crippled.

Manubhai Shah was certainly his right to draw the Prime Minister's attention to what he considered to be disabilities under which he was working. But his letter to the Prime Minister leaked out to the Press and provoked a debate in Parliament. Nehru denied that the Government's industrial policy was being implemented so as to encourage concentration of wealth. The details of Nehru's reply do not concern us here. What is significant is that a Minister of State should accuse the head of his own ministry of dereliction of duty and did not take care to keep his letter confidential.[11]

It is not surprising therefore that the Cabinet, lacking co-ordination, mutual understanding and team spirit, was unable to pull its weight in the country. The result was that efficiency in administration, at no time very conspicuous, deteriorated after the proclamation of the emergency. As B.M. Birla, the eminent industrialist, said in a speech in New Delhi in March 1963:

'There is no sense of urgency, whether in peace-time or in war. We are told that everything should be done on a war footing. I am afraid I do not find any difference between war-footing and peace-footing; it is the same footing. The foot does not move, it remains stationary. Therefore, there is no progress.'

In the meantime, the economic condition of the people was steadily deteriorating. Production was on the decline and prices were going up. The steep increase in taxation on individuals and companies, introduced in the Central budget for 1963-64, created considerable discontent in the country. The imposition of the super-profits tax hit the companies hard while the compulsory deposit scheme caused resentment among the low-income groups. The gold control rules also resulted in acute distress among some sections of the population. All these factors, it was believed, were responsible for the rout of the Congress in the prestige by-elections held early in 1963 when three of its powerful opponents—Acharya Kripalani, Minoo Masani and Ram Manohar Lohia were elected to the Lok Sabha with thumping majorities. The electoral verdict produced a shock to the Congress and many of its leaders came to realize that the time had come to revise its policies radically and adopt bold and imaginative measures to strengthen its hold on the masses.

It was in this background that K. Kamaraj, the Chief Minister of Madras, formulated his proposal that top Congress leaders should quit office and take to party work. Actually it was not his idea in the beginning that there should be a mass resignation of ministers. The Congress in Madras had suffered some reverses in the by-elections and Kamaraj felt that he should give up office and devote more time to organizational matters. The idea somehow caught on and it was thought that the Congress, which had become complacent as a result of being in power continuously for too long a period, should show some dramatic gesture to convince the country that its leaders were not eager to stick to office for all time and that they were still inspired by the Gandhian ideals of sacrifice and service to the people. Accordingly, the All-India Congress Committee adopted in July 1963 the so-called Kamaraj Plan by which all Congress ministers were required to submit their resignations to Nehru and he was entrusted with the responsibility for implementing it. Nehru alone was to decide who should remain in office and who should take up party work. Nehru also offered his resignation to the All-India Congress committee but the latter promptly and firmly rejected it and reaffirmed its faith in his leadership.

Phase III: Nehru availed himself of the opportunity to reorganize the Cabinet; and he accepted the resignations of six of his Cabinet colleagues; Morarji Desai, S.K. Patil, Lal Bahadur Shastri, Jagjivan Ram, Gopala Reddy and Shrimali.[12] The occasion was utilized to reduce the size of the Cabinet and to reallocate the portfolios in a more rational manner.[13] The important changes made were the following: Swaran Singh was made Minister of Agriculture and he was given overall charge of the Ministers of Irrigation and Power, and Community Development and Co-operation in respect of their activities connected with agricultural production.

With the transfer of Finance to T.T. Krishnamachari, the Ministry of Economic and Defence Coordination was abolished. But a Department of Coordination in Ministry of Finance was created, the other departments in this Ministry being the Department of Economic Affairs, the Development of Expenditure and the Department of Revenue and the Department of Company Law.

A single Cabinet Minister was placed in the charge of Education, Scientific Research and Cultural Affairs, the idea being to ensure the most effective utilization and training of the education manpower resources of the country. M.C. Chagla, formerly Chief Justice of Bombay, Indian Ambassador in the USA, and High Commissioner in the UK, was given this portfolio.

The importance of the Ministry of Industry was restored to some extent by transferring to it control over cotton textiles, handlooms and jute which were managed by the Minister of International Trade. Cement also was transferred to the Ministry of Industry from the Ministry of Heavy Industries.

Another major development was the appointment of Lal Bahadur Shastri as Minister without Portfolio. He was to perform such functions as might be assigned to him by the Prime Minister in relation to the Ministry of External Affairs, the Department of Atomic Energy, and the Cabinet Secretariat.[14]

The reallocation of portfolios[15] in the above manner was more rational than before. Nevertheless, there were some anomalous arrangements. For instance, subjects connected with industry and commerce, which were of crucial importance in a developing economy, came to be handled of four Ministers. C. Subramaniam was in charge of Steel, Mines and Heavy Engineering, and Humayun Kabir was given Petroleum and Chemicals, and both of them were members of Cabinet. Manubhai Shah and Nityananda Kanungo, both Ministers of State, were given charge of International Trade and Industry respectively. Manubhai Shah was once again reported to have protested to the Prime Minister in January 1964 when cotton and jute textiles were taken away from him, pointing out that he could not promote exports effectively if he was not given control over these major earners of foreign exchange. His protest, however, was ignored.

The Cabinet during the third and last phase of Nehru's Premiership was more compact and homogeneous than ever before. Never since the achievement of independence had Nehru enjoyed so much power as he did since September 1963. He wielded absolute authority in the Cabinet and was in a position to implement his policies without opposition from his colleagues.

'He is now the apex not only of a highly centralized powerful administrative machine. In both these machines, loyalty has become the supreme virtue, and independence of thought a dangerous adventure,' These words, used by R.H.S. Crossman to describe the present position of the British Prime Minister, seemed appropriate in the case of Nehru as well.

Nehru's role as Prime Minister has come in for criticism on several grounds. It is pointed out, for instance, that he sometimes took major decisions without consulting the Cabinet, that he was unable or unwilling to enforce discipline or ensure co-ordination, and that he deprived his colleagues of initiative by interfering too much with the details of administration. There is indeed a good deal of truth in these criticisms. But it is necessary to understand them in power perspective. It should be remembered that there is nothing unconstitutional if the Prime Minister on certain occasions first takes the decision and then gets it endorsed by the Cabinet. A study of the Cabinet system in other countries shows that nowhere is the Prime Minister able or willing to consult all his colleagues before taking every important decision.

Lloyd George and Churchill, it is well known, often took major decisions without consulting the Cabinet. So did Attlee in regard to the testing of the British atomic bomb and Anthony Eden in deciding to launch an attack on Port Said during the Suez Crisis of 1956. In these instances, the Prime Ministers concerned took into confidence only a few colleagues and permanent advisers. There have also been many similar examples in other countries. Indeed, R.H.S. Crossman goes so are as to say that 'a British Prime Minister is now entitled on really momentous decisions to act first, and then to face his Cabinet with the choice between collective obedience or the political wilderness.'

The lack of unity and team spirit in Nehru's Cabinet should not be exaggerated. The situation in this respect was far better in the final phase of his premiership than in earlier years; and moreover, in no country has it been possible for the Prime Minister eliminate entirely feelings of jealousy and misunderstanding among his colleagues.

Lord Beaverbrook, in his *Decline and Fall of Lloyd George,* recalls how Lord Curzon, the Foreign Secretary, had to face considerable embarrassment because his colleagues Winston Churchill, the Colonial Secretary, often made policy statements regarding foreign affairs without consulting the Prime Minister or Curzon. 'Winston', said Lloyd George, the Prime Minister, 'has always been in the habit of making these pronouncements on his own. He did it under the Asquith administration constantly whenever there was a chance of a real limelight effect.'

Sir Hugh Dalton in his Memoirs observes: 'Politics, whether democratic or dictatorial, is a most competitive trade and I doubt if in any British Cabinet or its counterpart elsewhere, there has been no jealousy, no incompatibility of temperament, no sincere difference of opinion on grave issues.' The same point was also made by Kirshnamachari when in April 1963, members of the Lok Sabha complained of serious differences between himself and the Defence Minister. Krishnamachari said: 'if two people do not have any differences all the time, one of them is useless.

Many of the honourable members, who have levelled that accusation against me and my colleagues, are married people, and I am sure they have differences with their wive. Still they live together and work together.'

In the course of his long career as Prime Minister, Nehru sometimes made mistakes or took the wrong decisions but every time he was able to come out unscathed because of his tremendous prestige. Even when India was put to shame by the Chinese invasion in October 1962 and the entire country felt indignant about it, Nehru was spared although, constitutionally and morally, he was responsible for the failure to defend the nation against external aggression. On this occasion, the people's wrath was directed against Krishna Menon, the Defence Minister, and the pressure of public opinion forced him to quit the Cabinet. The incident affected Nehru's prestige to some extent but only for a short time and, as we have seen after the Kamaraj Plan came into operation, he once again emerged as the nation's supreme leader with more power and prestige than ever before.

Another important occasion when the Indian Prime Minister displayed lack of firmness and foresight was in regard to India's agreement with the United States over the loan of a transmitter. Soon after the Chinese invasion of India, the Government felt that it needed a powerful transmitter to counter effectively Chinese radio propaganda. Such a transmitter was readily available only from the USA. Accordingly, an agreement was signed between India and the USA by which the latter agreed to give a transmitter on loan on condition that the Voice of America would be permitted to broadcast through if for two hours every day. Another condition was that India should not use the transmitted for broadcasting to Pakistan.

But when the agreement was published, the Communist Party strongly protested against it, pointing out that a foreign country should not be permitted to broadcast from Indian soil. Moscow too was reported be unhappy about it. Nehru, always sensitive to Russian reaction quickly to back out of the agreement.

At the Press Conference in New Delhi on October 9, 1963, Nehru was closely questioned on this subject. His defence was: 'Mistakes occur even in the best regulated families.' He explained that the agreement was brought to his notice, in bits, on two or three occasions but not as a whole. He was, moreover, heavily occupied with other matters and did not clearly understand its implications. 'When the deal came to me as a whole,' said Nehru, 'and I saw it as such, I reacted strongly to it. Immediately afterwards, the next day or the day after, we were having a Cabinet meeting, and I put it before them and they also reacted against it.'

Another remarkable revelation made by the Prime Minister at this Press conference was that Gopala Reddy, the Cabinet Minister in charge of Information and Broadcasting, had 'nothing to do' with the agreement. When a correspondent asked him whether it was not strange that a minister should be unaware of what was happening in his own ministry, Nehru replied: 'It is not strange. The same criticism could apply to me. The External Affairs Ministry was also concerned with it very much.'

It is necessary to point out that there was nothing unusual about this agreement in the sense that similar agreements had been concluded by the USA with a number of countries like the UK, Greece, Liberia, Morocco, the Philippines and Ceylon. The UK also had set up transmitters in West Germany, Malaya and Singapore, with arrangements for the sharing of time as was provided for in the Indian agreement with the USA. Nevertheless, India went back on the agreement and, curiously, its repudiation evoked hardly any serious protest in the country, which was another proof of Nehru's remarkable hold over public opinion.

NOTES

1. J.S. Dugdale in his book *The British Constitution says*: 'From the point of view of political power, *the phrase primus inter* pares is unsatisfactory and ambiguous: if it means that all ministers including the Prime Minister are equal, then it is obviously wrong; but if it means that all ministers, except the Prime Minister, are equal it is nearer the truth.'

   Peter G. Richards observers in his book Patronage in British Government that *primus inter pares* is 'a serious underestimate of the Prime Minister's position'.
2. However, Mrs. Gandhi was elected as Prime Minister in January 1966 although she was not a member of Lok Sabha. See chapter XII.
3. Now called Uttar Pradesh.

4. The only occasion when Jawaharlal Nehru came into contact with administrative problems, before he joined the interim government in September 1946 was in his capacity as Chairman of Allahabad Municipality. This experience to him was, in the words of Michael Brecher, 'highly instructive'. 'It brought the intellectual down to earth, into the realm of day-to-day administration with its many unsavoury features.'
5. Nehru wrote in his autobiography: 'Of one thing, I am quite sure that no new order can be built up in India as long as the spirit of the I.C.S. pervades our administration and public services. That spirit of authoritarianism is the only of imperialism and it cannot coexist with freedom. It will succeed in crushing freedom or will be swept away by itself. Only with one type of State it is likely to fit in and that is that fascist type. Therefore, it is essential that the I.C.S and other services must disappear completely as such before we can start real work on a new order.'
6. However, Krishnamachari joined the Cabinet in June 1962 as Minister for Economic Co-ordination. Later, in August 1963, he again became Finance Minister.
7. But in August 1963 Nehru accepted Patil's resignation which was submitted under the Kamaraj Plan.
8. Patil the fifth Minister to handle the Food Portfolio since independence. In December 1963, in a speech in Bombay, Patil expressed the view that frequent changes in the Food Ministry would not be helpful to solve the food problem. He added: 'It normally took a Minister about two years to acquaint himself with the complexities of the food problem. A Food Minister should be allowed about ten years before his ability to deal with the problem could be judged.'
9. Krishnamachary described his portfolio as 'this nebulous assignment'. When Lord Mountbatten who visited India in June 1963 enquired of Krishnamachari about his work, he replied: 'My duties? That, my Lord, is what I myself would like to know.'
10. Referring to newspaper reports of Parliament's criticism of his Ministry, Krishnamachari said: 'I read in a paper this morning that I have been under fire. Well, I did examine my coat today I saw that to part of it had been signed.'
11. When a member of the Lok Sabha asked Nehru how this letter had reached the Press, he replied that he had enquired into the matter and was satisfied that the leakage had not been caused by the Prime Minister's Secretariat.
12. Nehru also accepted the resignations of six chief ministers of States, namely Kamaraj of Madras, B. Patnaik of Orissa, B. Jha

of Bihar, B.A. Mandloi of Madhya Pradesh, G.P. Gupta of the U.P. and Bakshi Gulam Muhammad of Kashmir.

13. The reallocation was done over a period of five months, form September 1963 to January 1964.

14. Shastri's recall to be Cabinet became necessary because of Nehru's illness. Nehru started delegating his functions to his colleagues only when ill-health made it possible for him to carry on as before.

15. It is interesting to note that ministers did not always confine themselves strictly to their respective portfolios. For instance, Chagla, the Minister for Education, argued the case for India in the United Nations on the Kashmir dispute in the early months of 1964. Similarly, Swaran Singh, the Minister of Food and Agriculture, actively helped the Prime Minister on certain occasions in handling external affairs.

10

Constitutional Government

Indian are surprisingly conscious of constitutional probity. During the staggered 1991 elections which saw the likeliest prime ministerial hopeful Rajiv Gandhi assassinated, Vice-President Dr Shankar Dayal Sharma commented that 'constitutional functionaries must set an example of rectitude and perfect observance of constitutional and legal properties' (Datta-Ray, 1991a). In this chapter we propose to deal with the following questions:

1. What do mean by the terms 'constitution' and 'constitutionalism'?
2. What were the legacies bequeathed to India by British colonialism?
3. What is the structure of government established by the Constitution of India?
4. What is the structure and role of the judiciary in India?

Constitutionalism

A *constitution* lays down the rules of political game in order to ensure fair competition. It establishes the framework within which rival individuals and groups can engage in the struggle for power in a stable and orderly manner. Every political system needs clearly understood agents and rules for the authoritative allocation of values. The constitution does this by specifying the organs of government; the manner of their creation and organisation; their power and limits in relation to one another and to the citizens; the procedures for formulating and executing laws and resolving conflicts among members of the political community; and the conditions under which the polity may be defended against internal and foreign enemies. The constitutional relationship between the state and the citizens, it may be noted, contains the key to the organising principle of the political system (Marxism, democratic socialism, liberalism and so on). The Indian constitution has attempted to strike a balance between the liberty of citizens, the authority of the state and the cohesiveness of society.

Constitutionalism is the technique of striking the proper balance between establishing a system of government which has sufficient permissive authority and power to enable it to perform the necessary political tasks, and restricting the scope of governmental authority with a system of restrains to preclude the creation of a tyranny. Constitutionalism may not obtain even where there is a written constitution, if the latter does not act as an effective restraint on the government. In the former Soviet Union, for example, the constitution was minor inconvenience that could be overcome at the whim of the ruling communist elite. Constitutionalism may in a sense be regarded as the modern political equivalent of *dharma,* that ancient untranslatable Hindu concept which means religion, duty, responsibility and law all rolled into one. The word *dharma* was used often by the great Mauryan emperor Ashoka (269-232 BC), many of whose rock edicts survive. In his 26th year, Ashoka inscribed the following message: 'this is my rule: government by the law, administration according to the law, gratification of my subjects under the law, and protection through the law' (Wolpert, 1977, pp. 66-7).

Legacies of the Raj

Pre-colonial societies were usually authoritarian; loyalties were concentrated within clans and kinship groups; and systems of peaceful succession had not yet evolved. As the British progressively withdrew from former colonies, the political and economic institutions that they had established were in most cases managed in ways that were throwback to the earlier social patterns: authoritarian, clique-ridden and corrupt. India did not fit this pattern. An important reason for India departing from the norm for post-colonial societies was the legacies inherited form British India. Even so, claims of an enduring British heritage should be treated with a tinge of caution. During the early 1950s, social scientists began a comprehensive poll of villagers to determine how many Indians knew that British rule had ended in 1947. The survey had to be aborted when it was realised that a majority of villagers were not aware that the British had ever arrived (Manchester, 1983, p. 856).

The elective principle was introduced into local bodies in India in 1884 and into provincial councils in 1892. The progressive introduction and expansion of the principle was not without controversy in Britain. One group argued that representative government was alien to Indian society, incompatible with the social cleavages dividing Indian people and potentially disastrous for the Muslim community which had been loyal to British rule. Speaking to the Indian Councils Bill in the House of Lords on 23 February 1909, Lord Morley, Secretary of State for India, referred to 'the extremists, who nurse fantastic dreams that some day they will drive us out of India' (Hansard, *Parliamentary Debetes*, House of Lords, 23 February 1909, col. 118). British rule ended on 15 August 1947. In a memorable speech that captured the evocative and expectant mood of the infant country in this ancient land, Jawaharlal Nehru declared that 'At the stroke of the midnight hour, when the world sleeps, India will awake to life and freedom. A moment comes, which comes but rarely in history, when we step out from the old to the new, when an age ends, and when the soul of a nation, long suppressed, finds utterance' (Nehru, 1961, p. 13). On 26 January 1950, India adopted a new constitution and became a republic. How new was the constitution?

The British joined the struggle for a commercial foothold in India through the East India Company, which was chartered in London in 1600. As the Mughal empire waned, the British pushed for ever-expanding privileges and territories. By the end of the seventeenth century, the East India Company, was already aiming to establish a locally financed British-based system of civil and military power that would lay the foundation of a secure English dominion in perpetuity. Through the company, the British began to acquire India piecemeal with little regard for their own legal and contractual niceties. But if any of the native princes violated the terms of contract, then that was sufficient pretext to take over his territory. By the time of the great Indian mutiny/first war of independence in 1857, the Company's raj covered more than 60 per cent of the country. In the remaining 40 per cent, there were more than five hundred 'independent' princes. The East India co. was replaced by direct crown rule in 1858. A lasting legacy of the manner of the establishment of British rule in India was a deep-seated suspicion in Indian minds of multinational corporations.

The long-term economic consequences of imperialism remain a subject of debate. British imperial policies could be spectacularly cruel. The was a callous destruction of a flourishing textile handicrafts industry through a deliberate policy of favouring metropolitan economic interests. The British markets were closed to Indian textiles while the products of the Lancashire cotton mills were given free entry into India, a policy which led Lord Bentinck to remark in 1834 on 'the bones of the cotton-weavers bleaching on the plains of India' (Hanson and Douglas, 1972, p. 11.). The non-reciprocal opening of the Indian market to British goods destroyed the hopes of India emerging as a major manufacturing centre and produced an excessive dependence of the Indian economy on the agricultural sector. Agriculturists increased from 55 per cent of the total occupational workforce in the mid-nineteenth century to 74 per cent by 1939. Yet there was neither a modernisation of agricultural methods nor a growth of rural wealth. The natives provided the revenue for the entire British presence and activity in India as well as the string of military campaigns in and around the subcontinent.

The question of whether on balance British colonial rule retarded or accelerated Indian economic development remains contested and is perhaps inherently unanswerable. For against the exploitative policies must be set the economic, social and administrative infrastructural developments. The reforms introduced by the British, for example land reforms and the development of transportation and communications networks after 1857, were designed mainly to strengthen their rule. The intention may have been self-serving. The result of such activities as building railways, extension of irrigation works and the establishment of plantations brought the advantages of a developing market economy to the Indian merchants as well as to British traders. Still, had the British colonial masters had the interests of their words as their primary motivation, they would have attempted more positive steps to improve the system of production in India.

The rise of the middle class has been called the most significant creation of the British Raj (Spear, 1957, p. 110). It shifted the correlation of forces in class relations. Professional occupations—legal, medical, engineering, teaching- were Indianised rapidly. Many of them were sympathetic to the nationalist causeby sentiment and also because colonialism restricted job mobility. At the same time, many of them were government employees and had been exposed to Western values and training. The result was that they effectively constituted a mediating force both between different classes and between the British rulers and their Indian subjects. They were at the cutting edge of the tension between tradition and westernisation. They were also to be the transmission channel for the intellectual legacies of British rule, for example nationalism, Fabian socialism and an evolutionary belief in progress.

The long-term political impact of colonialism is similarly difficult to access with confidence. The paternalistic view that prevailed at the start of the colonial era held that the entire corpus of Indian literature was less valuable than a shelf of books in an ordinary Englishman's home. Lord Macaulay's justly famous minute of 1835 aimed to create 'a class of persons, Indian in blood and colour, but English in taste, in opinion, in morals, and in intellect' (Hardgrave and Kochanek , 1993, p. 32). English replaced Persian as the official language of government in 1835, and British advances in India continued to be based on assumptions of racial superiority. Thus Forbes, member of the Governor's Executive Council in Chennai, wrote in 1906 that.

> Administration in India will only be good administration so long as it is essentially British; that no in intellectual or educational attainments will even endow the Indian with the qualifications necessary to govern wisely and well... and that the Indian will fail in *character*, however brilliant he maybe in intelligence or erudition. (in Hanson and Douglas, 1972, p. 16; emphasis in original)

The political legacies of British rule are easier to identify. They include a rise in political consciousness; tools, machinery and experience of government; party politics; and civil disobedience as a legitimate technique of political protest. At the level of beliefs, the experience of the Raj was instrumental in instilling a belief in the importance of a strong and stable government. Hence the pragmatic concessions to 'reasons of state' in the new constitution of independent India: proportional representation, a fairer system of political democracy in such diverse a country, was eschewed in favour of first-past-the-post which promised to deliver more effective government ; fundamental rights were conditional, not absolute; the powers of state could be expanded in times of national emergency; and so on.

The British also bequeathed the basic organisational structure of government to independent India. The country inherited a unitary system of government, albeit with strong federal features. The Morely-Minto reforms of 1909 extended the elective principle to the state legislative council, extended the suffrage and introduced communal electorates. They also initiated a far-reaching debate on three constitutional issues: a further extension of the suffrage, and if so, the principles on which this was to be done; the further extension of the elective principle to all members of legislative bodies; and the appropriate power-sharing arrangements between provincial and national government.

The Montagu-Chelmsford reforms, (1919) had divided authority between central and state governments, and legislative functions between two chambers. The binary principle that infused British Indian rule was evident also in the system of dyarchy or dual government. The provincial governments were given responsibility for 'transferred' subjects such as education, health and local self-government. The governor retained authority over key 'reserved' subjects, including revenue and law and order. The suffrage was still limited to property taxpayers, landholders and men with educational qualifications, who together accounted for under 4 per cent of the population in the countryside and 14 per cent in municipal areas. But at least some power had been devolved and provincial authorities were not longer mere administrative agents of the central government . Even more important, the representation of Indians in provincial councils was increased.

The Government of India Act (1935) of UK parliament provided the structural link from the 1919 reforms to the 1950 constitution. The 1935 Act retained the federal features with different classes of constituent political units. Legislative functions were apportioned among them according to central, provincial and concurrent lists. The electorate was expanded from six to thirty million, covering about one-sixth of the adult population. On the one hand, there was an essentially conservative orientation to the franchise qualification, for example property ownership. On the other hand, from 1921 onwards, British tutelage gave many Indians direct experience with conventions, norms, practises and techniques of parliamentary debate and ministerial responsibility. The group that was to guide India through independence led the nationalist struggle by electoral means as well as civil disobedience.

As well as the organising principles, India inherited some of the actual institutions of government. Indeed the legacy that brought the greatest satisfaction to the British themselves is that of the bureaucracy. The elite Indian Civil Service (ICS) was an administrative aristocracy of fewer than 2000 officers. The 'steel frame' of British administration had been largely indianised by 1947, although not without problems. In theory, the Charter Act (1833) and the ICS Act (1861) outlawed discrimination against Indians. But something else bequeathed by the British, and at which Indians were to prove to be skilled pupils, was how legal requirements could be circumvented in practice. For example, for 'logistical' reasons, the ICS examinations could only be held in Britain. They virtually required studies in Britain. Surendra Nath ('Surrender Not') Bannerjea wrote the examinations in London in 1869 and performed better than most Britons who were accepted into the ICS, but was disqualified by the bureaucracy. He won his legal appeal against the disqualification, was admitted into the ICS, but was subsequently dismissed for a minor infraction for rules. As a results of such sharp practices, the proportion of Indians in the ICS was only 5 per cent in 1913. It had risen to 13 per cent by 1921 and to almost half the total intake by the time of independence. So again, with ill grace or good, in the end the British did leave behind a crops of Indians who had actual experience of administration at the elite level.

The virtues of the ICS were supposed to be many. They were generalist and non-technical and as such surprisingly adaptable. They were recruited from the educated elite by a difficult competitive examination process. Their sense of duty and *esprit de crops* kept them strangers to corruption. Most crucially, their loyalties were pan-Indian rather than regional, provincial or communal. This helped to foster a sense of centralised governance by officers who were widely dispersed all over India. Although assisted by specialised medical, engineering and police personnel, the ICS officers retained overall responsibility at each level of administration. Another distinctive feature was the fusion of judicial and administrative functions and personnel up to the district level.

Yet the ICS legacy was to prove a mixed blessing. The service was the administrative arm of an alien ruling power. After independence, the civil service became an instrument to implement public policies framed by democratically elected governments. Could the transition from master to servant of the people be made successfully without a major overhaul of the structure of administration? The problem was exacerbated by the very *esprit de crops* which had made the ICS such as valuable tool for the Raj. The elitism of the service detached it from the village heartland of India. Exclusiveness was useful asset when the primary purposes of the ICS were revenue collection and maintenance of law and order. It became a liability when the basic thrust of the service was changed to developmental tasks. The generalist orientation and the air of superiority over specialist personnel was to impede the progress towards functionalised task performance. Similarly, the sense of paternalism was to obstruct the move back from *dirigisme*.

In comparison with the pre-independence history of many other Third World countries, for example the Belgian Congo, India still had cause to be grateful for the legacy of a centralised, cohesive, dedicated and efficient administration which had been opened up significantly to 'the natives' by the time of independence. Another ambiguous legacy was that of civil disobedience, both in regard to the technique and legitimacy of political protest. Mahatma Gandhi launched his first *satyagraha* or civil disobedience movement in 1920. (The literal meaning of the term is urging of truth.) By providing an alternative channel of demand articulation, this has imbued the Indian political system with greater political legitimacy. It has enabled individuals and groups to challenge government policies, for example the planned construction of the giant Narmada dam project. It can be used to put pressure on governments for redressing injustices. On 22 September 1992, Bhanwari Devi, a worker with the Women's Development Programme promoted by the state government of Rajasthan, was raped by two men while three others assaulted her husband. The indifference of the state government to the attacks led women's groups to launch an agitation with the rallying slogan *Nyay Karo Ya Jail Bharo* ('Dispense Justice or Fill the Prisons') (*Manushi*, no, 72, 1992, pp. 18-20). And agitational techniques can be used by opposition parties. On 25 February 1993, the Bharatiya Janata Party (BJP) defied a government ban on a planned rally. BJP leader Lal Krishan Advani was among the many prominent people who were arrested in an unprecedented security operation in New Delhi. Speaking to reporters before his arrest, Advani said that courting arrest had been the traditional way of launching a political protest movement in India since the struggle for independence.

The person most responsible for the adoption and success of non-violent civil disobedience was Mahatma Gandhi. In this as in other respects. Gandhi demonstrated an uncanny ability to synthesise tradition and modernity and harness both towards specifically political goals. The tension between the two-Sanskritisation and westernisation (Seervai, 1990) was to transcend the transition to independence. Similarly, many other problems—domestic, regional and international; social, political and economic—survived the shift to independence status. There were two major challenges to national integration: the problem of the independent princedoms, and the communal divide between Hindus and Muslims. There was a powerful communist party that had shown itself singularly insensitive to the nationalist identity. The Congress Party faced difficult choices between gradual change and revolutionary transformation, and between the party-as-organisation and the party-as-government. It also faced an equally painful transition form a nationalist movement to the party of government.

In foreign relations, Indians inherited a healthy scepticism towards the fine phrases of Western leaders. A major fillip to the nationalist movement was given by the massacre at Jallianwalla Bagh. On Sunday 13 April 1919—the year of Woodrow Wilson's self-determination had idealism in world affairs, of Versailles and formal condemnation of Germans for war crimes—an unarmed crowd gathered in Jallianwalla Bagh square in Amritsar, the holy city of the Sikhs. Brigadier R.E.H. Dyer ordered his troops to fire 1650 rounds into the crowd whose avenues of escape had first been closed. The number of people killed was 379, with more than a thousand wounded. At a subsequent inquiry, Dyer explained that he had ordered 'the least amount of firing which would produce the necessary moral and widespread effect' (Wolpert, 1977, p. 299). In Britain the princely sum of £26000 was subscribed by the people as a testimonial to General Dyer's devoted gallantry as 'The Saviour of the Punjab'. In the dramatic Atlantic Charter of August 1941, US President Franklin Roosevelt and British Prime Minister Winston Churchill affirmed 'the right of all peoples to choose the form of government under which they will live'. Yet on 9 September Churchill explained in his House of Commons that Atlantic Charter did not apply to India, Burma and other parts of the British empire (Wolper, 1977, pp. 333-4).

India also inherited some enduring conflicts in its foreign relations as part of the ambiguous legacies from the Raj. There were border disputes with China and complications of relations with the mountain kingdoms along the Himalayas whose origins go back to certain sharp practices by British colonial authorities. The most important of the conflicts inherited with independence was the problems stemming from the partition of the subcontinent into India and Pakistan, with Kashmir today being both the symbol of the Indo-Pakistan conflict and the major bone of contention between them. The roots of the conflicts go back to desire of the British to protect the political rights of the Muslims against the encroachments of representative government. The Muslims believed that their representation should reflect not merely their numerical strength, but also their contributions to the maintenance of the Raj. They persuaded the British authorities that only communal electorates could assure them effective representation.

The system of communal electorates, in which Muslims could vote for their own candidates, was part of the package of the Morely-Minto reforms of 1909. The effect was to break the dependence of religious politicians on the support of the other community. Hindu politicians would reap maximum political rewards by enhancing their appeal to the Hindus, and Muslim politicians to Muslims. The discipline of moderation and accommodation imposed by the need to cultivate crossover votes from both major communities was thus removed. The impact of communal electorates was to ensure an emphasis on Muslim interests and loyalties; social cleavages were institutionalised in a system of political dualism (Weiner, 1987b, p.41).

India's Constitutional Structure

The structure of governance under the Indian constitution is shown in Figure 10.1 India is a republic, with no hereditary rulers. It has a representative and parliamentary system of government formed on the basis of periodic elections. Every adult citizen may vote in the elections and seek elective office. In essence, the 1950 constitution completed the democratisation of politics begun by the British. The retention of the basis axioms and structures of the Government of India Act of 1935 generated some criticism that the constitution was 'un-Indian' and democracy was a mere top-dressing. The Constituent Assembly, elected indirectly by the provincial assemblies in 1946, aimed to set up a system of government that would facilitate social change and economic development within a democratic structure. Reflecting the Congress triumphs in the provincial elections of 1945,

The Constituent Assembly was dominated by the Congress Party. The president of the assembly was Dr Rajendra Prasad, who was later to become the first president of the India. The drafting committee was chaired by Dr B.R. Ambedkar. Some of the other influential personalities in the Constituent Assembly were Jawaharlal Nehru, Sardar Vallabhbhai Patel and Maulana Abul Kalam Azad. The new constitution of independent India came into effect on 26 January 1950; the date is celebrated every year with due pomp and ceremony as Republic Day.

At 395 articles and eight schedules, India's Constitution was among the longest in the world. (By 1993, the Constitution had

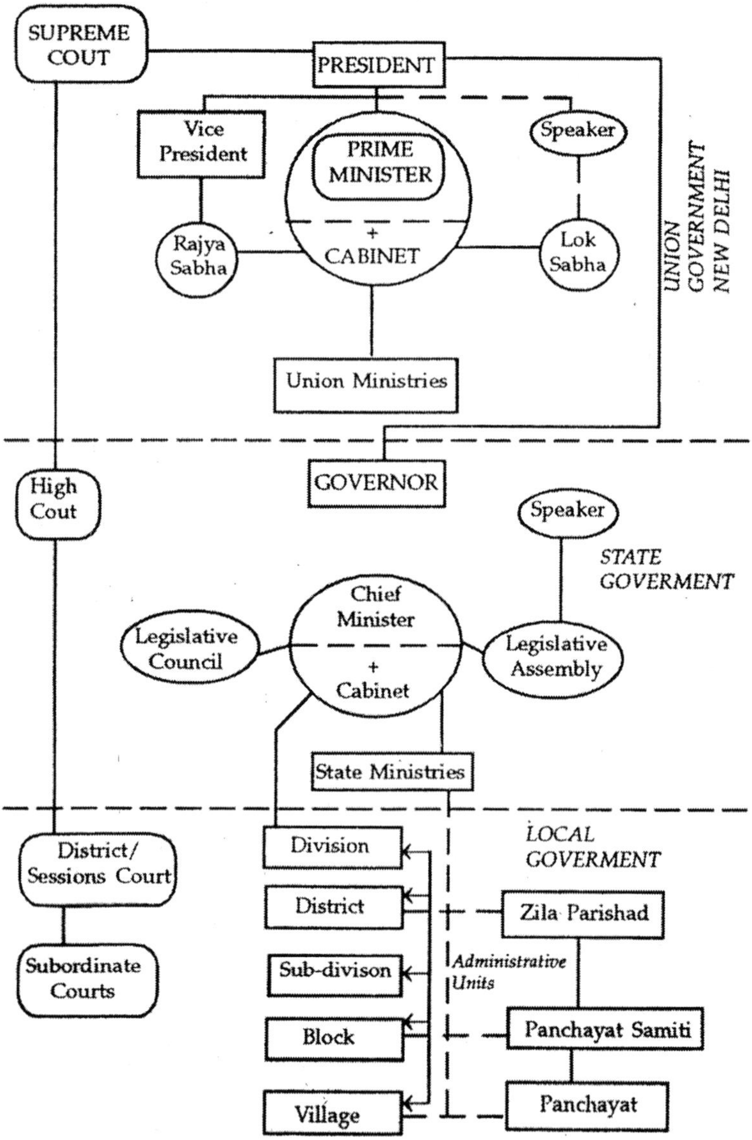

Figure 10.1
The three levels of government in India

been expanded to 441 articles and twelve schedules.) There were four main features of the political system set up by it: India is democratic, secular, federal and republican. While some members of the Constituent Assembly had been in favour of decentralised Gandhian state, most were comfortable with the system of parliamentary democracy that was familiar to them. A federal distribution of powers, again familiar from the colonial heritage, was believed to the best institutional means of accommodating India's diversity. Secularism was alogical corollary of the Congress Party's passionate rejection of the two-nation theory on which Pakistan had been partitioned off from India. The republican status was an expression of freedom and independence from the British crown. But India was keen to remain a full member of the Commonwealth of Nations if this could be done without proclaiming allegiance to the British crown. The creative formula adopted was to accept the British monarch as the symbol of the free association of the member-nations, and as such the head of the commonwealth.

India's founding fathers were at best ambivalent in their attitudes both towards Western ideals and Soviet experiments. In Nehru's own pithy assessment, 'all the evils of a purely political democracy are evident in the United States; the evils of the lack of political democracy are present in the USSR' (Nehru, 1960, pp. 562-3). Many influential personalities in the pre-independence Congress Party, while educated in the West, had flirted sentimentally with communism. The philosophy underlying India's Constitution reflects this dual attraction. The Preamble declares India to be a sovereign democratic republic and proclaims the following goals: social, economic and political justice; liberty of though, expression, belief, faith and worship; equality of status and opportunity; dignity of the individual; and unity of the nation.

Tension between Liberalism and Socialism

The simultaneous attraction of Western democracy and Soviet socialism is particularly apparent in the chapters on Fundamental Rights (Part III) and Directive Principles of States Policy (Part IV). In Britain, fundamental human rights are a product of a long political heritage rather than written constitutional guarantees. The chapter on fundamental rights in the Indian constitution essentially gives constitutional status and guarantee to the dignity and worth of individuals that Western liberalism emphasises. In sum, in enumerating the basic rights of Indian citizens, the framers of its constitution were influenced from abroad by the traditions of the English rule of law (for example in Article 14 of the constitution guaranteeing equality before the law and equal protection of the laws), the American Bill of Rights, and the Universal Declaration of Human Rights adopted by the UN General Assembly in 1948. Domestic influences included the caste system and the range of religious, linguistic and cultural minorities whose group rights needed safeguarding against majority encroachments. As a result, some features of the constitution are distinctly Indians.

The 'fundamental rights' are conditional rather than absolute, attempting to strike a balance between individual and community rights. Thus Article 15 of the constitution prohibits discrimination on grounds of religion, caste and gender; yet it also permits the enactment of special provisions designed to improve the lot of such disadvantaged groups as women and the outcastes. Moreover, the state may impose 'reasonable restrictions' on free speech and assembly in the interest of public order and morality (Article 19). Most important, the same article confers the right (freedom) to acquire, possess and dispose of property, yet permits the state to impose 'reasonable restrictions' in the general interest. Not surprisingly, the state found itself embroiled in number of court case in regard to property rights. Several constitutional amendments had to be enacted in pursuit of agrarian reform and the social control of the means of production.

The constitution does not recognise the doctrine of natural rights: no Indian can claim a right outside the chapter on fundamental rights. This contrasts sharply with the American conception, where the enumeration of rights is not be construed to deny or disparage other retained by the people. Another interesting feature of the fundamental rights in India is that they proscribe individual as well as state behaviour, for instance in an injunction against untouchability, Finally, it is constitutionally permissible in India to suspend various fundamental rights in times of emergency, and to enact preventive detention law;

judicial scrutiny is denied in either case. That is, necessity of state triumphed over due process of law.

Necessities of life, on the other hand, are notably absent for millions of Indians. Many Congressmen at the time of independence were impressed by the argument at the time freedom is possible only with economic security, and liberty is an empty abstraction to the hungry. As am influential member of Indian officialdom put it more recently, 'The immediate task (of the less developed countries) is to provide the mass of the people with bread: those finer aspects of human existence which are built on the foundations of a full stomach—and which are really relevant only to those who have one—can afford to wait'(Nehru, B.K., 1979, p.57).

If the state in India was to itself to task of maintaining the external conditions of public order, then civil rights would remain a hollow mockery for a majority of Indians. In the light of India's poverty, 'economic rights' (for example, the right to an adequate means of livelihood) could not realistically be enshrined as a basic rights; but they could be and were enshrined as ideals. The constitution accordingly incorporated them as directive principles, as a guideline for future public policy (Articles 36-51). Some of these are in the nature of socioeconomic rights, excepts that they are not enforceable through the courts, for example the right to an adequate means of livelihood. Others are in the nature of directives to the state on the manner of exercising its legislative and executive powers, for example in regard to promoting prohibition (Article 47). A third category articulated the ideals to be reached for by the state so as to nudge India towards a socialist society.

The directive principles were described as 'fundamental in the governance of the country and it shall be the duty of the state to apply these principles in making laws' (Article 37). But they were not justiciable (that is, to not enforceable through the judiciary). There would be instances where principles came into conflict with the rights. For example, the directive that the ownership and control of material resources be redistributed to subserve the common good (Article 39) cuts across the rights to property (Articles 19, 31). (The right to property under Article 31 was deleted from the chapter on fundamental rights by 44th

Constitution Amendment Act in 1978). In the event of a clash with directive principles, the courts would necessarily have to decide in favour of fundamental rights. The constitution explicitly provides that laws abridging the fundamental rights shall be void (Article 13). This is why during the Constituent Assembly debates T.T. Krishnamachari described the directive principles as 'a veritable dust-bin of sentiment' (in Austin, 1966, p. 75).

Since the constitution was adopted, fundamental rights have been steadily eroded and the balance has shifted markedly in favour of the directive principles. Once described as 'a formidable bulwark of individual liberty, a code of public conduct and strong and sustaining basis of Indian democracy' (Pylee, 1965, p. 325), they have been diluted and outflanked through such measure as the as Preventive Detention Act, the Maintenance of Internal Security Act, the Defence of India Rules, the Unlawful Activities Prevention Act. And so on. The main 'special laws in force in 1933 were the National Security Act (NSA), 1980; the Jammu and Kashmir Public Safety Act, in force since 1978; the Armed Forces (Jammu and Kashmir) Special Powers Act, 1990; and the Terrorist and Disruptive Activities (Prevention) Act (TADA), 1987.

The Judiciary

If there is to be constitutional government, then a political system must have a judiciary independent of and acting as a check on the arbitrary exercise of legislative and executive power. The functions of rule-making, rule-enforcement and rule-interpretation are separated into the three institutions of the legislaure, the executive and the judiciary. The judiciary is also the final arbiter on what the constitution itself means.

State-Level Judiciary

The structure of the Indian judiciary is shown in Figure 10.2 Unlike the US model of dual federal-state court system, India has a monolithic system. The base remains the same throughout the country, although the designations are not uniform from one state to the next. Article 214 of the constitution provides that there shall be a High Court in each state. In 1992, there were 18 High Courts in India in the hands of more than 500 judges. The state High Courts comprise a chief justice and other justices appointed by the president. The number of judges on a High Court ranges from 2 in Sikkim to 60 in Allahabad, court of the country's most populous state of Uttar Pradesh (U.P). Except in cases where the Supreme Court holds original jurisdiction, High Courts exercise full legal powers within their particular state (or group of states).

The district court is the principal civil court of original jurisdiction. It is subordinate to the High Court, and every lower-level court is subordinate to the High Court and district court. District judges and other subordinate judges in a state are appointed by the governor in consultation with the state High Court and public service commission. At the bottom rung of the judicial hierarchy, executive magistrates discharge functions of a criminal court as part of their administrative task of maintaining law and order. While executive magistrates are common to metropolitan and other areas, Figure 10.2 shows the pattern of judicial administration to be quite different in the two categories. City civil courts have been set up in metropolitan cities like Ahmedabad, Bangalore, Mumbai, Kolkata, Hyderabad and Chennai.

The constitution seeks to protect the independence of High Court judges through provisions broadly comparable to those affecting the appointment, conditions of office (except that the age of retirement is 60, not 65) and removal of Supreme Court judges. Although High Courts are placed under the jurisdiction of the Supreme Court, the latter does not have any direct administrative control over the former. A High Court is the apex body of a state's judicial system. But it is not as sharply separated from the federal government as the state supreme courts in the United States. The union government of India exercises control over High Court through powers of appointment and removal (Article 217 of the constitution), as well as transfer (Article 231). Also under central jurisdiction are the establishment and organisation of High Courts; the power to constitute a common High Court for two or more states, for example the Punjab and Haryana High Court (the jurisdiction of a High Court is normally co-terminous with the territorial boundaries of its state); to extend the jurisdiction of a High Court to a union territory (for example the High Court of Kolkata covers the Andaman and Nicobar

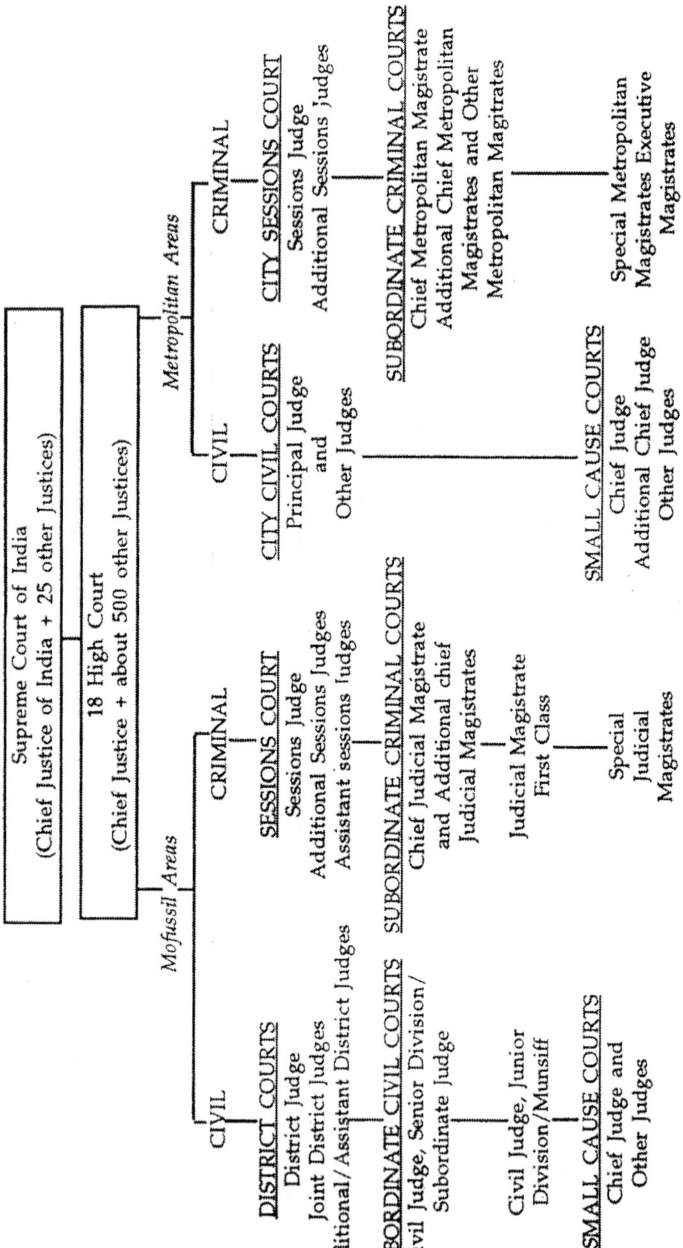

Figure 10.2 Organisational Chart of the Indian judiciary

Islands); or to exclude it therefrom. In addition, the Supreme Court can remove almost any case from a High Court and take it up directly. The aim of these provisions was a to remove the state judiciary from the realm of provincial politics; their effect is to blur the operation of federalism in the judicial sphere.

Under Article 227 of the Constitution, every High Court has court has a power of superintendence over all courts and judicial tribunals throughout its territorial, jurisdiction with the exception of military tribunals. Interestingly, this power of superintendence includes a revisional jurisdiction to intervene directly in case of gross injustice, or non-exercise or abuse of jurisdiction, even if the case should not fall within the high court's appellate jurisdiction. That is, the power of superintendence is both administrative and judicial. Furthermore, under Article 228, a High Court may transfer a case from subordinate courts to itself if a constitutional interpretation is germane to the disposal of the case. Having decided on the question of law in regard to the correct interpretation of the constitution, the High Court may either dispose of the case itself or return the case to the initial subordinate court. The latter is then bound by the high court's finding on the substantial question of law.

Six High Courts (Mumbai, Kolkata, Delhi, Himachal, Pradesh, Jammu and Kashmir, Chennai and Patna) exercise original or first-instance jurisdiction in civil matters. The appellate jurisdiction of a High Court in civil cases involves questions of fact as well as law. The power of first appeal directly to the High Court pertains to decisions of district judges and those of subordinate judges in cases involving amounts above a threshold pecuniary value. In addition, when a court subordinate to the High Court decides an appeal from an inferior court, then its decision in turn is subject to a second appeal to the High Court. In the High Courts of Allahabad, Mumbai, Kolkata, Chennai and Patna, an appeal to a High Court bench may be made against a decision of a single judge of the High Court itself. The criminal appellate jurisdictions of High Courts is similarly complicated.

There is one further power of High Courts that is worth noting. Article 226 of the constitution confers on every High Court the power to issues to any person, authority or government within its territorial jurisdiction directions, orders or writs, including writs in the nature of *habeas corpus*, for the enforcement of any of the fundamental rights or for any other purpose. Because this power derives from the constitution, it cannot be abridged or removed other than by a constitutional amendment. Moreover, while the Supreme Court can issue writs only where fundamental rights have been violated, the High Courts can issue them even where ordinary legal rights have been infringed, so long as a writ a is proper legal remedy in such cases.

The Supreme Court of India came into being on 26 January 1950 alongside the adoption of the Constitution. In its role as the supreme guardian of the constitution, the Supreme Court is vested with original, appellate and advisory jurisdictions. Moreover, its interpretation is binding on all other courts within the territory of India (Article 141), and all civil and judicial authorities throughout the territory of India are enjoined to act in aid of the Supreme Court (Article 144).

The Supreme Court has original jurisdiction firstly as a federal court. In a federal polity, both units of government derive their powers from and are limited by the same constitution. Differences of interpretation of the federal-provincial distribution of powers, or conflicts between state governments, require authoritative resolution by a judicial organ independent of both levels of government. Under Article 131 of the constitution, the Supreme Court of India is given exclusive original jurisdiction in a dispute between (a) the central government and any one or more states; (b) the central government and one or more state governments on one side, and one or more state governments on the other side; and (c) two or more states, if and insofar as the dispute involves any question about a law or fact on which the existence or extent of legal right depends. The court also has non-exclusive original jurisdiction as the protector of fundamental rights. Article 32 gives citizens the rights to move the Supreme Court directly for the enforcement of the any of the fundamental rights enumerated in part III of the Constitution.

The Supreme Court has comprehensive appellate jurisdiction in cases involving constitutional issues (Article 132); civil and criminal cases involving specified threshold values of property or death sentence (Article 133 and 134 respectively); and wide-ranging powers of special appeals (Article 136).

The Supreme Court of India has been vested with the power to render advisory opinions on any question of fact or law that may be referred to it by the President (Article 143). In December 1978, for example, an advisory opinion of the Supreme Court upheld the constitutional validity of special courts that had been set up to deal with offences committed during the 1975-77 emergency. This is different from ordinary adjudication in three sense: there is no litigation between two parties, and the advisory opinion of the court is not binding on the government and is not executable as a judgment of the court. The prevision is an interesting and conscious departure from the American precedent. The US Supreme Court decided early on against such a role, on the argument that it would encroach upon the legislative function and thereby negate the separation of powers that underpins the US constitution.

The availability of the provision gives a soft option to the Indian government on some politically difficult issues, for example the controversy surrounding the Barbi Masjid complex in Ayodhya. The government decided to refer aspects of the dispute to the Supreme Court for an opinion under Article 143 of the constitution. Unfortunately, since there was no legal point as such at issue, there was a danger that referral to the Supreme Court would further politics the judiciary instead of resolving what was essentially a political problem. The judiciary exist to interpret laws, expound the constitution and ensure that the rule of law prevails. Responsibility for maintaining law and order vests in the executive arm of government. Cabinet can weigh popular opinion the balance before deciding upon issues of public policy. The judiciary cannot decide upon questions of belief, opinion or political wisdom, nor pronounce upon question of history, archaeology and mythology. Cabinet cannot 'shift the responsibility to the courts for matters for which the government is too weak, too timid or too confused to decide for itself' (Palkhivala, 1993. P. 9). The judiciary cannot compensate for inadequacies of government or the failure of the political process. In a significant decision on 24 October 1994, a five-member bench of the Supreme Court ruled that the reference to it, of the question of a temple having existed at the disputed site in Ayodhya, was 'Superfluous, unnecessary and does not require to be answered' (*India Today*, 15 November 1994, pp. 29-30).

Independence of the judiciary

The independence of judges is safeguarded in the constitution by several means affecting their appointment, salaries and dismissal. But because a judiciary is formally independent does not mean that it is also socially neutral. Judges tend to be predisposed towards stabilsing the social order by upholding the dominant values of society (Hague, 1992, p. 281). With few exceptions, India's senior judges have come from the upper strata of society. They are generally held in high public respect. And many of the severest critics of the failings and shortcomings of the judiciary have been members of the legal profession itself.

The framers of the Constitution believed it would be unwise to leave the appointment of the judges to the president's discretion. But the alternative of making judicial appointments subject to legislative concurrence was through to be too cumbersome and vulnerable to political pressures. Instead, a middle course was adopted. The chief justice of India and 25 other justices of the Supreme Court are appointed by the president on the advice of the cabinet and after consultation with other persons. For appointing the chief justice, the president is required to consult such judges of the Supreme Court and High Courts as he deems necessary. In the appointment of other judges of the Supreme Court, consultation with the chief justice is mandatory (Article 124). These provisions clearly tried to apply lessons learnt from the American experience of the sometimes unseemly politicisation of the nomination and appointment process.

Despite this, over the years the appointment of High Court and Supreme Court judges, in including chief justices, became a focus of political controversy. In 1981, in case of *S.P. Gupta* v. *Union of India* (more commonly referred to as the *judges' Transfers case*), the Supreme Court itself conceded the last world on appointment of executive. In 1992, the lists of recommendations for appointments to the judges submitted by former Bihar's Chief Minister Laloo Prasad Yadav and Chief Justice B.C. Basak of the Patna High Court held no name in common. The resulting impasse frightened Judge Basak so much that he went to the Law Ministry in New Delhi seeking and being granted extra security (Pathak, 1992, p. 52).

The 1982 verdict was finally overturned in 1993. On 6 October, a special nine-judge bench of the Supreme Court ruled by a 7-2 majority, that no appointment of a judge to the Supreme Court under Article 124.2 of the constitution, or to any High Court under Article 217.1, could be made unless it was in conformity with the opinion of the Chief Justice of India. In the case of conflicting opinions among the respective constitutional functionaries, the judiciary's opinion would also have primacy in regard to the transfer of High Court judge, including High Court chief justices. The last was important because in fact transfer of High Court judges had become a favourite mode of executive influence over judicial decisions. During the 1957-77 emergency period, for example, Mrs Gandhi had transferred sixteen inconvenient judges to irrelevant posts in a largely successful attempt to intimidate the judiciary into submission to her will. The first instances of transferring High Court chief justices out of their home states against their wishes occurred in 1981 with the chief justices of Chennai and Patna High Courts. A Supreme Court decision on the *Judges' Transfer* case, delivered in December 1981, abdicated judicial responsibility in the appointment and transfer of judges to the executive. The judgement left the government free to hire High Court and Supreme Court, Judges first temporary judges and transfer High Court judges (except on mass scale). By the end of 1983 it was clear the power to transfer judges had been used to bend the judiciary to the government's will (Chawla, 1983). In 1985 a three-member bench of the Supreme Court itself accused the Rajiv Gandhi government of packing High Courts with 'sycophant judges' (*India today*, 15 June 1985, p. 78). In March 1993 the Supreme Court quashed the appointment of K.N. Srivastava to the Guwahati High Court, holding that he was not qualified to hold that post. This was the first instance since the constitution came into being that the apex court had quashed a presidential warrant on the appointment of a High Court judge.

Once appointed, justice hold office until the of judges retirement age of 65 specified by the constitution itself. A judge may of course vacate office voluntarily. A judge may also be removed from office on grounds of proven misbehavior or incapacity (Article 124.4). But the process of removal is quite rigorous, requiring a majority opinion of the total membership of the two houses of Parliament and a two-thirds majority of those present and voting in each house. In this case the precedent was England, were superior court judges are appointed by the crown but hold office on 'office behaviour' rather than 'the pleasure of the crown'. To shield judges from political controversy, the Indian constitution grants them immunity from criticism against decisions and actions made in their official capacity. While philosophical criticism are permissible, no motives can be imputed to any Supreme Court decision. The conduct of High Court and Supreme Court judges may not be discussed in parliament unless in the context of an address to move a judge from (Article 121). To keep judges free of temptation, the constitution further stipulates that retired Supreme Curt judges may be practise law in any Indian court (Article 124.7). But the scope for patronage has not been eliminated totally: retired judges are eligible for appointment for such specialised tasks as commissions of enquiry and university vice-chancellorships.

During office, the allowances, leave and pension rights of justices may be varied by parliament to their disadvantage (Article 125.2). The salaries of the justices are also fixed by the constitution. But the financial protection of the judges can be overridden by the president if a financial emergency is formally in force in the country (Article 360.4). Over the years, the salaries and conditions of judges have not kept pace with those of politicians. The constitution gives the Supreme Court the right to maintain its own establishment and staff independently of parliament. The associated expenses are chargeable on the consolidated fund, and therefore not subject to parliamentary vote.

The first motion of impeachment against a judge was not tabled in parliament until 1991. The case involved Supreme Court Justice V. Ramaswami. An audit report revealed several irregularities committed by him during his tenure as the Chief Justices of the Punjab and Harayana High Court. A three-man committee consisting of on serving and one retired Supreme Court judge and the Chief Justices of the Mumbai High Court concluded that there had been wilful and gross misuse of office, purposeful and persistent negligence in the discharge of official duties, intentional and habitual extravagance at the cost of the public exchequer, and moral turpitude by using public funds for private purpose in diverse ways. The committee observed that 'the acts, therefore, constitute 'misbehaviour' within the meaning of Articles 124.4 of the constitution'. Justice Ramaswami maintained that there were procedural irregularities in the notice of the motion, the constitution of the committee and its functioning. He survived the impeachment motion in the Lok Sabha on 10-11 May 1993. Of the 401 MPs in the house, 196 voted in favour of impeachment, not one voted against, but 205 abstained. The Congress Party, with the largest single bloc of votes in the house, issued a verbal whip late in the day calling on its MPs to abstained. The Congress Party, with the largest single bloc of MPs to abstain. The motion therefore failed (details of the case of in HIE, 22 May 1993, pp. 4,5 and 8). But , accepting reality, the judge subsequent resigned.

Judicial Review vs Parliamentary Sovereignty

In the United States, the Supreme Court assumed extensive powers of judicial review under 'due process'. By contrast, in India the constitution expressly provides for judicial review of legislation as to its conformity with the constitution. Rights enumerated in the constitution are made justiciable. Indeed, in India the right to constitutional remedy has itself been made a fundamental right (Article 32). Judicial review has been particularly significant and contentious in regard to constitutional amendments. The stability of the rarely amended American constitution contrasts markedly with the volatility of the amended-at-whim Indian constitution. Broadly speaking, any constitution may be said to have two goals. Positively, it codifies the values of a society and makes the state responsive to the aims and demands of society. Negatively, it erects safeguards which protect citizens from protect citizens from arbitrary actions of the state. That is, a constitution recognises that the state is simultaneously an embodiment of the pursuit of the civic good life by a collectivity and a threat to the pursuit of the good life by the individual. In keeping with the negative goal, a constitution should not be so flexible as to permit easy and constant modifications by an autocratically inclined government. At the same time, in accordance with the first goal, it should not be so rigid as to obstruct the legitimate demands and aspirations of the people. In sum, a constitution that can be amended only with then utmost difficulty risks atrophy, while one that does not differentiate between ordinary legislation and constitutional amendments risk losing credibility.

The Constitution of India laid down four methods for its own amendment. Some provisions may be amended by a simple majority of parliament, in consultation with or at the request of the states. A second class of provisions maybe amended by a simple majority in parliament. A third groups requires a majority of the total membership of each house plus a two-thirds majority of Members of Parliament present and voting in each house. The final category of clauses requires, in addition to the preceding, ratification by half the number of state legislatures. Between 1950 and 1990, the constitution was amended some seventy times, but without altering the basic structure of the system of government established in 1950.

Incontinent temperings with a constitution on the basic of overwhelming legislative majorities (see Table 10.1), in order to overcome constitutional obstacles, instil cynicism in the populace towards the principles of constitutional government. No constitution so wilful changed can command the necessary respect. Constitutional checks upon legislative powers are not antidemocratic in the sense of constituting checks upon sovereignty. In the Austrinian view sovereignty resides not in the elected body but in the electors, in the case of both the English and the American systems of government. The sovereign electorate may choose to make the legislature free from or subject to legal limitations (Hart, 1961, pp. 72-3). In Britain the First method is

TABLE 10.1
Constitutional amendments in India, 1950-93

	1950-59	1960-69	1970-79	1980-89	1990-1/6/93
No. of amendments	7	15	22	17	13

preferred, and the electorate exercises its sovereignty in electing legislators and thereafter delegates its sovereign power to parliament. By contrast, in democracies with legally limited legislatures, the electorate's sovereignty resides partly in the constitution and partly in parliament. The 'sovereignty of parliament versus constitutional checks' antithesis is a false equation that may, moreover, prove injurious to parliamentary democracy in its consequences. The dangers were well illustrated in the experience of India's Parliament during the 1975-77 emergency (Thakur, 1982)

Liberalism as the theory and practice of individual liberty is embodied in the constitutional state. A constitution is thus a formal statement of the liberties valued in society. In addition, however, the constitution is also a method of guaranteeing the liberties through enforcement mechanisms such as judicial review. An independent and powerful judiciary is one of the chief instruments for the attainment of the liberal goal of freedom from unrestricted state authority. The Indian constitution incorporated the principle in conferring substantial scope to the jurisdiction of courts and safeguarding the independence of their positions. As a result, the judiciary has been one of the most effective stabilising elements of democratic government in India.

Nevertheless, the evolution of tacitly recognised and mutually respected spheres of jurisdiction between the executive and the judiciary is an emergent necessity in Third World democracies. The complete insulation of the judiciary from governmental influence is an article of faith for liberal democracy. Yet the concept at best sits ill at ease in countries beyond the affluent West. Given the absence of a liberal society, is not an independent judiciary the most powerful bulwark of the entrenched elite against the democratic demands for equality?

The experience of the Indian emergency offer salutary warning against accepting such simplistic formulations. During the emergency, the Supreme Court effectively succumbed to governmental pressure and abdicated from its role as the guardian of individual rights against the state. In the historic *Golaknath* case (1967), the Supreme Court ruled, by a 6-5 majority, that fundamental rights could be abrogated by parliament even by means of constitutional amendments. In the landmark *Kesavananda Bharati* case (1973), the Supreme Court enunciated the doctrine that parliament, being a creature of the constitution, lacked the authority to amend 'the fundamental features' or 'basic structure' of the constitution. (Later, in the *Minerva Mills* case in 1980, judicial review was itself held to be an inseparable part of the basic structure of the constitution that could not be amended.) The judgement was delivered on 24 April 1973. Prime Minister Mrs Indira Gandhi's response on the very next day was to supersede three senior judges involved in the case and appoint Justice A.N. Ray as the next chief Justice of India. This was the first departure from the convention of appointing the senior-most judge of the Supreme Court as the Chief Justice.

During the 1975-77 emergency the same court under Chief Justice Ray's leadership failed to uphold the basic right of *habeas corpus*. Seven High Courts held that, despite the suspension of Article 21 by the declaration of the emergency, *habeas corpus* petitions were maintainable. On 28 April 1976, in a 4-1 majority verdict, the Supreme Court ruled that people detained during the emergency under the Maintenance of Internal Security Act (the notorious MISA) could not ask the High Courts to enforce their fundamental rights, including that of personal liberty. *Habeas corpus* petitions were no, therefore, admissible. The noted constitutional expert H.M. Seervai commented that coming 'at the darkest period in the history of independent India', the judgement 'made the darkness complete' (in Kapoor, 1984, p. 96). The lone but celebrated dissenting vote was that of Justice H.R. Khanna, who argued that the state had no power to deprive a citizen of his life or personal liberty without the authority of law. By contrast, Justice M.H. Beg talked about detainees being 'well-housed' well-fed and well-treated' with 'almost maternal care' (in Gupta, 1982, p. 297). In January 1977, after Ray's retirement as chief justice, the senior-most remaining judge was Khanna. He was superseded by beg as the new chief justice and resigned. (He was elected to parliament as part of the winning Janata coalition in the general election held shortly afterwards.)

In 1980, in the *Minerva Mills* case, the court overturned the 42nd Amendment Act that had sought to confer limitless power on parliament. The 59-clause bill, passed a pliant parliament during the emergency in 1976, had virtually rewritten significant parts of the constitution. It tried to overturn the *Kesavananda* verdict by declaring that there was no limitation of the power of parliament to amend the constitution, and that no constitutional amendment could be called into question in any court. Thus the power of judicial review would be severely curtailed. Fundamental rights were made subordinate to an expanded set of directive principles. In its verdict on the case in 1980, the Supreme Court held by a 4-1 majority that the Act. By converting a limited amending power into an unlimited one, deprived the courts of power of judicial review and thereby rendered fundamental rights into a 'writ in water'. In seeking to abrogate rights that give meaning to freedom and democracy, the Act disturbed the constitutional harmony between fundamental rights and directive principles and therefore contravened the constitution (OHT, 14 August 1980).

The fact that the emergency was precipitated in 1975 by the decision of the Allahabad High Court finding Mrs Gandhi guilty of corrupt electoral practices showed how the judiciary has sometimes found itself in the eye of the political storm. In 1982 the High Court of Kolkata and Supreme Court of India found themselves involved in electoral politics. The Marxist state government wanted to hold elections by the due date of June 1982, and Election Commission was agreeable. The state Congress Party and Mrs Gandhi argued that there were irregularities in the state's electoral rolls which made it impossible to hold free and fair elections. When Justice Sabyasachi Mukherjee of the High Court halted the electoral process, the state government appealed the Supreme Court, one of whose justices had some harsh things to say about the objectivity of the High Court judge. (Mukherjee was later appointed to the Supreme Court and is remembered for basing his judgements on the legal merits of each case, regardless of whether they helped or embarrassed the government.) The five-judge constitution bench of the Supreme Court issued a unanimous verdict removing all restraints on the Election Commissions from proceeding with the elections (SW, 3 April 1982, p. 1).

Laws and Mores

The subject of executive-judiciary demarcation can be subsumed within a wider philosophical discussion of the desirability of a colonially derived judicial system continuing to operate in an independent country. In this regard recent Commonwealth history is a fertile field of study of the embryology of legal systems. As sovereignty over former colonial territories no longer resides in the Westminster Parliament, so the ultimate rule of recognition shift and develops a local root. An independent legal system emerges. But the composition, mode of enactment, and structure of the post-colonial legal system may still be that prescribed originally by Westminster. As Morris-Jones notes (1971, p. 240), 'The system of law itself in India is basically derived from the "expansion" or "migration" of the English common law.'

A difficulty arises in societies where the imported legal system is not congruent with the indigenous sector of social life. In such circumstances the criteria of validity used in courts will diverge markedly from the criteria of morality in general usage in the wider society. The relation between law and morals may not exist; but neither can a legal system be said to exist in anything but a formal sense where there is no habitual obedience to official rules. Law cannot be based merely on power but must rest equally on authority. For law to be authoritative, the criteria of legal validity must include at least an implicit reference to social mores. In fact, even 'judicial decision, especially on matters of high constitutional import, often involves choice between moral values, and not merely the application of some single outstanding morel principle' (Hart, 1961, p. 200).

The English legal tradition of adversarial proceedings in court operates on the assumption that the one issue at dispute can be isolated from its context of wider controversies, that the evidence presented is the truth, the whole truth, and nothing but the truth, and that in each isolated dispute one party is right and the other wrong in accordance with law and precedent, and the court is duty bound to sift through the facts and find accordingly. Not all societies function within such a tradition, and many have quite different institutions and structures to regulate conflict and its arbitration. In India, thus, villagers recognise that a dispute involves not just one issue but a network of controversies; that each disputant presents only his side of the dispute; that all disputants must continue to coexist and therefore any settlement must satisfy both sides by being a compromise (Weiner, 1965, p. 214).

The adversarial approach in such society in both its legal

and political manifestations can appear to be a method for aggravating rather than settling conflicts. An uncritical imposition of one over the other can simply jam the smooth running of society. Alien systems of law can no more hope to be sensitised adequately to the full nuances of local culture, customs, and mores than can foreign political theories. In consequences of the political-legal framework governing their decisions, even judges sensitive to 'progressive' aspirations find their sympathies severely constrained.

It may be the case that such sympathies are misplaced rather than the scope for their expression curtailed. Liberal democracy does not create social and political cleavages. It simply recognises and legitimates the struggle for power in politics, and provides constitutional means of managing it. The Supreme Court of India is undoubtedly a centre of political power, and the judicial process is a subset of the political process. Unlike other centers of political power, however, the Court has no determinate constituency to shield it in times of crisis. Former Justice H.R. Khanna argued at a convention in New Delhi in March 1982 that 'There is no office which is so infinitely powerful and at the same time so frightfully defenseless as the judge' (OHT, 1 April 1982, p. 11). The Supreme Court is therefore vulnerable to encroachments upon its role as a *de facto* opposition in a political system dominated by one party (Baxi, 1980). Indeed at times the opposition parties treat it as a court of last *political* recourse. Despite having such a rule thrust upon it, the Supreme Court has generally deferred to the government's right to initiate broad socioeconomic reforms. Neither the political nor judicial correlates of liberal democracy pose insurmountable obstacles it either economic growth or egalitarian redistribution.

Problems

In a speech in 1992, P.D. Desai (1992, pp. 2-3), Chief Justice of the Mumbai High Court, remarked on the increasing restiveness of the Indian people with their judicial system based on four factors:

> The slowness and inaccessibility (due to the heavy cost of legal services and ignorance of the general public about their rights and obligations and their enforceability) of the judicial process;

The antiquated nature of court procedures and management practices;

Flaws in procedural laws, lack of effective control of court proceedings and availability of multiple remedies at different rungs of the judicial ladder which enable dishonest and recalcitrant suitors to abuse the judicial process; and

The lowered standards of conduct, character and competence of the legal profession and judges (Desai, 1992, pp. 2-3).

Probably the most serious shortcoming of the Indian judiciary is its excruciating slowness. In a speech on 8 May 1982, Justice V.R. Krishna Iyer of the Supreme Court remarked that 'In India law is on fighting terms with justice'. He went on to offer this advice: 'Once you start a litigation, please execute a will naming the person who will continue the case in court' (SW, 8 May 1982, p. 3). In 193l, there were about twenty million cases pending in the courts of India (TOI, 13 December 1993). While the Allahabad High Court was disposing of a little over one thousands cases each year, its backlog grew by fifty thousand cases in 1988-89 (Pathak, 1992, p. 56). The Supreme Court itself accepts some 100 000 cases each year (compared with the 100-150 cases of the 5000 filed that the are accepted by the US Supreme Court): perhaps it should be more selective go as to minimise the danger of being 'mired in judicial trivia' (Hardgrave and Kochnek, 1993, p. 103). Part of the explanation for the multiplying backlog lies in the politicisation of the judiciary at all levels, part in its corruption at lower levels: justice delayed can mean pockets filled. Is the Indians' fondness for litigation to be explained by the fact that they use courts not to settle disputes but to further them? Is the lag between judicial theory and practice to be explained by the relationship of judicial norms to the social structure of the judicial system or by their incongruity with indigenous values? A more charitable interpretation is that the frequency and number of resorts to the courts is testimony to the people's faith in their judicial system compared with the other institutional of government.

Conclusion

The key to the successful establishment of constitutional

democracy in India may lie in the gradualism of the British tutelage. India went through a comparatively long gestation period of democratic institutions. The principle of gradualism informed the widening of institutions. The principle of gradualism informed the widening of elective government form local to national levels and the broadening of power-sharing arrangements between elective and appointive bodies. But if independent India was going to give meaning to the fine sentiments expressed in its constitution-if it was to protect minorities, give content to equality of opportunity, establish that democracy meant that all votes and equal value and that all citizens were answerable in court-then the judiciary, led by the Supreme Court of India, was going go have to provide firm guidance. Despite occasional failures of nerve, by and large it has done so. At times this has meant that the Supreme Curt has had to fill a political vacuum. But in general, for the rule of law to prevail, the judiciary must be seen to be universal, impartial and impersonal. Its task is to expand individual rights and state power simultaneously. It is a delicate and challenging task, but not one beyond the capacity of India's learned judges.

REFERENCES

Basu (1993). A standard authoritative account that has been constantly revised and updated over several editions.

Baxi (1980). Examines the apex court as a political institution.

Pylee (1992). A clear and accessible exposition of the main features of India's constitution by a leading authority in the field.

Seervai (1990-1991). The book on the subject of India's constitutional law.

11

Relations with Rashtrapathi[1]

The office of the Indian President is a unique institution. His status and functions are neither like those of the British Monarch nor of the American President although the Indian Constitution incorporates important features form the Constitutions of both these countries. In order to understand his position correctly, it is necessary to recall the background in which the Constitution of India was framed in 1964-69.

Having provided for a quasi-federal structure, the fathers of the Constitution were anxious to ensure that the Head of the State was not an ornamental figure nor, at the same time, was he made as powerful as the American President. As K. M. Munshi, who played a prominent part in framing the Constitution, says,

> 'The provisions were the outcome of a definite decision that the President should not be the creature of the Parliament nor the nominee of the party in power at the center, nor a figurehead as the President of the French Constitution of 1875, but an independent organ of the State representing the whole Union and exercising independent powers.'

Mode of Election

The Indian President is chosen by indirect election. The Constituent Assembly decided against direct election because it was considered unnecessary since under the parliamentary system of government, the real power would vest in the Cabinet and not in the President. Moreover, direct election would be a costly and cumbrous procedure, involving the exercise of franchise by a vast electorate of over 300 million people. So the

President is elected by an electoral college consisting of the elected members of both Houses of Parliament and the elected members of the legislative assemblies of the States. The election is held in accordance with the system of proportional representation by means of the single transferable vote, the voting being done by secret ballot. A candidate for election as President should be an Indian citizen, should have completed thirty-five years of age, be qualified for election as a member of the Lok Sabha,[2] and shall not hold any office for profit. On entering upon his office, he has to take a solemn oath affirming that: 'I will faithfully execute the office of the President ... to the best of my ability, preserve, protect and defend the Constitution and the law and that I will devote myself to the service and well-being of the people of India.' The President is elected for a term of five years but he is eligible for re-election. There are two ways by which he may quit office within the term of five years; by tendering his resignation in writing addressed to the Vice-President of India or by removal by impeachment for violating the Constitution.

Powers of the President

The President's powers fall broadly into three categories: executive, legislative, and judicial.

Executive Powers

Under Article 53 of the Constitution, the executive powers of the Union are vested in the President and shall be exercised by him either directly or through officers subordinate to him in accordance with the Constitution. He has Council of Ministers to 'aid and advise' him in the exercise of his functions. He appoints the Prime Minister and, on the latter's advise, the other ministers. The ministers shall hold office during the pleasure of the President,[3] and he administers the oath of office and of secrecy.

Article 77 lays down that

> 'all executive action the Government of India shall be expressed to be taken in the name of the President, that all orders and other instruments made and executed in the name of the President shall be authenticated in such manner as may be specified in rules to be made by the President and the validity of an order or instrument which is so authenticated shall not be called in question on the ground

> that it is not an order or instrument made or executed by the President.'

The Constitution empowers the President to make rules for the more convenient transaction of the Government of India and for the allocation of business among ministers. It also enjoins upon the Prime Minister to

> 'communicate to the President all decisions of the Council of Ministers relating to the administration of the affairs of the Union and proposals for legislation; to furnish such information relating to the administration of the affairs of the Union and proposals for legislation as the President may call for: and if the President so requires, to submit for the consideration of the Council of Ministers any matter on which a decision has been taken by a Minister buy which has not bee considered by the Council.'

The President also appoints, on the advice of the Cabinet, the Attorney-General of the Union, the Comptroller and Auditor-General, the judges of the Supreme Court[4] and High Courts, the Chairman and members of the Union Public Service Commission and the State Governors. He also appoints the Union Public Service Commission, the Chief Election Commissioner, the Finance Commission, a Commission to enquire into the administration to scheduled areas, a commission to study the condition of the backward classes, and so on.

Legislative Powers

The legislative powers of the President are the following: he may summon the Houses or either House to meet at such time and place as he thinks fit; he may prorogue the House and dissolve the House of the people. He may address either House of Parliament or both Houses together. He may send messages to either House of Parliament whether which with respect to a bill pending in parliament or otherwise. His assent is necessary for bills passed by Parliament to become law. He may also return a bill, which is not a money bill, to the House with his suggestions for reconsideration; and if the bill is again passed with or without the suggested amendments, the President has no power to withhold his assent. The President also has the power to disallow bills passed by a State Legislature and reserved for his assent; or he may send them back to the Governor for reconsideration by the legislature.

The President shall cause to be laid, in respect of every financial year, the annual financial statement, showing separately the sums required to meet expenditure described by the Constitution as expenditure charged upon the Consolidated Fund of India, and the sums required to meet other expenditure proposed to be made from the Consolidated Fund. The President also shall cause certain reports to be placed before Parliament, such as the report of the Auditor-General concerning the accounts of the Government of India, the report of the Finance Commission together with a memorandum explaining the action taken thereon, the report of the Union Public Service Commission, the report of the Special Officer for Scheduled Castes and Tribes, the report of the Commission on backward classes; and the report of the Special Officer for linguistic minorities.

The President has the power the issue ordinance when he is satisfied that circumstances exist which render it necessary for him to take immediate action. Every such ordinance must be laid before both Houses of Parliament and it will cease to operate at the expiry of six weeks after the re-assembly of Parliament, or earlier if disapproved by both House. The President also may withdraw the ordinance.

The ordinance making power of the President has been criticized by some persons on the ground that it encroaches on the sovereignty of Parliament. But this criticisms is not justified because the President can exercise this power only on the advice of the Cabinet, and not in his discretion, and only when Parliament is not in session.

Judicial Powers

The judicial powers of the President include the right to grant pardons, reprieves, respites or remissions of punishment or to suspend, remit or commute the sentence on persons convicted by court martial and in cases in which the sentence of death has been passed. The President also has the power to refer any question of public importance to the Supreme Court for its opinion.

Emergency Powers

Apart from the normal powers of the President described above, he has been endowed with certain emergency powers, broadly of three categories. The President may issue a proclamation of emergency when he is satisfied that the security of India, or any part therefore, has been threatened by war, external aggression or internal disorder. Such a proclamation must be laid before each House of Parliament. It will cease to operate at the expiry of two months unless before that period it has been approved by both Houses of Parliament. The effect of the proclamation is that, for all practical purposes during the period of the emergency, the State Governments will be under the complete control of the central Government. The latter is empowered to give directions to any State Government regarding the manner in which its executive power is to be exercised; and Parliament will have the power to legislate on subjects in the State list as well. The financial relations between the Centre and the States may also be suitably modified if necessary by Presidential order. Moreover, so long as the emergency is in force, the right of citizens to move the Courts for the enforcement of fundamental rights remains suspended. For the first time the President issued a proclamation of emergency under Article 352 on October 26, 1962 when India was invaded by China; and the proclamation continues to be in force till the time of writing.

The second types of emergency relates to the failure of constitutional machinery in the states: when the President is satisfied that administration of a State cannot be carried on in accordance with the Constitution, he may issue a proclamation under Article 356 by which the Central Government may take over all the functions, expect judicial, of the State. Such proclamations have been issued on four occasions in Kerala in 1956, 1959, in 1964, and in 1965; and also once in the Punjab in 1950 and in Andhra in 1954.

The President is also empowered under Article 360 to issue a proclamation when he is satisfied that the financial stability or credit of India or of any part of the territory thereof is threatened. When such a proclamation is in operation, the Central Government has the power to issue directions to any State to observe suitable canons of financial propriety, which may include a provision requiring the reduction of salaries and allowances of all or any class of persons serving in connection with the affairs of the Union, including judge of the Supreme Court and High Courts as well as of a State Government. The proclamation may also require all bills or other financial Bills to be reserved for the consideration of the President after they are passed by the State Legislature.

The Constitution also vests the supreme command of the Defence Forces of Indian Union in the President, but he will exercise the powers in this respect in accordance with the law.

President's Secretariat

The President is assisted by two secretaries. One is designated as Secretary to the President and the other as Military Secretary to the President. Each Secretary has his separate establishment. The Secretary to the President is usually a very senior member of the Civil Service. He provides the liaison between the President and the Departments of the Government of India. He places before the President all papers that require his sanction or instructions, and conveys them to the appropriate departments. The Secretary also arranges interviews with the president and looks after the President's correspondence with State Governors as well as with the various non-official or organizations with which he is connected.

The main work of the Military Secretary is to make suitable arrangements for all functions that take place in the Rashtrapathi Bhawan or the Prime Minister's House, to draw up the tour programme of the President, to allot accommodation in the President's Estate and in the Rashtrapathi Bhawan, and to supervise the arrangements in connection with entertainments given by the President, Vice-President or the Prime Minister.

How The President Uses His Powers

It is thus clear that Indian Constitution vests the President[5] with vast powers over vital aspects of the administration. However, opinion, seems divided among constitutional experts about the actual status of the President. Some argue that whatever the Constitution may say, in practice, the President can, and should, act only in accordance with the advice of Cabinet in the interests of smooth administration. But others hold the view that if the President were to act always in accordance with the wishes of the Cabinet, it will ultimately results in the destruction of democracy. It will be useful to summarize briefly both these points of view.

The exponents of the first school of thought suggest that although the Constitution does not specifically law down that the President should act always on the advice of the Cabinet, it was expected by the authors of the Constitution that he would conduct himself on the model of the British monarch so as to maintain the sovereignty of the Indian Parliament. If the President did not do so, it would mean that Parliament would not be supreme, for under the Constitution, the actions of the President could not be discussed in Parliament.

It is interesting to recall that the Constituent Assembly had originally intended to incorporate in the Constitution an instrument, of instructions making it obligatory on the President to act always in accordance with the advice of the Cabinet. The instruction proposed was as follows: 'In all matters within the scope of the executive power of the Union, the President shall, in the exercise of the powers conferred upon him, be guided by the advice of his ministers.' But subsequently this proposal was dropped. B. N. Rau points out in his *Indian Constitution* in the Making that a number of members of the Constituent Assembly objected to this proposal dropped because it was not clear how far the conventions of the British Constituent would be binding under the Indian Constitution. But the Law Minister categorically assured them that the conventions would be binding on parliament. He was specifically asked: 'If in any particular case the President does not act upon the advice of his Council of Ministers, will that be tantamount to a violation of the Constitution and will he be liable to impeachment?' To this question the Law Minister's answer was: 'There is not the slightest doubt about it.' The Constituent Assembly, on this assurance, agreed to omit the clause.

B.N. Rau also makes the important point that 'acting on ministerial advice does not necessarily mean the immediate acceptance of the Ministry's first thoughts. The President can state all his objections to any proposed course of action and ask his ministers in Council, if necessary, to reconsider the matter. It is only in the last resort that he should accept their final advice.'

Rajendra Prasad also expressed the view in the Constituent Assembly that the President should conduct himself as a constitution monarch. He said:

> 'Although there is no specific provision in the Constitution itself making it binding on the president to accept the advice of his ministers, it is hoped that the convention, under which in England the king always acted on the advice of his ministers, would be established in this country also and that the President would become cons‘‘itutional President in all matters.'

But other eminent constitutional experts, including Patanjali Sastri, a former Chief Justice of the Supreme Court, have asserted that the President is under no obligation to act always on the advice of his minister. The Constitution, they argue, has provided for a Council of Ministers to aid to advice the President but nowhere is it laid down, as it has been done in the Irish Constitution, that the should always be guided by them. They point out that unlike as in Britain, the Indian Constitution provides for a quasi-federation where there is a clear demarcation of powers between the Centre and the States. Both the Central and State Legislatures participate in the election of the President, who has the responsibility to ensure the autonomy of the States against encroachment from the Centre. 'If the powers of the President are passed on to the Prime Minister and the President becomes a figure-head', says K. M. Munshi, 'the character of the Union as a quasi-federation will be destroyed. The Union will become a unitary one and its powers maintaining the unity of the country will also be materially impaired,'

The exponents of this view quote in their support Article 61 which provides for impeachment of the President if he violates the Constitution. The charge can be initiated by either House of Parliament, after giving at least 14 days' notice in writing, signed by no fewer than one fourth of the total number of members of the House, and the resolution should be passed by a majority of not less than two-thirds of the total membership of the House. A charge so preferred by either House of parliament will be investigated by the other House and the President has the right to appear and to be represented at such investigation. The President will be removed from office if, as a result of the investigation, a resolution is passed by a majority of not less than two-thirds of the total membership of the House by which the charge was investigated, sustaining the charge against him.

In view of this clear provision for impeachment, it is suggested that the president has a personal responsibility to preserve and protect the Constitution—a responsibility which cannot be passed on to the Cabinet. It is, therefore, contended that there is not, and cannot be any legal obligation on the President to accept the advice of the ministers. Munshi in fact argues that some of the President's powers are 'super-ministerial' where the Cabinet 'could not be relied upon to advise him'. These include the power to dismiss a Prime Minister who does not enjoy the leadership of the Party, to remove a ministry which lost the confidence of the Parliament, to dissolve the Lok Sabha when it cease to command the confidence of the people, and to exercise the authority of the Supreme Commander in an emergency where the ministry has failed to defend the country. Munshi also recalls the opinion expressed by Nehru in the Constitution Assembly: 'We did not want the president to be just a mere figurehead like the French President.'

President and Prime Minister

From the strictly constitutional point of view, Munshi's interpretation seems correct.[6] But what ultimately matters is the personality of the president as well as his personal relationship with the Prime Minister. So far, the Constitution has worked smoothly because of the cordial relationship between the President and the Prime Minister and because the same political party, namely the Congress, has been in power both at the Centre and in the States even since the Constitution came into force in January 1950.[7]

India's first President was Rajendra Prasad, veteran Congressman and a close associate of Mahatma Gandhi. Before the attainment of freedom, Prasad had served as the Congress President for three terms and as member of the Congress Working Committee for a number of the years. He was Minister of Food and Agriculture in the Interim Government of India set up in September 1946 but resigned the post on being elected President of the Constituent Assembly. His election as President of the Indian Republic in January 1950 was opposed by the late

Professor K.T. Shah, an eminent economist. But Prasad was elected by 2,896 votes out of the total of 3,486 votes cast.

Prasad and Nehru had been intimate colleagues in the Congress for many decades and both had great respect and affection for each other, although their outlook on political and economic problems was not always identical. While Nehru favoured radical and rapid reforms in the country's economic and social structure, Prasad wanted to go slow so that the Government could carry public opinion with it. It was, therefore, unsurprising that sometimes differences arose between the President and the Prime Minister on certain major issues.

For instance, when the Government wanted in 1950 to rush through the Hindu Code Bill, which sought to bring about drastic changes in the marriage and property laws of Hindus, Prasad advised the Prime Minister against its hasty legislation. The President's view was that there was no urgency to take up the reform of only one community and that, moreover, the Constituent Assembly did not have the mandate from the people to introduce social legislation of a revolutionary nature. The Bill met with strong opposition both from within the Congress and other sections of Public opinion and the Government, therefore, was compelled to postpone its consideration.

Food policy was another major question on which the President and the Prime Minister did not see eye to eye. The Government's proposals to impose ceilings on landholdings, to introduce co-operative farming and to resort to State trading in foodgrains created uncertainty in the country, particularly in the rural areas. Prasad, who had an intimate acquaintance with India's agricultural problem, felt that these measures were likely to disrupt production, dislocation the trade and dampen initiative and enthusiasm on the part of the people, especially among those engaged in agricultural pursuits. Therefore, in a letter to the Prime Minister in June 1959, Prasad gave expression to these views and advised a reconsideration of the proposals. He pointed out that food production should not be mixed with the programme of social legislation. State trading in foodgrains would result in multiplying and aggravating difficulties because, apart form other factors, it required a tremendous organization and trained personnel. He urged the encouragement of the existing large agricultural farm for utilizing mechanized methods. He also recommended the formation of service co-operatives of small farmers by providing the necessary credit, improved seeds and irrigation facilities. The President added that positive action to discourage hoarding would achieve better results than the price control.

Nehru in his reply welcomed the President's suggestions and pointed out that while State trading in foodgrains had resulted in immediate difficulties, including an increase in price, the Government had no alternative. He also laid emphasis on the service co-operatives though he would like co-operative farming to develop gradually.

Although the correspondence between the President and the Prime Minister was meant to be strictly confidential, its contents leaked to the Press; and K. L. Punjabi, who was Secretary to the President, records in his biography of Prasad, that the publication of the President's letter.

> 'strengthened the hands of the State governments which were reluctant to undertake State trading. . . . The President's views were generally supported by the Press and by thoughtful people, among whom were numbered many Congressmen whose voices could not be heard in the party'.

Another important letter from the President to the prime Minister, which also found its way into the newspapers, was in regard to corruption in high places. C. D. Deshmukh, a former Finance Minister, had suggested, in a speech in Madras towards the end of 1959, the need for a high-powered tribunal to examine the charges of corruption against ministers and other influential persons. He also asserted that he had concrete evidence to confirm charge of corruption, against some top people in the government but he would disclose it only to an independent tribunal. Prasad observed that the Government should consider seriously Deshmukh's suggestion and take prompt and effective measures to root out corruption. Nehru, however, regretted his inability to set up a tribunal although he fully shared the President's anxiety to put down corruption.

The introduction of Hindi for official purposes was another major issue on which the Prime Minister and the President differed. Prasad felt that the use of Hindi in Government offices should be speedily and vigorously encouraged so that it might become the sole official language as early as possible. Nehru, on the other hand, was of opinion that the Government should not force the pace of Hindi if offices because, first, there were practical difficulties in using it at all levels of administration and secondly, such a course would meet with stiff opposition from non-Hindi areas, especially from the South.

These instances clearly how that India's first President did not function like a figure-head and that he did try to influence the Cabinet on major decisions. In fact, Prasad even suggested in his address to the Indian Law Association in 1961 that there was need to consider what exactly were the powers enjoyed by the President under the Constitution. The President's remarks caused some surprise in the country because he himself had played a conspicuous part in framing the Indian Constitution, and many wondered what was the purpose in having the relevant provisions examined. When Nehru enquired of Prasad as to what it was all about, the latter was reported to have told the Prime Minister that it was only a casual suggestion he had made while addressing a gathering of lawyers.

Although the President and the prime Minister did differ on some a major issues, the relationship between them was perfectly cordial; and when prasad retired in May 1962 the Prime Minister and Parliament paid him warm tributes for the ability and tact with which he had conducted himself in this high office for twelve years. The address presented to him on May 8, 1962 said

> 'By your qualities of unostentatious grace, your utter simplicity, clarity of outlook, keep humility and broad humanity, you invested a special meaning and significance in your choice as President. As the first President of India, you have enriched and embellished the office and are leaving behind inspiring traditions'.

Prasad was succeeded by S. Radhakrishnan who had served as Voice-President of India since 1952. As scholar, professor and philosopher, he had won great renown both in India and abroad. He had also been India's Ambassador in Moscow for three years. Within a few months after his election as President of India came the massive invasion by China in October 1962, and the President, therefore, proclaimed an Emergency in November under Article 352 of the Constitution.

During the four years he has been President, Radhakrishnan has shown courage and statesmanship of a high order. He made no secret of the fact the Chinese invasion had greatly hurt the prestige of India. In a speech in Bombay in January 1963, he described India's reverses in NEFA as 'a matter of sorrow, shame and humiliation'. His speeches in the United States and the United Kingdom, which he visited in 1963, helped to create a better understanding of India's foreign policy, and strengthened India's friendship with the Western world.

Radhakrishnan often been quite frank in expressing his views on important problems. For example, in his address to the first convocation of the Uttar Pradesh Agricultural University in November 1963, he attributed the stagnation in India's agriculture to administrative inefficiency. India's farmers, he said, were intelligent, capable of accepting new methods, and applying them to the development of agriculture. So, if the farmers were good and the land was there and the Government was improving the irrigation facilities, what was it that had led to this deterioration in agricultural production? The President raised this question and pointed out that the failure in agriculture indicated nothing more than 'lack of true' wise leadership and administrative efficiency'.

Again in his broadcast to the nation on Republic Day in January 1964, Radhakrishnan cautioned the country against complacency towards corruption. 'It would be well to recognize', he said, 'that the tolerance of our society for weak, inefficient and unclean administration is not unlimited'.

As in the case of India's first President, Nehru and Radhakrishnan also got on together very well indeed. In his Republic Day message in January 1964, Radhakrishnan expressed his pleasure and that of the people of India in Nehru's rapid recovery from his illness, and paid a warm tribute to the Prime Minister's leadership. The President said: 'He has brought a modern, secular and scientific outlook to our difficult and diverse problems and has, indeed, reflected the national purpose over these years. More than anyone, our Prime Minister has helped us to put us on the right track in our quest for national integration and orderly growth.' And on the death of Nehru, the President, in the course of a broadcast to the nation, said:

> 'Nehru held the office of the Prime Minister of our country ever since the dawn of independence; and in the long years of his Premiership, tried to put our country on a progressive, scientific, dynamic and non-communal basis. His steadfast loyalty to certain fundamental principles of liberalism gave direction to our thought and life. . . He used the existing social and political institutions and breathed into them a new spirit, a new vitality.'[8]

The war with Pakistan was the major event during the eighteen-month tenure of Shastri as the Prime Minister. During the twenty-two days when the fighting want, on the President kept himself in close touch with military developments and gave his full support to the Prime Minister. As the Supreme Commander, the President encouraged the armed forces to give of their best and also inspired the people through broadcasts to keep their morale high. And when the cease-fire was proclaimed on September 22nd , he publicly congratulated Shastri and the Chiefs of Staff. He said:

> 'I should like to congratulate our Prime Minister and the Government and our Chiefs of Staff, General Chaudhuri, Air Marshal Arjan Singh and Vice-Admiral Soman, on the hard and excellent work which they and those working under their leadership have done in these difficult days. We have today retrieved our prestige and it is my hope that our Army, Air Force and Navy will continue to function with daring, heroism and skill and be treated as a force to be reckoned with'.

NOTES

1. Rashtrapathi, a Hindi word, means President of the Indian Republic.
2. But the President shall not be a member of either House of Parliament or of any State Legislature.
3. In practice, as we have seen earlier, the choice of ministers is solely at the discretion of the Prime Minister. The President is bound to appoint as Prime Minister the leader of the majority party in the Lok Sabha and accept his nominees as ministers.

4. While appointing judges of the Supreme Court, the President has to consult also the Chief Justice of the Supreme Court.
5. The Constitution provides for a Voice-President who is *ex-officio* the Chairman of the Rajya Sabha. He is elected by members of both House of Parliament assembled at a joint meeting in accordance with the system of proportional representation. The Vice-President shall act as President in the event of any vacancy caused by the latter's death, resignation, or removal until the new President is elected. But the Vice-President does not automatically become the President when a permanent vacancy occurs. He merely acts as President, till the election is held. The Vice-President, when he acts as President, shall have all the powers of the President.
6. The following comments on the President's constitutional position, made by India's Supreme Court, in *Ram Jawaya* V. *State of Punjab* (1955), are significant: 'Under Article 53 (1) of our Constitution, the executive power of the Union is vested in the President, but under Article 75 there is to be a Council of Minister with the Prime Minister at the head to aid and advise on his functions. The President has thus been made a formal head of the executive and the real executive powers are vested in the Ministers or the Cabinet. The same provisions obtain in regard to the Government of States: the Governor occupies the position of the head of the executives in the State, but it is virtually the Council of Ministers in each State that carries on the executive Government. In the Indian Constitution therefore we have the same system of parliament executive as in England, and the Council of Ministers, consisting as it does of the members of the Legislature, is like the British Cabinet - "a happen which joins, a buckle which fastens the legislative part of the State to the executive part".
7. In Kerala, however, the communist party was in power for a brief period of twenty-seven months in 1957-59.
8. The role of the President in forming a caretaker government, following the death of Nehru, has been described in Chapter X.

12

Democracy and the Multiplicity of Religious Sects in India

It is very often said that democracy is not suited to India because it is inhabited by people of different creeds and religious sects. This argument is made use of by the people of Christian countries from the experience they have had of their own countries. In those countries, secularisation of politics is a thing not many centuries old. Because in Europe members of different denominations used to persecute one another, hence they argue that such must be the case in other countries also whose inhabitants are not composed of one religious sect. But the natives of India have been always comparatively tolerant. India should not be judged by the standard of the Christian countries and Christian nations of the West. The great German thinker and philosopher Schopenhauer has very truly observed:.

> "In comparison with the Christian centuries that followed, the ancient world was undoubtedly less cruel than the Middle Age, with its death by frightful torture, its countless burning at the stake; further, the ancients were very patient, thought very highly of justice, and frequently sacrificed themselves for their country, showed traits of magnanimity of every kind, and such genuine humanity, that up to the present time, an acquaintance with their doings and thoughts is called the study of Humanity. Religious wars, massacres inquisition as well as other persecutions, the extermination of the original inhabitants of Christianity, and among the ancients one cannot find anything analogues to this, anything to counterpoise it.

> Think of the fanaticism, of the endless persecutions, the religious wars that sanguinary frenzy of which the ancients had no idea; then, think of the Crusades, a massacre lasting two hundred years, and perfectly unwarrantable, with its war-cry. It is God's will, so that it might get into its possession the grave of one who had preached love and endurance; think of the cruel expulsion and extermination of the Moors and Jews from Spain; think of the massacres, of the inquisitions and other heretical tribunals, the bloody and terrible conquests of the Mohammedans in these different parts of the world, and the conquests of the Christians in America, whose inhabitants were for the most part, and in Cuba entirely, exterminated: according to Las Gasas, within forty years twelve million persons were murdered of course, all in *majorem deigloriam*, and for the spreading of the Gospel, and because, moreover what was not Christian was not looked upon as human.
>
> As a matter of fact, intolerance is only essential to monotheism; and only god is by his nature a jealous god, who cannot permit any other god to exist. On the other hand polytheistic gods are by their nature tolerant: they live and let live; they willingly tolerate their colleagues and being gods of the same religion, and this tolerance is afterwards extended to alien gods, who are accordingly, hospitably received, and latter on sometimes attain even the same rights and privileges; as in the case of Romans, who willingly accepted and venerated Phygian, Egyptian, and other foreign gods. Hence it is the monotheistic religions alone that furnish us with religious wars, persecutions, and heretical tribunals, and also with the breaking of images, the destruction of the idols of the gods: the overthrowing of Indian temples and Egyptian colossi, which had looked on the sun three thousands years; and all this because a jealous God had said: "Thou shalt make no graven images."

Schopenhauer has placed Muhammadanism also on the same level with Christianity as having caused murder and bloodshed in the world. That may have been so in other parts of the,world, but certainly not so in India under Musalman rule. When the

Muhammdans settled in India as rulers, they generally showed every scrupulous regard for the religious susceptibilities of their Hindu subjects. Much of the proselytising zeal and fanaticism of the followers of the Crescent had disappeared when they came to India. This was mainly duet to Islam being tempered with *sufism*, which is allied to *Vedantism*. Persian poets were *sufis*, and Muhammadans having settled in India were indirectly influenced by the teachings of the *Vedanta*, for no one living in India can avoid its subtle influence. Says Max Muller:

> "This Vedanta spirit pervades the whole of India. It is not restricted to the higher classes. It lives in the very language of the people, and is preached in the streets and in the forest by mendicant saints."

The Christian English have not come under its influence because they have not settled in India and do not mix with the natives of this country. Just as "conquered Greece conquered her conquerors," so the conquered Hindus had conquered their Muhammadan conquerors by infusing into their minds the spirit of the Vedanta. It is expressed in that formula in Sanskrit *tatvamasi*, i.e., "Thou art He." Professor Deussan says:

> "The Gospels fix quite correctly: as the highest law of morality: 'love your neighbour as yourselves.' But why would I do so, since by the order of nature I feel pain and pleasure only in myself: not in my neighbour? The answer is not in the Bible (this venerable book being not yet quite free of sematic realism), but it is in the *Veda*, is in the great formula *'tat tvam asi,'* which gives in three words metaphysics and morals together. You shall love your neighbour, and mere illusion makes you believe, that your neighbour is something diffent from yourselves. "And so the Vedanta, in its unfalsified form is the strongest support of pure morality, is the greatest consolation in the sufferings of life and death-Indians, keep to its!"

Yes, Indians, wether Hindus or Muhammadans, have always kept to it. And because the Muhammadans came under its influences they lost their fanaticism and became tolerant. What spirit of catholicity breathes in the poems of the Mohammedan poets!

It must be admitted that Aurangzib was a bigot. But then he was an abnormal specimen of a man. He ill-treated his father by making him a captive, murdered his brothers.

There is a pretty story in the *Mantiq-ut-Taiq* of Farid-ud-din, which shows the religious tolerance of Persian poet. It runs thus: One night the words "I hear" came from the presence of God. Gabriel said, "there must be some servant of God, calling on Him, a man of pure heart and subdued passion. I must know who he is." The Angel sought in vain through the seven heavens, on sea and on land, in the hills and in the plains. At last by command of God Gabriel went to Rum. There he found the man he sought praying before an idol. " O thou source of all good," cried the angel, "unveil to me this mystery. This man is invoking an idol, and Thou in thy grace answerest him." Then God said, and sapped the foundation of the Moghul Empire by his unprovoked wars in the Deccan. From a man of his nature, it was too much to expect toleration or good government. However his bigotry and want of toleration may be accounted for, if we remember the fact that he spent the most impressionable years of his life in Southern India and thus came more or less under the spell of the Portuguese who were notorious for their Inquisition and persecution of the non-Christians. Aurangzib imbibed their spirit. Many a Hindu temple did he demolish and many a Hindu did he cruelly persecute. Regarding his zeal for breaking Hindu temples, one of his Hindu courtiers once said to him:

> "Behold, my lord, the miracle of my house of idol; when it becomes useless, it becomes the house of God."

This observation of one of his Hindu courtiers made such a deep impression on him, that he gave up the practice of breaking temples and idols.

It is not true then that the Muhammadans made a business of cutting the throats of the Hindus. India is about equal to Europe minus Russia. Period for period, there has never been greater bloodshed in India than in Europe. Until they came under the influence of Europeans, Moslem and Hindu were living in comparative peace and harmony and as brothers, because they were all children of the Indian soil. Many a Hindu prince built mosques for the Muhammadans, and this feeling was reciprocated by the latter also. In the provinces which contained the capitals of the Muhammadan sovereigns of India, and where anti-Muhammadan feeling should have been very; predominant had the Hindus been generally persecuted by Muhammadan subjects. Thus in Bareilly which was founded by Raja Makaranda Rai, a Jama Masjid was erected by that prince for the use of the Muhammadans.

In an article on "*Swaraj* or self-rule in Oriental Countries," we have shown how Hindus are well treated by their Muhammadan neighbours. "If from ignorance he has missed the way, shall I who know the way not teach him? My grace shall plead for his pardon and bring him to the truth."

This is no isolated utterance as all who have any acquaintance with Persian literature will testify. Over and over again we are told that all who earnestly seek God, whatever be their religion, will find Him. Nor is Muhammadan tolerance a mere matter of theory.

It has always been displayed in practice by the best Muhammadan rulers. The Omeyyads might almost be said to have carried tolerance to an excess, for they discouraged the conversion of their Christian subjects.

The Indian people have neighbours in Afghanistan. We know the Afghans are an illiterate class of people and, therefore, given to blood feuds and quarrels. If they were religious fanatics, then there would be nothing to prevent them from polishing off the Hindu inhabitants of Afghanistan in no time. But they do not molest or ill-treat the Hindus.

The fact is that Europeans judge others by their own standard. They imagine that the votaries of one creed would behave towards those of another creed, as they themselves are in the habit of treating non-Christians or even Christians who do not belong to the same sect as they do. Because they themselves lack toleration, they imagine that others must likewise do the same.

But a homogeneous population in a country is not necessarily an advantage from the point of view of the political progress of that nation. In his "Dialogue on the best form of government," the Right Honorable Sir George Cornwall Lewis, Baronet, M.P. puts the following in the mouth of Aristocraticus:

"It is mainly by the existence of parties powerful enough to secure attention to the interests and arguments of a minority that political improvement is accomplished. Entire unanimity on political questions is in general an evil: political discord, is to a certain point an advantage to a State. All received opinions on political subjects cannot be right; all existing laws cannot be wise and expedient.

Even unity in matters of religion is, for civil purposes, disadvantageous. The existence of various sects is a guarantee for religious liberty, and a protection against ascendancy of various sects is a guarantee for religious liberty, and a protection against religious tyranny and persecution. Nothing, in a political and intellectual point of view, would at present be more beneficial to Italy and Spain than the formation of religious sects, strong enough to resist the dominant Church. If Charles V, Philip II, and Lonis XIV, had understood the true interest and duty of a civil ruler, the would, instead of extinguishing religious dissent by force, rather have thrown, like Cadmus, a stone into the midst of the conflicting parties."

Nature abhors monotony and discord, but loves diversity and harmony. India has been the home of different religions and creeds, but because there was always comparative harmony amongst them, so there was always religions liberty and not much religious persecution. It is because of the existence of this toleration and religious liberty, that it has been possible for India to have given to the world Comparative Philology and Comparative Mythology. Says Sir Henry Summer Maine:

"It may yet give us a new science not less valuable than the sciences of language and fold-lore. I hesitate to call it Comparative Jurisprudence, because, if it ever exists, its area will be a so much wider than the field of law. For India not only contains (or to speak more accurately, did contain) an Aryan language older than any other descendant of the common mother-tongue, and a variety of names of natural objects less perfectly crystallised than elsewhere into fabulous personages, but it includes a whole world of Aryan institutions, Aryan beliefs, in far earlier stage of growth and development than any which survive beyond its borders."

It would have been quite impossible for India to have given all these sciences to the world had there been one common religion in this country as it is in many other lands.

No, varieties of religion do not stand in the way of swaraj or self-rule, if some one does not try to create mischief by pitting the followers of one religious sect against those of another.

Let us now take a specific episode of religious prosecution in the history of India. The Sikhs were badly treated and persecuted by the fanatical Maghul Emperor Aurangzib and his effeminate descendants. This accounts for the retaliatory spirit of the Sikhs. The sect founded by the mild and meek Baba Nanak was forced by circumstances to become a church militant under Guru Govind. Sir John Malcolm in his sketch of the Sikhs, says:

> "Though the Sikhs had already, under Har Govind, been initiated in arms, yet they appear to have used these only in self-defence: and as every tribe of Hindus, from the Brahman to the lowest of the *sudra*, may, in cases of necessity, use them without any infringement of the original institutions of their tribe. No violation of these institutions, was caused by the rules of Nanak; which formed with a view to conciliation, carefully abstained from all interference with the civil institutes of the Hindus. But his more daring successor, Guru Govind, saw that such observances were at variance with the plans of his lofty ambition; and he wisely judged, that the only means by which he could ever hope to oppose Muhammadan Government with success, were not only to admit converts form all tribes, but to break, at once, those rules by which the Hindus had been so long been chained; to arm, in short, the whole population of the country and to make worldly wealth and rank an object to which Hindus of every class, might aspire.
>
> In the character of this reformer of the Sikhs, it is impossible not to recognise many of those features which have distinguished the most celebrated founders of political communities. The object he attempted was great and laudable. It was the emancipation of his tribe from oppression and persecution: and the means which he adopted, were such as a comprehensive mind could alone have suggested. The Muhammadan conquerors of India, as they added to their

territories, added to their strength, by making proselytes through the double means of persuasion and force; and these, the moment they had adopted their faith, became the supporters of their power against the efforts of the Hindus, who bound in the chains of their civil and religious institutions could neither add to their number by admitting converts, nor allow more than a small proportion of the population of the country to arm against the enemy. Govind said that he could only hope for success by a bold departure from usages which were calculated to keep those, by whom they were observed, in a degraded subjection: to an insulting and intolerant race. 'You make Hindus Muhammedans,' and are: justified by your laws,' he is said to have written to Aurangzeb: 'now I, on principle of self preservation, which is superior to all laws, will make Muhammedans Hindus. You may rest,' he added, 'in fancied security security: but beware! For I will teach the sparrow to strike the eagle to the ground.' A fine allusion to his design of inspiring the lowest races among the Hindus with that valor and ambition which lead them to perform the greatest actions."

It is true that Guru Govind gave the following injunctions to his followers: "It is right to slay a Muhammedan wherever you meet him. Employ your constant efforts to destroy the countries ruled by Muhammedans; if they oppose you, defeat and slay them." But had the Sikhs acted on his injunctions, it is not too much to say, that not a single Muhammedan would have been this day left in the Punjab. Maharajah Ranjeet Singh was never intolerant to the Muhammedans. He appointed Muhammedans to positions of trust and responsibility. The most noted of his ministers was a Muhammedan.

It is often alleged by those who ought to know better, that the Sikhs destroyed the mosques of the Muhammedans. Had this been so, not single mosque would have been seen in the Punjab to-day. On the other hand, the following instances of Sikhs religious tolerance are mentioned by Mr. R.W. Trafford in the Punjab Notes and Queries:

"The principal queen of Maharajah Ranjit Singh, lived in Shekhupura (Gujranwala District), where she built a Masjid for her Muhammedan subjects. In a similar spirit of liberality a Masjid was created at Botala Sivalay by Sikh sardar."

Aurangzib was no doubt a fanatic Muhammedan king. But even he was so tolerant to the Hindus, that he entrusted them with high and responsible posts for the management of his vast Empire.

That the Hindu revival of the later seventeenth and the early eighteenth centuries under Shivaji and his descendants was not due so much to religious as political caused will be evident from the fact that the faithful servants of the Moghul empire when that empire was in extremis were Hindus and not Muhammadans. For it was the Hindu governors and viceroys who were loyal and exerted their utr :ost for the safety and greatness of the Moghul Empire. The rise of the Marathas was not a little due to the help accorded to them by the treacherous Moghul Viceroy of the Deccan, the first Nizam-ul-Mulk. When the assistance and connivance of the Nizam, the Marathas were ravaging the territories then under the sway of the Moghul Empire of Delhi, it is recorded in the Siyar-ul-Mutakherin, that the Hindu Viceroy of Malwa, named "Raja Giridhar,: who commanded in the country with a small body of troops, would not suffer his country to be ravaged; and being an officer of character, he engaged Baji Rao several times, after having in vain requested assistance form the capital. His repeated representations to the throne and to the ministers availed nothing, and that brave man, having, wasted his small force in endless skirmishes, at last fell . . . himself in one of them."

The Hindu governor of Gujarat who also loyal to the Moghul Emperor. But compare and contrast their conduct with that of the Nizam-ul-Mulk and other Muhammadan viceroys and governors of that period.

Had there been persecution of the Hindus by their Muhammedan rulers, does it not stand to reason that in the hour of need of the latter, they would have one and all conspired against them and tried to throw off their yoke?

English historians have described Tippoo as almost an incarnation of Satan and very intolerant to non-Muhammedans. If such were the fact, how was it that he suffered a Hindu to be his Prime Minister? Purneah, the Talleyrand of Mysore, was his Chief Minister, and the country flourished under him.

13

The State Executive: The Governor

The machinery of government in the States is organised on the same pattern as that of the Union Government. Hence, in the light of our discussion on the machinery of the Union Government, the task of analysing the organisation and working of the State Government becomes comparatively easy. As in the Union, the government in the State also is organised on the parliamentary model. The Head of the State is called the Governor who is the constitutional head of the State as the President is for the whole of India. The Chief of the State Government is called the Chief Minister who is at he counterpart in the State, of the Prime Minister of India. There is a Council of Ministers for each of the States as in the Union. The organisation of the State Legislature is also more or less on the model of the Indian Parliament. In the judicial field, the High Courts, for all practical purposes, occupies the same position within the States as the Supreme Court does for the whole of India. Thus, the Sate Government is a true copy of the Union Government within the jurisdiction of each States; this helps the States to draw examples and inspiration from the working of the Union Government in almost every field of activity.

The executive power of the State is vested in a Governor who is appointed by the President and who holds office during the pleasure of the President. The vesting of the entire executive power of the Sate in the Governor shows that he occupies the same constitutional position within the State as the President does with respect to the Government of India. Normally, the

Governor holds office for a period of five years from the date on which he enters upon his office.

The qualifications for appointment as a Governor are simple and few. He should be a citizen of India and must have completed the age of thirty-five years. The Governor cannot be a member of either House of Parliament or of a State Legislature. Nor can be hold any other office of profit. He is entitled to a free official residence, a regular monthly salary and other allowances. At present, his salary is fixed at Rs. 5,500 per month. His salary and allowances cannot be reduced during his term of office. These are charged on the Consolidated Fund of the State and, as such, are non-votable. Before entering upon his office, the Governor has to make and subscribe, in the presence of the Chief Justice of the High Court of the State, an oath or affirmation to preserve, protect and defend the Constitution.

Why the Governor is Appointed and not Elected

In the beginning, the framers of the Constitution had decided upon an elected Governor for each of the States. This decision was in conformity with their idea of giving each State the maximum autonomy as units of a federation. The position of the State Governor in the United States must have been the greatest influence upon them in this connection. However, within two years, they decided to abandon this idea in favour of an appointed Governor. What made them to do so deserves some consideration.

(1) In a Parliamentary system of Government a popularly elected Governor does not fit well. If the Governor is elected directly by the people, he becomes a direct representative of the people and may very well exercise his powers not as the constitutional head of the State, but as its real head. Such a position is very likely to create a rivalry between the Governor and the Council of Ministers whose members also are directly elected by the people. Since the American State have a Presidential system of Government just as in the case of the Federal Government in the United States, they do not face a problem of rivalry between the Governor and his Cabinet.

(2) Instead of the Governor being elected directly by the people, if he is elected by the State Legislature, there seems to be not much chance of a rivalry between him and the Ministry. This is because the Ministry is responsible to the same legislature which has elected the Governor. But a serious defect of such an arrangement seems to be the danger of the Governor becoming a pawn in the hands of a political party or parties that secure his election. Since he is not elected to the office on a permanent basis, the temptation for him to play into the hands of a legislative majority for the sake of re-election is, indeed, irresistible.

(3) Either a directly elected or an indirectly elected Governor is unlikely to fit into a highly centralisd federal system of government. For, the Governor in either case is a representative of the State who receives his authority form the people of the State. In case of a conflict between the State and the Union, such a Governor may not very likely prove an obedient servant or a convenient instrument of the Union Government. On the other hand, the Governor may create difficulties in the path of the Union's authority extending in any form to the State's sphere. This is not something in harmony with the idea of emergency powers under which the Union becomes all-powerful and the federal system ceases to function.

The original idea of the framers to have a *weak* Union and *strong* States had yielded place to one of a strong Union and *weak* States. A number of causes contributed for this major change in the basic structure of the Constitution. Among these were the partition of the country, the various problems created by the partition, the food crisis, the urge for economic and social planning for the country as a whole, the upsurge of provincialism and the fear of possible instability of State Ministeries. It was thought that both for the preservation of the newly won independence and the planned development of country, central direction was essential. For this purpose, an elected Governor was not desirable. The Governor should be one who could be commanded by the President in times of emergency for translating the will of the Union into action within the State.

(4) It was thought that in the wake of a newly established self-government, the emergence of rival groups and factions was inevitable within the State Legislature and the State as a whole. Under such conditions, a Governor who was resident of the State might become an interested party rather than an impartial and independent mediator or conciliator of the rival factions. When the Governor is the President's nominee there is very little possibility for such a danger.

(5) Even if the Governor is appointed by the President, so long as the State politics is of a stable character, so long as the Ministry has a solid backing within the legislature, he is bound to function as a constitutional head of the State just as the President himself. The change in his role is envisaged only under exceptional circumstances. Hence, this is a provision that arose out of abundant caution and the Constitution-makers have been fully justified by events in some of the State during the last few years.

The Canadian Constitution which has a strong Centre seems to have particularly influenced the Constituent Assembly in this connection. There, the Governor-General appoints all the Governors who hold office during his pleasure. But this provision as such has not affected the smooth working of the Canadian federation. On the contrary, it has on several occasions proved beneficial.

As Alladi Krishnaswami Aiyar said in the Constituent Assembly:

> "On the whole, in the interests of harmony, in the interests of a good working, in the interests of sounder relations between the Provincial Cabinet and the Governor, it will be much better if we accept the Canadian model."

Thus, the Constitution vests complete power in the President for the selection and appointment of the Governor. This means in effect that he is a nominee of the Central Government. But a healthy convention has grown up during the last few years which make the Governor not merely a nominee of the Central

Government but also one who is agreeable to the State concerned. Such a result is obtained by the Central government consulting the State Cabinet prior to the appointment of a new Governor. This enables the selection of an agreed candidate who is capable of discharging his responsibilities as the head of the State and "a sagacious counsellor and adviser to the Ministry, one who can throw oil on the troubled waters" of the State politics. Thus, the present method of selection has removed the evils which would have otherwise resulted from any of the alternative methods of selection originally contemplated by the Constituent Assembly.

Another convention has also been fairly well established and this too has contributed to making the position of the Governor one above party and group politics within the State. According to this, the person selected as the Governor of a State is normally an outsider, a resident of another State, on who has had no political entanglements within the State. This has, on the whole, proved to be of great advantage. Not only does this keep the Governor out of the local politics, but it also enables him to look at the problems of the State and the problems of Union-State relationship with detachment and objectivity.

Powers and Functions of the Governor

The executive power of the State is vested in he Governor who is empowered to exercise it either directly or through officers subordinate to him. And the executive power of the State extends to all matters on which the State Legislature has the power to make laws. In the discharge of his responsibilities as the Head of the State, the Governor exercises functions similar to those of the President as the Head of the Union. He appoints the Chief Minister and other members of the Council of Ministers who hold office during his pleasure. He allocates the business of the Government among the Ministers and makes rules for the more convenient transaction of such business. All executive actions of the Government are taken in his name. He appoints the Advocate-General and other offices of the State. In the States of Bihar, Madhya Pradesh and Orissa, it is the special responsibility of the Governor to see that a Minister is placed in charge of tribal welfare. In Assam, the Governor is given certain special powers with respect to the administration of the tribal areas as provided in the Sixth Schedule of the Constitution.

Like the President's power of pardon, the Governor too is empowered to grant pardons. This applies to all persons convicted of any offence against any law relating to a matter to which the executive power of the State extends.

In the legislative field, the Governor has considerable powers. He is an integral part of the State Legislature. He convenes the State Legislature, addresses it in person or sends messages to it, and can prorogue or dissolve it. During every financial year, he causes the budget to be laid before the House. Demands for grants in the Legislature can be made only on his recommendation. Every Bill that is passed by the State Legislature has to be presented to the Governor for this assent. The Governor has three alternatives before him with respect to such a Bill. He may give his assent to it, in which case it becomes law. Or, he may return it to the Legislature with a message suggesting alterations or modifications. The Governor has, however, no power to return a Money Bill. Or again, he may reserve the Bill for the assent of the President if, in his opinion, it contains provisions which might endanger the position envisaged for the High Court under the Constitution.

The Governor has also the special legislative power of promulgating Ordinances during the recess of the State Legislature, if he is satisfied that there exist circumstances which make it necessary for him to take immediate action. But with respect to three matters, the Governor is prohibited from promulgating Ordinances without prior instructions from the President. These are : (1) if the Ordinance contains provisions which, if embodied in a Bill, would require the previous sanction of the President for introduction in the State Legislature; or (2) if the Governor would have deemed it necessary to reserve a Bill containing the same provisions for the consideration of the President; or (3) if an Act of the State Legislature containing the same provisions would be invalid without the assent of the President.

Every Ordinance promulgated by the Governor has the same force and effect as an Act of the State Legislature. But every such Ordinance should be laid before the State Legislature when it reassembles and if the Ordinance is not upheld by the Legislature, then it becomes invalid. The Governor is empowered to withdraw the Ordinance any time he likes. The Ordinance will be invalid if it has provisions which would not be valid if enacted in an Act of the State Legislature to which the Governor gives his assent.

During a period of emergency, the Governor comes into his own as the real head of the executive in the State. With the proclamation of an emergency by the President, the entire State administration comes directly under the control of the Union. Being the 'man on the spot' and the 'agent' of the President in the State, the Governor during the period of emergency, takes over the reins of administration directly into his won hands and runs the State with the aid of the civil service.

14

The Governor and the Council of Ministers

In the exercise of all his functions, except when he is expressly required to act in his discretion, the Governor is aided and advised by a Council of Ministers headed by a Chief Minister. But if there is a conflict of opinion between the Governor and the Ministry as to whether or not a particular matter falls within the scope of the Governor's discretionary power, the decision of the governor in his discretion shall be final. Further, the validity of anything done by the governor cannot be called in question on the ground that he ought not to have acted in his discretion. Although the Governor has to act on the advice of the Ministers, the question whether any, and if so what, advice was tendered by the Ministers to the Governor cannot be enquired into in any Court.

The Governor appoints the Chief Minister and on the advice of the Chief Minister he appoints the other Ministers. The ministers hold office during the pleasure of the Governor. The Ministers are collectively responsible to the Legislative Assembly of the State just as the Central Ministers are responsible to the Lok Sabha. The Governor administers the oath of office to each Minister before the enters upon his office. The Governor can appoint as Minister a person who is not a member of the State Legislature at the time of the appointment. But such a Minister should become a member of the Legislature within six months after entering upon his office.

We have already noticed that all executive action of the State Government is taken in the name of the Governor. In this connection the Governor is authorised to make rules for the more convenient transaction of the business of the State Government. He is also empowered to allocate among the Ministers the business of the Government except where he is expected to act in his discretion. It is the duty of the Chief Minister as the head of the Council of Ministers to communicate to the Governor all decisions of the Council relating to the administration of he affairs of the State and proposals for legislation. He has also to furnish any information which the Governor calls for and which is connected with any administrative or legislative matter of the State. Again, it is the duty of the Chief Minister to place before the Council, if the Governor so requires, any matter on which a decision has been taken by a Minister but which has not been considered by the Council.

These provisions of the Constitution vest in the Governor a fairly long list of powers which, if taken on their face value, will add up to formidable proportions. Yet, as we have already seen from statements made in the Constituent Assembly, the Governor normally is only the constitutional head of the State. This means that although he is the 'Chief Executive', in the exercise of his functions, the real power is in the hands of the Council of Ministers. This was pointed out again and again by authoritative spokesmen in the Constituent Assembly.

Interpreting the scope of the provision that "the Ministers shall hold office during the pleasure of the Governor", Ambedkar said: "I have no doubt that it is the intention of this Constitution that the Ministry shall hold office during such time as it holds the confidence of the majority. It is on this principle that the Constitution will work. The reason why we have not so expressly stated it is because it has not been stated in that fashion or in those terms in any of the Constitutions which lay down a parliamentary system of Government. 'During pleasure' is always understood to mean that the pleasure shall not continue notwithstanding the fact that the Ministry has lost the confidence of the majority, it is presumed that the Governor will exercise his 'pleasure' in dismissing the Ministry and, therefore, it is unnecessary to differ from what I may say the stereotyped phraseology which is used in all responsible governments."

It is difficult to think of a Governor under a fully responsible system of government established on the broadest possible popular basis, to behave in an authoritarian manner. When a Cabinet composed of popular Ministers, collectively responsible to the Legislature, is to aid and advise the Governor in the discharge of his functions, occasions are almost non-existent for him to over-rule them or act in a manner contrary to their advice. But does this mean that he is a mere figure-headed, "a rubber-stamp of his Cabinet or a post-office between his Cabinet and the President or between his Cabinet and the official gazette?" A careful reading of the constitutional provisions and an appreciation of them in the perspective of the totality of the constitutional scheme, will show that the Governor is neither a figure-head nor a rubber-stamp but a functionary designed to play a vital role in the administration of the affairs of the State.

The occasions which will give such an opportunity to the Governor to act in his discretion seem to be the following: (1) the selection of a Chief Minister prior to the formation of a Council of Ministers; (2) dismissal of a Ministry; (3) dissolution of; the Legislative Assembly; (4) asking information from the Chief Minister relating to legislative and administrative matters; (5) asking the Chief Minister to submit for the consideration of the Council of Ministers any matter on which a decision has been taken by a Minister but which has not been considered by the Council; (6) refusing to give assent to a Bill passed by the Legislature and sending it back for reconsideration; (7) reserving a Bill passed by the State Legislature for the assent of the President; (8) seeking instructions from the President before promulgating an ordinance dealing with certain matters; (9) advising the president for the proclamation of an emergency; and (10) in the case of the Governor of Assam, certain administrative matters connected with the tribal areas and setting disputes between the Government of Assam and the District Council (of an autonomous District) with respect to mining royalties.

It should be pointed out however that the Governor's discretionary powers cannot in reality be absolute. For, absolute discretion is an element of autocracy. The Governor can under no circumstances be an autocrat, so long as he functions within the framework of a democratic Constitution. What, then is the check on his discretionary power? Neither the Ministry nor the

State Legislature can control the Governor in this respect; but the President can. This means that the Governor is not a free agent in the exercise of his discretion. If he misuses it either as a result of personal; ambitions or as a partisan in ;the currents and cross-currents of State politics the President can always check him and if necessary he may even dismiss him. Thus, in the final analysis, the Governor is not a free agent, either during normal times or abnormal times. For, in the discharge of his functions, normally he is aided and advised by the Council of Ministers. So long as the Council has the confidence of the State Legislature, the Governor will not be able to substitute his discretion for the advice of the Council. If he attempts to do that, it will lead to political complication which will ultimately lead to his dismissal. On the contrary, under abnormal conditions such as an emergency caused by war, internal rebellion or breakdown of the constitutional machinery in the State, he will be acting as an agent of the President and not as the absolute master of the situation himself. No doubt, during such times his powers are more real than during normal times when his powers are practically nominal.

All things taken together, the emphasis on the Governor's office seems to be on his role as an adviser. On the one hand, he is a non-partisan adviser to the Ministry. By virtue of his position as the Head of the State he has a right to be consulted, the right to encourage and the right to warn. He is a detached spectator, from a position of vantage and authority, of what is going on in the State. Placed in that position, he maintains the dignity, the stability and the collective responsibility of the State Government. On the other, he is the agent of the President, his adviser on the affairs of the State and the 'representative' of the Union in the State. He is the link that fastens the federal-state chain, the channel which regulates the Union-State relationship. Thus, he is an essential part of the constitutional machinery, fulfilling an essential purpose and meandering an essential service. In the words of one who was privileged to know the position form inside: "A Governor can do a great deal of if he is a good Governor and he can do a great deal of mischief, if he is a bad Governor, in spite of the very little power given to him under the Constitution we are framing."

The Advocate-General for the State

Like the Attorney-General who is the legal adviser to the Union Government, the Constitution provides for a legal adviser to the State Government known as the Advocate-General for the State. He is appointed by the Governor and holds office during his pleasure. To be appointed as Advocate-General, a person should have the same qualifications as would make him eligible for appointment as judge of the High Court. The Advocate-General will receive such remuneration as the Governor may determine.

It is the duty of the Advocate-General to give advice to the State Government on legal matters referred to him as well as to perform certain other duties of a legal character which are assigned to him from time to time. In the discharge of these duties he is entitled to appear before any court of law within the State or address the State Legislative as and when required.

15

The State Legislature

The Constitution provides for a Legislature for every State in the Union. But it does not adhere to the principle of bicameralism in the case of every State Legislature. There are ten States, namely, Andhra Pradesh, Bihar, Jammu and Kashmir, Maharashtra, Madhya Pradesh, Madras, Mysore, Punjab, Uttar Pradesh and West Bengal, each of which has two Houses in the Legislature, while the remaining States have unicameral legislatures. Where there are two Houses of the Legislature, one is known as the Legislative Assembly and the other the Legislative Council. Where there is only one House, it is known as the Legislative Assembly. The Governor of the State is an integral part of the Legislature.

The State Legislative Assembly is modelled on the House of the people while the Legislative Council has a resemblance to the Council of States. Although the Constitution provides for bicameral Legislatures for certain States and unicameral ones of others, the question of the organisation of State Legislatures in a single House or two Houses is still left an open one. For, Article 169 provides a special procedure for the creation and abolition of Legislative Councils in the future. According to this, Parliament is empowered to create a Legislative Council in a State having no such Council or abolish the Council where it exists, provided the Legislative Assembly of the State passes a Resolution to that effect supported by the House and majority of the total membership of the House and a majority of not less than two-third of those who sit and vote. Any law passed by Parliament in this regard should contain the necessary amendments to the provisions of the Constitution which are affected by such law.

But these amendments will not be considered as regular amendments to the Constitution for which a special procedure is prescribed.

The Legislative Assembly

Composition

The Assembly is composed of members chosen of direct election. The only exception is this rule is the representation of the Anglo-Indian community. If no member of that community secures election to the Assembly, the Governor is empowered to nominate one or more members on behalf of it as members of the Assembly. The Constitution has fixed a maximum number of 500 members for any State Assembly and minimum of 60 members. For purposes of election, the State is divided into as many territorial constituencies as there are seats in the Assembly. As for as possible, the ratio between the population of each constituency and the number of seats allotted to it will be the same throughout the State. At the end of each decennial census, the constituencies will be recast to make the necessary adjustments to meet the variations in population. At present, the number of voters in each constituency is about 75,000. The number of members in each State Legislative Assembly may be seen from the following table which contains the figures both before and after the reorganisation of States in 1956:

Legislative Assembly

	Total Members		
Name of the State	Before reorganisation	After reorganisation	Nominated
Andhra Pradesh	196	302	1
Assam	105	105	
Bihar	330	318	
Gujerat	..	133	
Jammu and Kashmir	75	75	
Kerala	109	127	1
Madhya Pradesh	332	289	1
Madras	234	205	
Maharashtra	..	264	1
Mysore	105	209	1

Name of the State	Total Members		
	Before reorganisation	After reorganisation	Nominated
Orissa	140	140	
Punjab	126	154	
Rajasthan	160	176	
Uttar Pradesh	431	431	1
West Bengal	238	258	4

The Legislative Council

Composition

Several members in the Constituent Assembly were opposed to the idea of constituting an Upper House for the State. They thought that an additional House to the Legislative Assembly in the State was superfluous. Some of them even doubted the financial ability of several States to maintain this "costly ornamental luxury". These criticisms were mainly responsible for the assembly allowing the members from different State to decide the question themselves, and leaving the future of the Council in a fluid state in the Constitution itself. The basis of the composition of the Council is as follows:

1. The total number of members in the Legislative Council should not exceed one-third of the total number of members in the Legislative Assembly. But in any case, it should not be less than forty.
2. There are five different categories or representation to the Council. These are:
   (a) one-third of the total membership to be elected by electorates consisting of members of self-governing local bodies like Municipalities, District Boards etc. in the State.
   (b) One-third to be elected by the members of the Legislative Assembly of the State.
   (c) One-twelfth to be elected by electorates consisting of University graduates (of at least three year' standing)

or others recognised as possessing equivalent qualification and who are residing in the State.

(d) One-twelfth to be elected by electorates consisting of secondary school teachers or those in higher educational institutions with at least three year's experience in teaching.

(e) The remainder to be nominated by the Governor on the basic of their special knowledge or practical experience in literature, scien‿e, art, the co-operative movement or social service.

3. The election of the first four categories is to be held in accordance with the system of proportional representation by means of the single transferable vote.

4. voting shall be by secret ballot.

5. Parliament is empowered to make any change with regard to the nature of representation detailed above.

These provisions, it must be said, are not the result of sufficient thinking on the question. As it stands at present, there is a combination of direct election, indirect election and nomination which make the Council a hotchpotch of representation. The right of franchise given to teachers and members of local government bodies indicate that the emphasis is primarily on functional representation. But, from that point of view, the representation is too narrow. There are many professions and interests in addition to these whose representation in the Council is desirable and likely to prove of great benefit. Too much weight has been given to the members of the Assembly by providing for one-third of the Council membership to be elected by them. The percentage of seats reserved for nomination, no the other hand seems to be too small. Men of merit from the fields of art, science, literature and social service should have formed a larger number among the members of the Council in order to make it a body of meritorious elders who can effectively help in the work or legislation, supervise or watch over the administration with the wisdom born of their maturity and experience.

Legislative Council

Name of the State	Total number of members	Elected by Legislative Assembly	Elected by Local Authorities	Elected by graduates	Elected by Teachers	Nominated
Andhra Pradesh	90	31	31	8	8	12
Bihar	72	25	23	6	6	12
Jammu and Kashmir	36	21	7	Nil	2	6
Madhya Pradesh	90	31	31	8	8	12
Madras	50	16	16	6	4	8
Maharashtra	78	31	21	7	7	12
Mysore	63	21	21	6	6	9
Punjab	42	18	10	3	3	8
Uttar Pradesh	72	24	24	6	6	12
West Bengal	51	17	17	4	4	9

The following table shows the membership of the Legislative Councils in different States with a detailed statement of the constituencies from which they are elected.

The normal life of the Assembly is five years; but it may be dissolved earlier by the Governor. In case of an emergency, its life may be extended by a law of Parliament, one year at a time, but in any case not beyond six month after the Proclamation of Emergency has ceased to operate. The Council, on the other hand, is a permanent body which renews one-third of its membership after every two years. In this respect, it follows the pattern of the Council of States.

There is hardly any special qualification fixed for election to the State Legislature except one of age. As in the case of a member of the House of the people, a member of the Assembly should have completed the minimum age of twenty-five years at the time of election. In the case of a member of the Council the minimum age prescribed is thirty years.

The Assembly has two elected officers, the Speaker and the Deputy Speaker, to conduct its business. The position of these two officers in the conduct of the business of the House, and their powers and functions in the Assembly, are respectively the same as those of the Speaker and the Deputy Speaker of the House of the People. They may be removed from office by a resolution of the House supported by at least a majority of all the existing members of the House. The Council has Chairman and a Vice Chairman both elected by the Council, and they have the same powers and functions as their counterparts in the Assembly. They also can be removed from office by a resolution of the Council supported by a majority of the existing members in the Council at the time of passing such resolution. The Constitution provides for each House of the State Legislature a separate secretarial staff whole members are independent of the Executive in matters of recruitment and conditions of service.

Conduct of Business

There is hardly anything special to be pointed out in this context which is different from that of the two Houses of Parliament. Most of the articles in this part of the Constitution are a reproduction, almost verbatim, of those which deal with corresponding provisions regarding the two Houses of Parliament. Ambedkar acknowledged this in the Constituent Assembly and pointed out that that was one the reasons why there were very few amendments to the various articles in that part of the Constitution. In view of the detailed discussion on Parliamentary procedure given in an earlier chapter, it is not considered necessary to go into any details regarding the procedure in the State Legislatures. A brief resume of the is given below.

The State Legislature must meet at least twice a year and the interval between any two sessions should not be more than six moths. Usually, a new session begins and with an opening address by the Governor which outlines the policy of the State Government. The address is then subjected to a debate and finally voted upon in the form of a resolution expressing thanks to the governor. It is during this debate that the Opposition Parties get the best opportunity to criticise in general the policies and programme of the Government.

Every Bill, except Money Bills, may be introduced in either House of the Legislature. The Bill is finally passed with its third reading. Then it goes to the Governor for his assent. But the Governor may send it back for reconsideration. When it is passed again by the Legislature, the Governor cannot withhold his assent. But he may reserve it for the consideration of the President, who may ask the Governor to place it before the legislature for reconsideration. When it is passed again, with or without amendment, it goes to the President for his consideration. The President is not bound to give assent even though the Bill has been reconsidered and passed for a second time by the State Legislature.

Assembly Vs. Council

A significant point of difference between the relationship of the two Houses of Parliament and that of the two Houses of the State Legislature (wherever the two Houses exist) is the comparatively less important role which the Legislature Council plays in contrast to that of the Council of States. As we have already seen, the Council of States has, excepting in the field of Money-Bill, co-equal powers with the House in all legislative matters. When there is an irreconcilable conflict between the two, the deadlock is resolved in a joint sitting of the two Houses. In the State Legislature, on the contrary, the Council is designed to play a definitely inferior role. Its functions are of an advisory nature only. Ambedkar point out in the Constituent Assembly that the provisions adopted by the Constitution to resolve conflicts between the two Houses of the state Legislature were based on the provisions of the (British) Parliament Act of 1911.

According to this, a Bill can have only two journeys from the Assembly to the Council. When a Bill goes to the Council for the first time from the Assembly the Council has four alternative courses of action: (1) it may reject the Bill; (2) it may amend the Bill; (3) it may take no action on it; (But when three months have elapsed since its receipt by the Council and the Council does not inform the Assembly as to what action it has taken on the Bill, it is deemed to have been rejected by the Council); and (4) it may pass the Bill as sent by the Assembly. In the first three cases the Assembly takes up the consideration of the Bill for a second time. It may or may not accept the amendments made by the Council which and pass the Bill. It now goes for the second time to the Council which can adopt any of the above alternative courses of action except that it can delay the Bill only for a month instead of the three months in the first instance. The Assembly acts again according to the same procedure as before, if the Council does not again agree with it. Thus, only twice will the Bills travel from the Assembly to the Council and the latter has only the power of a suspensory veto, the first time for a period of three months and the second time for a moth. These provisions clearly establish the absolute superiority of the Assembly over the Council. In respect of Money Bill, the powers of the States Assembly are the same as the House of the people, which we have already dealt with. There is also a special procedure prescribed for financial matters on the same pattern as what obtains in Parliament.

Privileges

The powers, privileges and immunities of the State Legislature, its committees and their members are the same as those of Parliament, its committees and its members. Members are entitled to receive such salaries and allowances as are determined by the Legislature. At present, there is no uniformity with regard to these among the various States. Nevertheless all of them give regular monthly salaries and certain allowances to their legislators.

The question of the privileges and immunities of the legislature and its members figured prominently in three cases where an attempt was made to persuade the High Courts and the Supreme Court to interfere with the working of the State Legislative Assemblies. Of these, Misra Vs. Nand Kishore was a case which came up before the Orissa High Court in which the petitioner challenged the action of the Speaker who disallowed certain questions which he asked on the floor of the Orissa Assembly.

The High Court declined to interfere as this was a matter which fell within the exclusive rights of the Legislature to regulate. In the case of Sing Vs. *Govind,* the Allahabad High Court was asked to determine the legality or otherwise of certain disciplinary action taken against the petitioner as a member of the Uttar Pradesh Assembly. Here again, the Court refused to interfere. Speaking on behalf of the Court, Justice Sapru said: "Obviously, this Court is not, in any sense whatever, a Court to appeal or revision against the Legislative or against the rulings of the Speaker, who as the holder of an office of the highest distinction, has the sole responsibility cast upon him of maintaining the prestige and dignity of House". He added that under Article 194, the legislature has the right (1) to be the exclusive judge of the legality of its own proceedings, (2) to punish its members for their conduct in the House, and (3) to settle its own proceedings.

The matter came before the Supreme Court for the first time in the case of The Searchlight and the Court gave its verdict in favour of the legislature. The case arose out of the publication by *The Searchlight*, an English language daily newspaper, of certain references in the Legislative Assembly of the State of Bihar relating the conduct of the Chief Minister of the State and an ex-Minister. The newspaper reported that a member of the Assembly made a bitter attack on the Chief Minister and his ex-colleague with respect to their activities regarding the selection of Ministers and the glaring instances of encouragement of corruption by the Government. Soon after, the Secretary, Bihar Legislature, issued a notice to the Editor of *The Searchlight* for the breach of privilege of the House in as much as he was alleged to have published a perverted and unfaithful report of the proceedings. The notice asked the Editor to appear before the Privileges Committee which had found a *prima facie* case against him, and show cause why action should not be taken against him. The Editor challenged the validity of the notice by a petition filed in the Supreme Court under Article 32 of the Constitution.

The Court said that it was called upon to answer two question: (i) whether the House of the Legislature could prohibit the publication of publicly seen and heard proceedings. (ii) Whether the privileges of the House under Article 194 (3) prevailed over the Fundamental Rights of the citizen under Article 19 (1) (a). A four to one majority of the Court answered both the questions in the affirmative. Speaking on behalf of the majority, Chief Justice S.R. Das held that in the absence of a law made by the Legislature, the Legislature shall have all the privileges, power and immunities enjoyed by the House of Commons in England at the commencement of the Constitution of India and the citizen could not insist on the faithful publication of the proceedings of the Legislature if the Legislature chose not to permit him to do so. The Fundamental Right of freedom of speech guaranteed to a citizen under Article 19 (1) (a) could not override the privileges of the Legislature. It must not be overlooked that they (the privileges) were conferred by constitutional laws and not ordinary laws made by Parliament and, therefore, they are as supreme as the Chapter on Fundamental Rights.

In his dissent, Justice Subba Rao said that the reasoning adopted in the majority judgment would unduly restrict and circumscribe the wide scope and content of one of the cherished Fundamental Rights, namely, the freedom of speech in its application to the press. The learned judge asked: "Why should Article 194 be preferred to Article 19 (1) (a) and not *vice versa?*" According to him if there is a conflict between a legislative privilege and Fundamental Rights, the former should yield to the latter to the extent that it is necessary to uphold the

Fundamental Right. The legislature has only the privilege of preventing *mala fide* publication of the proceedings. Article (19)2 gives ample scope for such reasonable restrictions to be imposed by a duly enacted law. The privilege of the legislature can be adequately protected by applying the test of reasonable restrictions envisaged under Article 19 (2). Hence it is unnecessary to accord a preferred position to the privilege of the legislature over the Fundamental Right of the citizen expressly guaranteed by the Constitution.

16

New Patterns of Diplomacy

Neutralism or Non-Alignment?

Vast and complex as were the problems India faced after 1947 in reorganizing its political life, its economy, and its social order, its leaders at least could draw for inspiration on the country's ancient traditions as well as on its more recent experience with British rule. There was need for reorientation of thought, for renovation of institutions, for new construction-but these tasks, urgent as they were, could be carried out in a familiar environment, and an environment, too, over which the Indians themselves had control. The materials, they had at their disposal-climate, resources, population growth, grinding poverty, the restrictions of the caste system, illiteracy, lack of technical skills, shortage of capital-were hard to work with, often seemingly unyielding. Yet, the Indians had won their long struggle to become molders of their own destiny. However inadequate the end result of their efforts might be, they would have the satisfaction of knowing that, at last, after three centuries of foreign rule, it was of their own making.

The problems they faced in world affairs were far less malleable. At the peak of their power and glory, Hindu emperors and Mogul rulers had welcomed trade and what we would call today cultural exchanges with lands outside their borders. Greeks and Syrians, Persians and Chinese, English and French and Portuguese successively left their imprint on India-some through influence on the arts, some on languages, others on religious beliefs, still others on political ideas and administrative practices. Visitors from the Middle East and from China, impressed by the high level of civilization they found in India, bequeathed to us the best available descriptions of achievements in administration, education, religious tolerance, and the arts of living as reflected in day-to-day occurrences among rich and poor. The most enlightened of India's rulers—Asoka and Akbar—were eager to learn the rule of their neighbors and to benefit by their experience.

But in a vast subcontinent which, until the development of naval power in the sixteenth century was difficult to reach except by long journeys overland-and in the case of China by perilous travel over the passes of the Himalayas - there was relatively little need to seek the military support of neighbouring countries through alliances, as France and England and other European nations had done in a comparable period of national growth. It was not with other countries that the Indian princes fought or made pacts before the coming of the British. It was among themselves that they waged bloody wars such as shocked Asoka and drove him to reject the use of force and to accept the "middle path" preached by Buddha. And once the British came, they soon took over the direction of India's contacts on the world scene and the protection of its frontiers, which after 1858 had become the frontiers of the British Empire. India had no foreign policy of its own. The British made its foreign policy. And even when the lines of India's struggle for independence had been clearly laid down, and it was increasingly apparent that the final parting of India and Britain was not far off, the British did not consult leaders like Gandhi and Nehru about taking their country into World War II on Britain's side. In world affairs India was an object, not a subject.

Thus, when independence came, India had not choice but to start with a clean slate in foreign policy. And it started at a time when the international landscape was undergoing seismic changes which even the more experienced powers—Japan and the Western Nations—found it difficult to assess and to fit into existing patterns of policy. India, a newcomer to the world scene, was confronted with not only the need to initiate relations with dozens of countries of which it had no recent direct knowledge but the necessity of doing this at a time when its attention, perforce, had to be concentrated on domestic problems of staggering difficulty which brooked no delay.

World War II, like a tornado, had overturned empires, cast national idols from their pedestals, shattered age-old alignments, destroyed untold wealth of manpower and resources. Communist Russia, despite the losses it had suffered at the hands of Nazi Germany, had emerged as one of the two great powers to survive the holocaust. Britain and France had been gravely weakened at home and lost colonial domains overseas. Germany, Italy, and Japan, the defeated nations, had experienced grave psychological as well as economic disasters. The nationalist aspirations of peoples liberated from colonial rule or struggling to be liberated-as in the case of India-were remaking the map of the globe with dizzying speed. China, racked by Japanese depredations and torn by civil strife, came under Communist rule within three years after India had won independence. The Arab lands were striving to complete the process of self-determination that had started with the breakup of the Ottoman Empire after World War I, but had been temporarily checked by British and French administration in the area under League of Nations mandates. The United Nations had been in existence for two years, and had barely begun to function. Everywhere one looked around the world, change seemed to be the only common denominator. The cold war was emerging before the debris of the hot war had yet been swept up. The United States, alone untouched by foreign invasion, had enhanced its power, and had reluctantly but resolutely assumed responsibilities in world affairs it had hither to sought to avoid.

As the curtain rose on this bleak scene, worthy of the brush of a Brueghel or a Goya, the Indian leaders, overwhelmed by anxieties at home, had to make far-reaching decisions abroad. What was to be the fulcrum of the new nation's policy? Was it to align itself unquestioningly with its former ruler, Britain-or become its opponent? Was it to assert its faith in democracy, and reject relations with all non democratic countries, but particularly with the totalitarian Communist regimes of Russia and, later China? Was it to support the aspirations of people who, just as the Indians had done before 1947, were still struggling to achieve independence, or counsel them to move cautiously, for fear that they might merely aggravate postwar confusion and disorder? Was it to accept unreservedly the leadership the United States had assumed in the cold war, or plead its domestic problems as a legitimate excuse for isolationism? Was it to make clear that the independence it had won after so many years and at such great sacrifice would mean just what the word said-freedom to choose its own course in world affairs, as seemed best for its national interests?

Varied and bitter as have been the many criticisms made of India's foreign policy, particularly in the United States, it would be difficult to argue that India, confronted with this list of harsh ineluctable choices, adopted a dogmatic and rigid position. Far from it. The new nation, instead of irrevocably choosing "this or that" developed a policy based'on a continuous acceptance, adjustment, interweaving of "this and that".

This policy, for lack of a more precise term, has been defined as "neutralism". It has also often been described as non-commitment and nonalignment. The most accurate description for these shorthand terms would have to be phrased something like this: "Don't any of you great powers push us into a corner. We find something good in each of you, but by no means everything, and we feel we have the right, as an independent people, to choose those things which we find good and reject those we find bad. Having just succeeded in obtaining our freedom, we naturally object to any form of colonialism, but this does not make us any less friendly toward Britain, many of whose qualities we greatly admire-al-though, understandably, we sympathize with all those who are still trying to emulate our example and become free. The totalitarian pattern of Russia and China is unsuited to our national temperament and is alien to our traditions-but we want to be free to learn what we can from the Communist experience with industrialization. We admire the many achievements of the United States, but we do not see why our admiration should make it inevitably for us to join the American-led bloc in world affairs when we do not share some of the American estimates about the future of Russia, China and, above all, of the uncommitted nations of Asia, the Middle East, and Africa. We increasingly believe in the value of the United Nations, which offers the best hope of avoiding a polarization of the world into two contending blocs-led by the United States and the U.S.S.R.-whose clashes could sooner or later unleash a nuclear war which would jeopardize, if not destroy, all the efforts we, who are underdeveloped and objectly poor, have been painfully making to improve the lot of our people. Let us make more and more use of the United Nations, and other international agencies, to stabilize a world wrenched out of balance by two world wars, and to help the underdeveloped nations achieve the modicum of well-being which modern science and technology make possible for mankind."

This definition, although obviously unsuitable for crisp and vivid newspaper headlines, may make in possible to understand the inner coherence of what seems like contradictory decisions by India in world affairs. The newly independent nation, a republic which owes no allegiance to the British Crown, far from becoming an opponent of Britain, voluntarily joined the Commonwealth, and has proved loyal to this loose yet closely knit alignment, in spite of the strains imposed by the Suez crisis of 1956, and the controversy over the Greek Cypriotes' demand for self-determination to be followed by self-government. In this case, India's decision not to challenge Britain about Cyprus in the UN was facilitated not only by concern for British interests, but more so by the belief in India that the Greco-Turkish struggle was not between a while nation and a people of colour, but between two white and comparably advanced peoples-and therefore, according to the Indian yardstick, did not constitute a case of colonialism. At the 1958 United Nations General Assembly, however, Krishna Menon, on behalf of India, reversed this position, and attacked Britain's policy toward Cyprus.

India, however, was shocked by Britain's military intervention, along with France and Israel, against Egypt in the Suez zone in 1956, and made no secret of its dismay that its partner in the Commonwealth, which had shown its willingness to relinquish colonial possessions in Asia, should be reverting to colonial practices in Middle East. Although Mr. Nehru firmly resisted demands in parliament for termination of India's association with Britain through membership in the Commonwealth, the Suez crisis left in its wake a felling of uneasiness on both sides-with the Indians becoming more cautious in their belief that Britain had turned its back on colonialism, and the British feeling resentful about the attitude taken at that time by India, as compared with the more friendly attitude of Pakistan which, as a Muslim country, might have been expected to back Egypt without qualifications. In this case, as contrasted with that of Cyprus, India saw a conflict between an overseas white colonial nation with a people of color striving to achieve independence from past colonial rule.

India's anticolonialism, a product of its own experience which is still fresh in the minds of the generation now ruling the country, has also caused it to demand the withdrawal of remnants of Western colonial possessions on its own territory. France, under the premiership of Pierre Mendes—France, voluntarily relinquished in 1954 it two small territories—Chandernagore and Pondicherry-under friendly circumstances, and India took that occasion to assure France that its cultural influence in these areas would be respected. In keeping with its sympathy for peoples who are struggling to free themselves from Western domination, India has been sympathetic to the cause of the Algerian nationalists. Yet, when, in 1956, France walked out of the United Nations General Assembly, refusing to be present during discussion of the Algerian problem which it regards as an issue of domestic affairs, it was India's delegate, Krishna Menon, usually known for his intransigence towards the United States, who initiated moves in the UN to make possible France's return to the Assembly. Similarly, Mr. Menon not only forbore from attacking Britain's administration of non-self-governing territories in Africa, notably British Togoland, in the UN Trusteeship Council, but actually praised Britain for its policies.

India, however, has vigorously denounced Portugal for its determination to retain its colony of Goa, which Portugal describes as an integral part of its territory, but which Mr. Nehru has described as "a pimple on the face of India". In spite of repressive measures taken by the Portuguese authorities against Indians in Goa who oppose their rule-including the jailing and deportation of critics to Portuguese Africa and rising demands in India for measures of retaliation, Mr. Nehru has determinedly resisted that use of violence, even though it is generally recognized that a small Indian force could easily occupy Goa and oust the Portuguese. But the Indian government has been shocked and disturbed by what it regards as Washington's unqualified support of Portugal's claim to Goa, which the Indians find it difficult to reconcile with the traditional American opposition to colonialism.

India's resentment on this score came to a climax in 1956, when, at the close of a conference between Secretary of State John Foster Dulles and the foreign Minister of Portugal in Washington, a joint communique was issued in which the United States declared its concern for the preservation of Portugal's rule over its colonies in the Far East. Although it was eventually explained by the department of State that the communique was intended to refer to the Portuguese colony of Macao, bordering on Communist China (this seems to have been indicated by the use of the term Far East, instead of Southeast Asia where India is located), the damage had been done; and the United States made no subsequent official gesture to dispel the impression that it was taking the side of Portugal against India. This American stand, which seemed incomprehensible to the Indians, was assumed to have been determined by the fact that Portugal is a member of the North Atlantic Treaty Organization (NATO), and that the United States wanted to retain the goodwill of the Portuguese in order to assure maintenance of its bases in the Azores.

The issues of Cyprus, Algeria, and Goa are examples of the difficulties India has faced in steering its newly established foreign policy among the shoals of the cold war. Mr. Nehru has often been accused, particularly in United States, of using neutralism in such a way as to embarrass and damage the cause of democracy, and to enhance the prestige and influence of communism. American commentators have frequently asked India: "Are you with us or against us? Why don't you stand up and be counted on the side of democracy?

If the issue is narrowed to the question, "Is India against democracy?" then it can be answered in the negative. For there is no doubt that no sooner had India achieved independence them it joined the Commonwealth of its own free will-when, presumably, had it desired to strike a blow against the Western democracies, it could have chosen to co-operate closely with the Union of Soviet Socialist Republics. Nor has India, in spite of tremendous domestic problems and frequent lack of understanding of its views on the part of the United States, departed from its initial determination to maintain a democratic society.

But, if the question is, "Does India intend to deal exclusively with the democracies, and to support the Westernled bloc against the Communist bloc?" then the answer is again in the negative. Responsible Indians do not believe it is in the interest of their country to join one military alliance against another. This view is due not only to the Indians' traditional predilection for nonviolence, or to fear that a nuclear war would destroy all they are trying to achieve. It is due, at a far deeper level, to a prevailing conviction that neither side in the cold war has a monopoly of virtue and wisdom, and that each has legitimate interests and aspirations which, amidst the rigors of the cold war, either are not seen, or if seen are rejected, by the other. India's response to the cold war is, first, negative-an overwhelming desire to be left out of a struggle which, Indian leaders are convinced, can only lead, if unchecked, to the greatest catastrophe in human history; and second, positive-a profound conviction that if the potential combatants can be kept apart, India, together with order like-minded countries (high on the list are Tito's Yugoslavia and Nasser's Egypt) could eventually bring about a reconciliation between seemingly irreconcilable ideologies and national ambitions.

Undeterred buy foreign, most frequently American, criticism, Mr. Nehru, as principal spokesman for India, has endeavored to maintain a balance-not between East and West, a common Western phrase which makes no sense to India, since it is an integral part of the East, and sees Russia as a Eurasian nation-but between democracy and communism on the ideological plane, and between the two power blocs on the plane of politics and military force. Here still another question arises: "If, as India claims, it is neutralist, has it kept the balance even? Or, in spite of its best intentions, has it shown greater partiality toward the Communist nations-if not by choice, then because of fear for its own safety?"

The answer to this question is complex, and must be given in three parts. First, there is no doubt of India's special regard for Britain and the Commonwealth-and this in spite of the fact that one of the members of the Commonwealth, the Union of

South Africa, pursues a policy of rigid discrimination against all people of colour among its population, including Indians and Pakistanis. If India is partial, it is partial to Britain-and that means to democracy, assuming that we regard Britain as a democracy. Yet this point is not always clearly understood in the United States where adherence to democracy is usually equated with unquestioning support of this country and its policies - although it could be equally and, in this case, more easily equated with support of Britain. It sometimes seems as though American did not realize the democratic quality of Britain and of other members of the Commonwealth, and did not give them due credit for the role they play in world affairs.

The second part of the answer is that India, although it has grown increasingly friendly toward the United States in the past or three years, is not as much at ease with this country as it is with Britain, or Canada, and is much more ready to question the motives of the Americans than of the British. This is understandably puzzling to Americans. For we know-and the India's leaders know - that on country in the world so outspokenly and unremittingly supported the cause of India's independence, and so openly denounced British "imperialism" as the United States, to such an extent that it could be convincingly argued it was the Americans, rather than the Russian Communists, who did most, before 1947, in bringing about the disintegration of the British Empire, sealed during World War II by Japan's victories in Asia. What, then, caused what can only be described as the estrangement between the United States and India after independence? How could the Indians, instead of showing eternal gratitude for the backing their cause had received in the United States, display aloofness, at times downright suspicion, toward this country's foreign policy?

For this seemingly mysterious transformation there are several explanations. First, Britain, shorn of its imperial power, was no longer a threat to India's national interests, and the Indians, once free, found that they could benefit by a new-found friendship with their former ruler, whose political ideals and administrative methods they had admired in the past. No such ties exited between India and the United States and, to make the situation more difficult, it was now the United States which, replacing Britain as the premier Western nation, had assumed, albeit with great reluctance, the role of a great world power and, many Indians feared, might proceed to become a new empire-builder. While suspicions about the intentions of the United States might not prove, caution seemed to be indicated until the policies of the new great power had been clarified. And this attitude of caution was confirmed when, as the cold war succeeded the hot, the United States, particularly at the time of the Korean war, began to press Asian nations to align themselves with the West in the struggle against not only Russia, but also Communist China.

Second, the Indians were disappointed to find that the United States, which they had regarded as the champion of anticolonialism, yielding to the pressures of the cold war, appeared to be tempering its former support of self-determination of nations, proclaimed by Woodrow Wilson in World War I, so as not to disturb the remaining overseas possessions of its NATO allies. From the point of view of the Indians, NATO, although designed for the defense of Western Europe against aggression by Russia, had the aspect of a coalition in which the United States would be enlisted by its allies for the defense of their interests in the Middle East, Asia, and Africa. This fear was strengthened by the Suez crisis, in which Britain and France were reported to have used American weapons; by the seeming indifference of the United States toward the long-drawn-out war in Algeria, which reportedly took a toll of several hundred thousand lives; the diversion to Algeria of four French divisions which had been placed under the command of NATO, and were said to be using American equipment and planes provided to NATO forces; and in 1958 by the use of NATO airfields in West Germany for the transport of American troops and equipment to Lebanon. To Indian critics of the West, it seemed as if NATO was a new instrument of Western intervention in non-Western areas.

But the most serious, because most direct, threat to the development of Indo-American friendship was the decision of the United States, at the end of the Korean war, to create a series of bases along the periphery of Russia and Communist China which would serve to implement the policy of "containment" first initiated at the suggestion of George F. Kennan. Washington had hoped to enlist all China's neighbours in this containment task, and had offered military as well as economic aid to a number of Asian countries, including India and Pakistan. India adhering to its policy of noninvolvement, declined military aid, although it welcomed, and has since increasingly made use of, American economic aid. Pakistan accepted both, and subsequently became a member of two military alliances sponsored by the United States—the Southeast Asia Treaty Organization (Pakistan, Thailand, the Philippines, as well as Britain and the United States), and the Baghdad pact (Pakistan, Iran, Turkey, and Britain, with Iraq a member until the July 14, 1958 coup which toppled the Hashemite dynasty of King Feisal).

Pakistan's acceptance of American military aid struck a severe blow at India's relations with the United States. Even thoughtful and well-informed Indians found it difficult to believe, in spite of American efforts to explain the sequence of events which had led to this decision, that the United States was concerned solely with its over-all policy of containing Russian and Chinese communism. They deprecated the possibility of attack by Russia and /or China, or the capacity and willingness of Pakistan to fight off such an attack if it occurred. They contended that the United States, fully aware of the hostility between India and Pakistan since partition, was deliberately arming India's potential enemy and, since the principal controversy between the two nations was the problem of Kashmir, was in effect intervening in the Kashmir issue on the side of Pakistan. Even those Indians who took the time to hear the American side of the case pointed out that, whatever the motives of the United States, the mere fact that modern weapons were being supplied to Pakistan made it imperative for patriotic Indians, who had hitherto opposed the creation of a large military force, to demand an increase in India's defenses and, consequently, an increase in defense expenditures which the country, faced with mounting difficulties in fulfilling its second Five-Year plan, could ill afford to spare.

The anxiety created in India by publicity about the arrival of American tanks and other equipment in Pakistan which, it was argued, could hardly be used in the visible future against

Russia or China, redounded, according to our friends in India, to the benefit of Krishna Menon, close associate of Mr. Nehru and regarded by some of his critics as sympathetic to the Communists, who as his representative in the United Nations had antagonized American public opinion by his unconcealed attacks on the United States. Mr. Menon, who on his return to India in 1957 had been appointed Defense Minister, responded to demands in Parliament for modernization of the country's armed forces, and thereby not only appeared in the role of champion of national security, but won the sympathy of the armed forces, whose requests for re-equipment he readily met. Thus, Indian friends of the United States contended, by giving military aid to Pakistan, Washington, in effect, was enhancing the importance and influence of the principal political leader who had unmistakably indicated his hostility to American policy.

But, American might ask, if it is true that India had some reasons to be concerned about the role played by the United States in world affairs, and particularly about the course it was following in Asia, is it not true that India, far from acting impartially between this country and the Communist bloc, actually bent its neutralism in favor of Russia and China?

This is the third aspect of the question raised above about the impartiality of India's neutralism. It is true and thoughtful Indians, although few in number but on occasion influential would be the first to admit this-that the Indian leaders have seemed more ready to give the benefit of the doubt to the two great Communist powers than to the United States. For this, too, there are several explanations.

First, and this is something that is difficult for Americans to understand, the Indians have a fellow-feeling for chines-far more than for the Russians, only a minority of whom are Asians-not because of admiration for totalitarianism, but because they seen in China a struggle comparable to their own to achieve independence from Western intervention and to create a new economic and social order. Unlike most Americans, the Indian cannot bring themselves to regard Communist China as an outlaw from international society. They are aware of the danger that China might try to infiltrate or dominate neighboring areas-they have ready seen this happen in Tibet, and hope to prevent it in Nepal, the Himalayan kingdom whose foreign policy and defense are controlled by India. But, in contrast to Americans, they believe that the wisest way of dealing with Communist China is to recognize Peiping and admit it to represent China in the United Nations, where the power of world public opinion could then be brought to bear on the Chinese, no longer isolated from the West by the American economic boycott and Washington's refusal to grant recognition. Consequently, the Indians, are not prepared to adopt the policy of intransigence and nonintercourse followed by the United States with respect to Communist China. Nor do they agree with the United States in regarding Taiwan as the spokesman of mainland China.

Second, India, although committed to the democratic way of life, and convinced that the totalitarianism of Russia and China is unsuited to its economic and social needs, nevertheless believes that it can learn many useful lessons from the experience of Russia, and even more of China, in it efforts to achieve rapid industrialization. The Indians see no advantage in isolating themselves from their two great neighbors to the north. And, while it has become increasingly apparent that in order to fulfill its series of economic plans it will have to depend more and more on aid from the West, it wants to be free to accept aid also from the Communist bloc.

Third, India, fearful of war, has desire to antagonize Russia and China by actions which might bring about military reprisals. With an army of 400,000 as yet inadequately equipped with modern weapons, India would in any case be no match for its neighbors. Nor does India see any advantage in joining the United States-led bloc, which might conceivably give it the military protection it does not command itself, but would at the same time, it believes, greatly increase the danger of a clash with Russia and China.

Fourth, the Indians are not, as sometimes appears, insensitive to ruthless deeds committed by Russia and China. The Hungarian revolution of 1956 brought protests from many leading Indians, among them the Socialist Jayaprakash Narayan, and although Mr. Nehru was slow to express his own views until an inquiry on the spot had been made by his Ambassador to Moscow, who was also Ambassador to Budapest, he did indicate his concern when the results to this inquiry became available. Even sharper was the reaction of Indian opinion to the execution of former premier Imre Nagy and other Hungarian leader in 1958, which was widely condemned by the press, by spokesmen of various points of view, and by Mr. Nehru. Condemnation of Russia and China, however, would be far more prompt and vigorous if it were not for the fact that many Indians are apt to compare what the Russians and Chinese do with what they know of a past and present actions by Westerners in colonial areas. And, while the West points out that the days of colonialism are over, the Indians insist on discussing current or recent happening in Algeria or Kenya which, in their opinion, are no better than the actions of the Russians. As they see it, both the Western nations and the Communist powers do not hesitate to use force and violence when they believe it necessary for defense of what they consider their national interests. And here again, the Indians are apt to be more sympathetic to the sufferings of people of color than to those of the white peoples of Eastern Europe.

A sharp reassessment of India's foreign policy, however, was precipitated by the March 1959 events in Tibet. The Tibetan revolt against the rule of Communist China, news of which began to seep out through Indian sources in mid-March, promised to a mark a historic turning point in the triangular relationship of non-Western countries with the West, on the one hand, and the Communist bloc on the other. Experts on Chines affairs did not expect that, over the long run, this revolt would affect the power of the peiping government in mainland China. But peiping's treatment of the Tibetans deeply affected the attitude of India, as well as other Asian countries, toward Communist China as a world power.

It is important for the West to understand the reason for this change. Hitherto, many Asians had regarded "imperialism" as synonymous with "colonialism". This, in turn, was associated with the Western nations-Britain, France, the Netherlands, Belgium, Spain, Portugal-which in the Age of Exploration, and Expansion had acquired territories in Asia and Africa, and, after the breakup of the Ottoman empire in 1918, in the Middle East as well. Thus, in non-Western eyes imperialism became a symbol of the unequal treatment accorded by the white man to his non-white colonial subjects. What Westerners referred to as "the white man's burden" was regarded by non-Westerners as the white man's yoke.

Japan's conquest of Southeast Asia in the 1930s did not dispel this conviction; for the Japanese, being Asians who challenged and, for a time, seemed on the point of defeating the West, were regarded by many Asians as harbingers of their own long-hoped-for liberation from western rule. Had the Japanese consolidated their victories and retained power they would doubtless have suffered the onus of being regarded as new imperialists-as was the case with Japan's domination of Formosa and Korea, and its aggression against China in the 1930s . Their defeat and withdrawal left the Asian colonial peoples once more face to face with white rulers, some of whom made an orderly peaceful withdrawal (the British in India, Pakistan, Burma, Ceylon, Malaya), whole others relinquished their possessions with marked reluctance (the Dutch in Indonesia) or after bloody struggle (the French in Indo-China as late as 1955).

Meanwhile, China had long been regarded by Asians not as a colony of the West-even in years of most far-reaching internal disintegration China preserved its own government-but as a victim of the kind of intervention and unequal treatment by Western powers which colonialism had come to represent.

Given these circumstances, the assumption of power by the Chinese Communists in 1949 was viewed by many Asians not merely as an internal revolution but as a legitimate national liberation from Western encroachments. Nor was peiping's military occupation of Tibet in 1950 regarded as an imperialist move, because this remote land high in the Himalayas had been dominated in the eighteenth century by the Manchus of China who, after a brief invasion of Tibet by the British in 1904, restored their hegemony in 1910, and suppressed a revolt at time, quartering troops in Lhasa. Thus, historically, Tibet, which in the nineteenth century had been a bone of contention between Britain and the Tsarist Empire, was regarded as having been under the suzerainty of China.

Tibet

Tibetans, however, in their mountain retreat difficult of access, had developed a society of their own, dominated by Lamaism, a form of Buddhism, whose high priest, the Dalai Lama, with his seat the Tibetan Capital, Lhasa, is believed to be a living god, the incarnation of Lord Buddha himself. Thus, the present Dalai Lama, aged 23, is a national as well as religious symbol. The rival *Panchen* Lama, aged 21, who head smallest sect of Shigatse, is regarded as an incarnation of a lesser Buddha, Amitabha.

When the Chinese Communists, in their drive to assert their rule over all areas historically claimed by China, occupied Tibet, they imposed a treaty in 1951 in which they pledged autonomy to Tibet, with no change in the political position, status, or power of the Dalai Lama. Under the treaty a Chinese military and administrative committee was to be established in Tibet, the Tibetan army was to be absorbed into that of China, and peiping was to control Tibet's external relations.

Peiping, however, found it difficult to establish its authority over the Dalai Lama and the Buddhist monks who comprise a considerable portion of the population of about 1,300,000. The Chinese Communists tried to strengthen the influence of the Dalai Lama's rival; the Panchen Lama, who is believed to be more amenable to peiping's influence. The *Khambas*, a warlike tribe located in the southeast area of the country, had revolted against peiping in the summer of 1956, and had established their own local authority. When the population of Lahasa joined the Khambas, peiping tried to arrest the Dalai Lama in March 1959. At the time some 13,000 Buddhist monks-whom the Chinese Communists, intent on secularizing Tibet, had described as "unproductive" elements-joined the revolt, which subsequently spread to the neighboring Chinese province of Sinkiang, where many Tibetans are settled. Fierce fighting broke out in Lhasa, and the Dalai Lama, accompanied by members of his family and four members of his cabinet, fled southward. The Tibetan cabinet, on March 25, denounced the treaty with China and proclaimed the Country's independence. On March 28, Peiping, in turn, proclaimed the end of the Dalai Lama's rule and his replacement by the Panchen Lama. The Chinese then charged that revolt had been sparked by Western "imperialists" abetting the Chinese Nationalists on Formosa (who had meanwhile stated they had made air-drops in Tibet and had pledged aid, and ultimate independence, to the area); and that Tibetans settled at Kalimpong, on India's territory, had played a part in the uprising.

They also declared that discussion of Tibet in the Indian Parliament constituted intervention in China's internal affairs.

The Asian country most immediately concerned with events in Tibet is India, which borders on that area. Prime Minister Jawaharlal Nehru had questioned China in 1951 about the status of Tibet, and had urged peiping to give kit autonomy. While peiping had not directly answered Mr. Nehru's suggestion, the pledge of autonomy contained in the 1951 treaty had been accepted by India as satisfactory. Subsequently, India had endeavored to maintain friendly relations with its powerful neighbor, China, and had encouraged other Asian countries-notably at the conference of Asian-African countries at Banding in 1955 to accept the Five Principles of peaceful coexistence (*Panchsheela*) which India and China had agreed on in New Delhi in 1954. The Five Principles are mutual respect for territorial integrity and sovereignty, nonaggression, noninterference in one another's internal affairs, equality and mutual benefit, and peaceful coexistence.

Peiping's ruthless suppression of the Tibetan revolt came as a shock to India. Speaking in Parliament on March 30, Mr. Nehru, who had previously rejected peiping's complaint about parliamentary discussion of Tibet, said that the Chinese Communists had violated their pledge of autonomy. Mr. Nehru also expressed India's sympathy for the Tibetans, and subsequently declared that the he was seeking to bring about a peaceful settlement through diplomacy. On April 2, it became known that the Dalai Lama had taken refuge on Indian's territory, and was to reside at a hill-station, Mussoorie. On April 18, in his first public statement, the Dalai Lama accused peiping of having broken all its promises to respect Tibet's autonomy. Again, the Socialist leader Jayaprakash Narayan, was more outspoken than Mr. Nehru, and in July 1959 urged that the case of Tibet should be discussed in the United Nations.

Whatever may be the outcome of the Tibetan revolt, it has had the effect of causing Asians, even those who follow a neutralist policy, to assert that the non-white rulers of Communist China are practicing "imperialism," which was once associated solely with Western whites. For example, *The Daily Times of* Jakarta in Indonesia said: "The picture of Asians kicking Asians is not a pleasant one." Another Indonesian newspaper said that this event "may cause Communist China to lose all her friends." *The Hindustan Times*, in an editorial entitled "The Rape of Tibet," declared: "Much else could die with Tibet if we do not even now need the warning," and urged reassessment of "the basis of our foreign policy."

What happened in Tibet stirred Asians far more than events in Hungary, because the Hungarian revolt was regarded as struggle between two white peoples. This does not mean that the Asian countries will intervene militarily on behalf of Tibet. India, the most powerful of them, with an army of 400,000, is not in a position to attack Communist China, with an army of 2,500,000. It should be borne in mind that the United States, the strongest military power in the world, did not issue a military challenge to Russia in the case of Hungary, in spite of its promise of "liberation." Nor will china's actions in Tibet make Asians less sensitive to Western methods in Algeria or South Africa, where whites continue to treat non-whites in a colonial manner.

The significance of Tibet is that is has aroused Asians to put moral pressure on peiping, as they had previously done on the West, for independence or autonomy of peoples under foreign rule. Paradoxical as it may seem to Americans, many Asians believe that this pressure could be more effectively applied if Communist China was in the United Nations.

Meanwhile, India does not contemplate a change in its policy of nonalignment, as demonstrated by Mr. Nehru's rejection of a bid by Pakistan for a military alliance. Some observers, in fact, believe that the events in Tibet may have reinforced India's belief in nonalignment, on the ground that, as the threat of China grows, India should more than ever shun foreign entanglements and concentrate on its own economic and political progress. At the same time, it is expected that that India will view Communist China with increased suspicion and distrust; will take precautions against possible Chinese encroachments, both political and military, along India's Himalayan frontier, where peiping has long been conducting a "cartographic war" by including some of the border areas of India within the boundaries of China as represented on Chinese maps; and will increasingly identify the Indian Communist party with international communism.

Nehru's Foreign Policy

Indian critics of Mr. Nehru's foreign policy, although agreeing with him on the desirability of keeping the country free of what George Washington called "entangling alliances," contend that government is not genuinely "neutralist," because of its marked tendency to be more lenient about the mistakes and misdeed of the Communist dictatorships than about those of the Western democracies. To this contention government supporters replay that the Indian leaders expect far more the advanced industrial democracies of the West, with their long tradition of freedom, than from Russia or China, which have grappled with the problems of industrialization only in recent years, and, having lived for centuries under autocratic regimes, had little or no opportunity to acquire the habits of though and action that are prerequisites for democracy. This argument may sound specious to Westerners, particularly in moments when India seems more shocked by Suez than by Hungary. Yet, whatever we in the West may think of its merits, it ,too, reflects a deep-seated belief that India may be in a position to act as mediator between the West and the Communist dictatorships just because its own experience is a unique synthesis of Asia's past and the West's present which, it hopes may prove to be the world's future. It is only after several years of American condemnation of India's neutralism that the *New York Times* (one of the principle critics) said editorially on July 29, 1958, speaking of the Arab states: "Nationalism and even neutralism do not automatically mean victory for communism and Soviet imperialism."

The role of mediator between democracy and communism and of activator if not acknowledged leader of the new nations of Asia, the Middle East, and Africa to which Nehru has aspired since he came to office, might have been more readily attainable had India itself escaped the dilemmas of power politics for which it has been quick to criticize other great nations. These dilemmas are a direct result of its as yet unadjusted relations with Pakistan which, through the accidents of geography, borders on it in West and East Pakistan-separated by one thousands miles of Indian territory.

The failure of the two religious groups, Hindus and Muslims, who had found accommodation between their faiths and their way of life under Mogul rulers such as Akbar, to restore their coexistence on the eve of Britain's withdrawal was not only tragedy for the subcontinent, but also cast a dark shadow on Asia and, to the extent that Asia is now inextricably part of the international community, also on the world. Unlike India, a secular state which promptly reorganized its political life and adopted a democratic constitution three years after independence, Pakistan, a religious state, has found it difficult to reconcile the interests of its two wings: the western sector, with a predominantly conservative leadership drawn from big landowners, and with militant tribes a long the border of Afghanistan, and the eastern sector, with a socially and economically more advanced population which has pressed for increasing autonomy from the central government in Karachi.

As in India, the political group which led the fight for independence and, in this case for partition—the Muslim League founded by Jinnah, a brilliant Bombay lawyer—has found it necessary to adapt itself to the tasks of developing a new nation. In Pakistan, however, the influence of the religious leaders, the *ulema* or priests, slowed down the process of reorientation. But, in the course of forging the constitution political scientist, economists, and other leader of secular though who believed that a narrow interpretation of the Koran was not suited for the needs of a modern state, sought to achieve a synthesis of modern ideas with Islamic principles. The constitution, adopted on March 23, 1956, nine years after partition, had a preamble which began with the words: "In the name of Allah, the Beneficent, the Merciful...," and declares "The Pakistan would be democratic state based on Islamic principles of social justice."

According to constitution, democracy, freedom, equality, tolerance, and social justice were to be observed, but as enunciated by Islam. There was provision, however, assuring freedom to minority groups-the most important of which are the ten million Hindus-in the practice of their religion and guaranteeing their fundamental rights. But a Hindu could not be elected be to the presidency of the Islamic state-although it is also unlikely that in India a Muslim could hope to become president of predominantly secular India. The extent to which the constitution could have operated as an instrument for the modernizing of Pakistan depended on its future interpretation by experts who favor the country's secular development. Meanwhile, however, the ruling Muslim League headed after Jinnah's death by Premier Liaquat Ali Khan *and*, after his assassination, by Premier Mohammed Ali, later Ambassador to the United States, gradually began to disintegrate, and was succeeded by the more liberal-minded Awami League, with its principal strength in East Pakistan, headed by the former Premier, Hussein S. Suhrawardy, who before partition had been governor of Bengal. The Awami League and other political groups were disbanded on October 7, 1958, when President Iskander Mirza abrogated the constitution and established a military government, only to be subsequently ousted from office by his aide General Mohammed Ayub Khan on October 27, 1958. With the abrogation of the constitution, the secular-religious issue may once more be reopened.

The travail of partition, which wreaked human misery on both sides of the new frontiers, and left each country economically crippled –with Indian factories deprived of Pakistan's jute, producers deprived of India's manufacturing facilities-was further compounded by the as yet unresolved controversy about division of the subcontinent's canal waters.

Kashmir

Next to Kashmir, the problem of the canal waters is the most difficult issue between India and Pakistan. The background of the problem is that, in the undivided Punjab under British rule, 26 million arid acres a had been brought under irrigation by thirteen complex canal system. Ten of these system, 88 per cent of the irrigation water, were on the Pakistan side of the frontier at partition, and nearly all of them depend on river flowing from India of from India-held Kashmir. Pakistan has charged that India could, at will, divert these canal waters from its territory, had leave it to face a disastrous drought-a charge which India has vehemently denied. The fact that the sources of some of the waters needed for the irrigation of Kashmir are involved in the controversy has added to the bitterness on both sides.

The controversy was submitted to the World Bank which, after a careful study, made four proposals in its report published in February 1954:

1. Ultimately, Pakistan should have the exclusive use of the waters of the three rivers (Indus, Jhelum, and Chenab), and India those of the three eastern rivers (Ravi, Beas, and Sutlej).
2. This division should take effect after a transitional period, estimated at about five years, during which link canals would be built to bring surplus-flow water from the western rivers across to be Pakistani area that now depends on the eastern rivers.
3. India could progressively reduce deliveries to Pakistan as replacement water from these link canals became available.
4. India would pay for the building of the link canals.

India accepted the 1954 proposals in principle, but Pakistan expressed doubts about the adequacy of the link canals and the time required to build them. After further discussion, the Bank adjusted its proposals by an *aide-memoire* in May 1956. Its experts reported that link canals alone could not free Pakistan from severe water shortages, and advised that more reservoirs on the western rivers would therefore have to be built too. This time Pakistan agreed, but India objected, largely on the ground that bill for link canals and reservoirs, which it would have to pay and which was then estimated at over a billion dollars, was too high.

Eventually, at the advice of the Bank, Pakistan trimmed its programme down to $700 millions, but India offered only $150 million, and complained that Pakistan was delaying a payment of normal water charges and was slow in building the link canals. India contends that it must put into operation without further delay its Bhakra dam and its Rajasthan Canal, slated to start functioning full-scale in 1962, when deliveries of water to Pakistan would have to be discontinued. Pakistan, for its part, fears the shortage of water which, it insists, would result from the operation of India's new dam and canals, and expresses suspicions about India's ultimate motives in withholding water deliveries to which, India retorts, Pakistan has no right in any case.

In spite of these controversies, on April 18, 1959 the governments of India and Pakistan announced that they had signed in Washington a one-year agreement regulating the use of the Indus River and its main tributaries for irrigation. This agreement, reached through the good offices of the World Bank, was to cover "transitional arrangements" for the period between April 1,1959 and March 31, 1960. The bank was to send a mission to India and Pakistan to discussion new proposals.

Important as settlement of all these problems it, if both countries are to cohabit peacefully in the subcontinent and to heal the wounds left by partition, none of them has threatened to create the threat of war-although there has been a good deal of sabre-rattling by Pakistan, particularly since General Ayub's rise to power and, occasionally, on India's side by Krishna Menon in his capacity as Defense Minister. Mr. Nehru, however, has firmly opposed a policy of hostility toward Pakistan. According to an urban opinion poll taken in 1958 by the Indian Institute of Public opinion, nearly 48.7 per cent of the urban population in all age, education, income, and occupation groups is inclined to believe that India's expenditure on defense - which in 1958-59 constituted 35 per cent of the national budget, is not excessive—apparently because of concern about the uncertain state of Indo-Pakistan relations. Of those who regarded defense expenditure as excessive, 11.5 per cent did so on the ground that it is not appropriate to a country which is supposed to be following the Gandhian policy of nonviolence; and 15.4 per cent on the ground that India cannot afford it because of the five-Year Plan. Of the total polled 23.1 answered, "Don't know."

In the case of military defense, as in the case of foreign policy, the Tibet revolt marked a sharp turning-point. As late as February 28, India's Finance Minister, Morarji Desai, in presenting his budget to Parliament for the next fiscal year, which begins on April 1, announced a $50 million cut in defense spending-the only significant reduction in expenditures. Spending on the army and navy was to remain unchanged. The saving was to be effected by cutbacks in the purchase of planes and spare parts for the Indian air force.

Yet, when the Parliament debated this cut on April 9, following the Tibet revolt, many members both of the Congress party and of the opposition demanded assurances that the government was not taking a "calculated risk" by cutting expenditures this year in view of Chinese Communist military operation in Tibet, and asked whether the government was taking adequate steps to protect the frontier with Tibet. One Congress party member raised the possibility that peiping might not be satisfied with the conquest of Tibet, and might have ambitions to extend its influence in other neighboring countries, including Nepal, Sikkim, and Bhutan, India's neighbors to the north, whose foreign policy and defense are controlled by New Delhi. The Defense Minister, Krishna Menon, replied that defense spending for 1959-60, estimated at $510,300,000 compared with $560,700,000 for 1958-59, meant no sacrifice of combat effectiveness and had been made possible by improved planning and the greater availability of trained manpower.

In practice, one of the most striking aspects of relations between India and Pakistan are the good spirit and the mutual respect displayed by the representatives of the two countries whenever they have met on the level of experts concerned with specific technical problems. Not only are the civil servants of India and Pakistan former colleagues in the civil service of India under the British, with the same tradition and intellectual formation, but several of the political leaders on both side have tried to overcome mutual resentments and fears, aware that if this task is not accomplished now, while those who remember undivided India are still living, it may prove much more difficult for the next generation, accustomed to an atmosphere of hostility. This was the view of Ghulam Mohammed, the late Governor-General of Pakistan, who even when he was on the point of succumbing to a mortal illness, strained his ebbing strength to find a basis for agreement with India. This has also been true of Mr. Nehru and of several of his associates, in spite of their profound opposition to partition.

All these efforts at accommodation, however, have so far foundered on the issue of Kashmir, the one princely state which bordered on both Pakistan and India and was not originally incorporated into India at the time of partition. In the case of Kashmir, all the emotions which in the past have hampered the settlement of territorial problems in other areas of the world, are present on both sides: the nationalist sentiments of both Pakistan and India; the fundamental split between the secular and the religious state which in the first place brought about partition; the attempt, in which both Muslims and Hindus among the Kashmiris have played a part, to transform a backward agrarian community into a welfare state; the struggle of the great powers over the control of a strategic area which lies at the crossroads of Pakistan, India, Russia, and China, and could be an important jumping-off place for military operations; and the desire of the Kashmiris to determine their own destiny. Unfortunately for Kashmir, as well as for Pakistan and India, it is one of those territories which, because of their desirability, seem destined to be bones of contention between neighboring nations. The list of these territories is long and repeatedly marked by bloodshed; Alsace-Lorraine, the Saar, Trieste, Danzig, the Polish Corridor, Korea, Vietnam.

Both Pakistan and India claim Kashmir, a beautiful state, with its jewel-like lakes set among Himalayan peaks and its sturdy population, which in its long history has known the passage of many conquerors. Neither has shown signs of yielding its claim in the past decade, which is strewn with abortive bilateral negotiations and the failures of successive efforts of United Nations mediators, from Sir Owen Dixon of Australia to Dr. Frank P. Graham of the United States.

As India sees it, Kashmir was one of the 562 princely states of undivided India which were advised by Britain to choose between India and Pakistan. After considerable initial hesitation, its Hindu Maharajah, Sir Hari Singh opted for India at the last minute. The Muslim leader, Sheikh Abdullah, a member of the National Conference, the political party of Kashmir associated with the Indian National Congress, and a close friend of India's prime minister, Jawaharlal Nehru, who was at that time in jail because of his efforts to democratize the Maharajah's absolutist government, favored accession. According to India, Hari singh acceded after Pakistan had committed aggression by furnishing arms and military direction to "tribesmen" who invaded the western portion of the state, coming within five miles of its summer capital, Srinagar. India, therefore, say its spokesmen, had no choice but to send armed forces to Kashmir, at its ruler's request, to protect a state which had signified its desire to become part of the Indian Union.

True, at that time Mr. Nehru, at the suggestion of India's last Viceroy, Lord Mountbatten, agreed that the people of Kashmir should have an opportunity to express their views about the accession, but only after the Pakistanis had with drawn from the territory they had occupied—a condition Pakistan has so far not fulfilled. Lord Mountbatten's proposal was due to two factors: Kashmir's contiguity to both India and Pakistan, and the presence of population of 4 million, 77.11 per cent of whom are Muslims concentrated in the Vale, 20.12 per cent are Hindus, and the rest are Buddhists (concentrated in Ladakh in the north) and Sikhs. In retrospect, Mr. Nehru's agreement to a plebiscite is regarded as a political mistake, not only in India but also by some outside observers. For no arrangements were made about plebiscites in any of the other 561 states, and none were held, even though after 1947 India experienced difficulties with Hyderabad, were a Muslim prince ruled a population with a Hindu majority, and with Junagadh. Neither of these states, however, is contiguous with Pakistan, and it is difficult to imagine how, had they signified their desire to accede to Pakistan, they would have established a link with the country.

Mr. Nehru now takes the view that a decade later, when conditions in the subcontinent and in the world have changed, a plebiscite in Kashmir would become a new test of the two-nations theory he vigorously opposed in 1947; and that, if it should favour Pakistan, would lead to renewed turmoil and bloodshed among Muslims and Hindus in both Pakistan and India, and might jeopardize India's very existence. However, this view, strongly held by the Prime Minister, whose family are of Kashmiri origin and who has an emotional attachment to Kashmir, is disputed by some leading Hindu experts, who say that the assumption they would maltreat Muslims in India because of Kashmir is a libel on Hinduism.

Many Indians feel puzzled and aggrieved that the Western powers, quick to denounce aggressors elsewhere, have refused to recognize Pakistan's aggression in Kashmir. Other urge the government to have a plebiscite in the Vale of Kashmir for the sake of improving relations with Pakistan while retaining predominantly Hindu Jammu and Buddhist Ladakh. The Vale, they claim, whatever its economic, strategic, and sentimental value to India, is not worth perpetuating a dangerous quarrel with a neighbor whose support in Asia would be valuable for the Indians.

As the debate over Kashmir waxed and waned, the Indian government in August 1953 summarily deposed and jailed Sheikh Abdullah, once its trusted friend, who by that time was the actual ruler of Kashmir, since the Maharajah, son of Hari Singh meanwhile deposed by the Sheikh, had been reduced to the role of a constitutional monarch, appointed for a five-year period. This high-handed action, taken in the dead of night, was justified on the ground that the Sheikh had shown he favoured an independent Kashmir which, New Delhi feared, might have gone over to Pakistan. In 1956, Kashmir's Constituent Assembly, under the leadership of the Sheikh's successor, Muslim Prime Minister Bakshi Ghulam Mohammed, voted to make Kashmir a state of the Indian Union, thereby officially confirming the existing situation. This vote is regarded by many Indians as a consultation of the will of the people, tantamount to the plebiscite which had been promised but never held-although, in fact, this is not the case.

Pakistan, as India known well, disagrees with all these arguments. It takes the view that the predominantly Muslim population of Kashmir was not consulted about its wishes; that the Pakistanis did not commit aggression, as claimed by India, since the armed action which frightened the Maharajah into opting for India was carried out by "tribesmen" over whom Karachi had no control; that India high-handedly took over Kashmir, and failed to abide by its own promise to hold a plebiscite; that it added insult to injury by disregarding the decisions of the United Nations Security Council before which it had itself brought the Kashmir case; that it rules the Muslims by force; and that is obligated hold the plebiscite, which Karachi contends, would result in an overwhelming vote fore accession to Pakistan.

Impartial observers believe that of Kashmir's component parts Jammu-with its predominantly Hindu population—Buddhist Ladakh, and Gilgit would go to India, and that the crucial decision would have to be made only in the Vale of Kashmir. But the Vale, often called India's Switzerland, with its scenic prize for both countries, quite aside from religious and political considerations.

Gunnar Jarring, former president of the United Nations Security Council, as Sweden's permanent delegate to the UN, undertook a study of the Kashmir problem at the Council's request. In his report of April 30, 1957 he expressed his awareness of "the grave problems that might arise in connection with and as a result of a plebiscite". He called to the council's attention that "the implementation of international agreements of an *ad hoc* character, which has not been achieved fairly speedily, may become progressively more difficult because the situation with which they were to cope has tended to change." He added: " I could not fair to take note the concern expressed in connection with the changing political, economic and strategic factors surrounding the whole of the Kashmir question, together with the changing pattern of power relations in West and South Asia."

This statement was interpreted in New Delhi as suggesting that, given the state of the world in general and the unabated tensions between India and Pakistan in particular, the best that can be done is to maintain the *status quo.* Although these tensions emerged in the course of the partition of the subcontinent, in which the United States was not involved, they have been seriously aggravated by American military aid to Pakistan since 1950.

But, even if it were possible, and advisable, to maintain the *status quo* internationally, will it be possible to do it within Kashmir itself? So far as can be ascertained, the Kashmiris are uneasy about their present situation. Recurring attempts to review the case in the UN and threats broadcast by the Pakistani radio create a sense of insecurity which has an unfavorable effect on business and particularly on its most important component-tourism. People in Kashmir say, "Let's get this settled once and for all."

Sheikh Abdullah remains a highly popular leader in spite, or perhaps because, of his four-year imprisonment-from which he was temporarily released in 1958 only to be put in jail again, and than, in October of that year, brought to trial on charges of treason. If he is released once more, he might rally around him those Kashmirs who-although they welcome its economic aid and benefit by it-are discontented with India. The future is further clouded by the struggle for power which developed in the summer of 1957 between Bakshi Ghulam Mohammed, Prime Minister and president of the National Conference (Kashmir's counterpart of India's congress party), and G.M. Sadiq, believed by his critics to be a fellow traveler, if not a Communist, who after an open break on August 9 left the conference and formed a party of his own. New Delhi has backed Bakshi, but Sadiq also has some support in India-although he was weakened by the outright stand of the Indian Communist party in his favour.

In contrast to the Sheikh, who is believed to remain favourable to independence, Bakshi, a forceful personality, contends that Kashmir could not long survive without India. It is economically weak, he argues, and depends on India for both economic aid and military security, with 100,000 Indian troops, one quarter of the army, stationed in Kashmir. According to Bakshi, if Kashmir won independence, it would promptly become a pawn in cold war. And India continues to fear that independence would ultimately mean that Kashmir would go over to Pakistan.

Supported of Mr. Nehru point to the achievements of Kashmir, under the Sheikh and under Bakshi, both of whom could be described as Socialist-minded reformers. The state has carried out a land reform more far-reaching than that of India (in fact, Mr. Nehru regards it as a model for Indian study-although, in contrast to the situation in India, no provision was made for compensation), and has made a good start with its Six-Year Plan for economic development, which has included the construction of an all-weather road between India and Kashmir, and of a hydroelectric project. The Indian Planning Commission assisted Kashmir with the drafting of its plan, and India provided three-quarters of the necessary funds in the form of grants and /or loans. With its considerable known mineral resources, Kashmir, it is contended, will be able to achieve a diversified economy and raise the now low living standard of its people. These achievements, say the pro-Indian Kashmiris, would be lost if Kashmir were integrated into Pakistan. Meanwhile, the Pakistanis rule the section of Kashmir conquered by the "tribesmen" in 1947, which is now called Azad (Free) Kashmir.

In India itself there is a feeling of guilty about Abdullah. It was expressed most clearly by the Socialist leader Jayaprakash Narayan on August 27, 1957 when he said that "the policy followed with regard to Kashmir has led to the deterioration of relations with Pakistan." He favoured the release of Abdullah who, he thought, would then be able to persuade the Kashmiris to accept an independence and sovereign Kashmir which could be guaranteed by both India and Pakistan. The Sheikh, however, when he briefly regained his liberty, did no succeed in solving the problem.

For an outside observer the Kashmir problem is fraught with poignant contradictions. If one believes in democracy, then, one asks, is it not wrong, and even hypocritical for Mr. Nehru, who upholds the democratic character of India, to block a plebiscite in the Vale of Kashmir and thwart the inhabitants' right to self-determination? If the Kashmiri Muslims want to join Pakistan, then what right has India to prevent them from doing so? Yet, immediately, the question arises in one's mind: But would the Kashmiris including the Muslims, be better off with Pakistan-politically, economically, and socially-then they are now with India? Is it possible, in this case, that self-determination might aggravate, rather than remedy, the problems of the Kashmiris?

No solution so far proposed for Kashmir is local from the point of view of either of the two nations that emerged from partition. But one thing is clear: responsible persons no both sides, as well as in the UN, believe it is essential to find as soon as possible a basis for restoring good relations between Indian and Pakistan, which are crucial for the peaceful development of both. Otherwise, both will tend to dissipate their limited financial resources on piling up of more and more armaments, instead of concentrating on their urgent economic and social needs.

India's failure to find a *modus vivendi* with Pakistan has weakened its influence in international councils, where otherwise its voice has become increasingly heard and listened to since 1947. On a wide range of issues, from a settlement in Korea to the war in Indo-China, from the suspension of nuclear tests to reconstruction of the Middle East, Mr. Nehru intervened again and again with efforts to bring about a reconciliation of conflicting interests or, as in the case of the American prisoners held by Communist China, to speed the settlement of tense situations.

While many Americans have resented the "holier than thou" moral tone of Mr. Nehru (not like our own) on a number of critical occasions in which the United States was involved, there has been a growing respect for his broad view of world affairs, his philosophical outlook, and his willingness to work on preventing head-on clashes, as in the case of the Suez crisis, and of France's decision to leave the UN General Assembly over the issue of Algeria. In this respect India's neutralism has served the interests of clashing nations, since India is one of the few countries of the world which is regarded as an impartial arbiter.

That India cannot consider itself immune to the frailties of other nations has been clearly shown by the Kashmir case. Painful as this is for India and Pakistan, and for friends of both in other countries, it may have the negative merit of convincing the Indians that in the long run they, too, may benefit by the kind of impartial advice which they are always ready to give in world affairs. Humility is a quality seldom possessed by great powers. India, a power great in size, in numbers of population, in the imagination and vision of its leaders, but weak in resources and military strength, has discovered early in the history of its independent foreign policy that it, too, is not without fault. In the years ahead this discovery may prove an asset rather than a liability.

Nor should the prospect for improvement of Indo-Pakistani relations be regarded as entirely bleak. In the past Mr. Nehru has urged a "no-war" pact between the two countries, which could allay the fear, real or imagined, of attack by one on the other-fear, it should be added, which is discounted by the military leaders of both, who believe that either has the capacity to occupy the other's territory.

Hitherto Pakistan had firmly opposed such a pact. But, in July 1958 Pakistan's then Prime Minister, Firoz Khan Noon, who had previously served as its foreign Minister, declared at a press conference at Lahore that his country would not go to war with India to settle its disputes. He described the talk of war between the two nations "as nothing short of lunacy," and asserted that he would try to seek a solution of Indo-Pakistan problems through peaceful means only, indicating willingness to consider India's no-war pact offer if Mr. Nehru should make it again. When it is recalled that Mr. Noon has previously spoken in menacing tones about the "unfriendly and unhelpful" attitude of the Western powers about Kashmir, threatening to "shake hands with the Communist countries" if necessary to win the controverted state, and that cries of *jihad* (holy war) had been uttered in Karachi by no less a person than Jinnah's sister, Fatima Jinnah, Mr. Noon's statement appeared to open a new approach toward settlement of Indo-Pakistani controversies. *The Eastern Economist*, recalling that, "only until the other day we were a single family," said: "If we cannot reunite politically, there is no reason why we cannot effect unity of the hearts. The next best thing to unity is friendship as between two grown-up brother." The Noon-Nehru negotiations, however, ended in October 1958 when Premier Noon was thrown out of office by the military government of Iskander Mirza.

If leaders on both sides of frontiers reach the conclusion that the urgent needs of their peoples for economic and social development are more important, over the long run, than preparation for a war which, in their hearts, they do not believe will occur, and decide to divert the funds they now spend on defense - 70 per cent of Pakistan's budget and 35 per cent of that of India-than both would be able to proceed far more rapidly with their development. And, instead of calling on the United States for armaments which serve to inflame the wounds between the two nations of the subcontinent, Pakistan might ask for an increase of American aid commensurate with the armaments funds it was relinquishing. For, while India has vigorously opposed American arming of Pakistan, it has strongly favoured economic assistance to its neighbour. And, in both countries thoughtful men and women realize that, in the race between democracy and communism, those countries have the best chance of success which show most concern for the welfare, rather than the military preparedness, of their people.

APPENDIX I

LIST OF POLITICAL PARTIES

Party type Abbreviation	Party
NATIONAL PARTIES	
AIIC (T)	All India Indira Congress (Tiwari)
BJP	Bharatiya Janata Party
CPI	Communist Party of India
CPM	Communist Party of India (Marxist)
INC	Indian National Congress
JD	Janata Dal
JP	Janata Party
SAP	Samata Party
STATE PARTIES	
ADMK	All India Anna Dravida Munnetra Kazhagam
AGP	Asom Gana Parishad
ASDC	Autonomous State Demand Committee
BSP	Bahujan Samaj Party
DMK	Dravida Munnetra Kazhagam
FBL	All India Forward Bloc
FPM	Federal Party of Manipur
HVP	Haryana Vikas Party
ICS	Indian Congress (Socialist)
JMM	Jharkhand Mukti Morcha
JPP	Jammu & Kashmir Panthers Party
KCP	Karnataka Congress Party
KEC(M)	Kerala Congress (M)
MAG	Maharashtrawadi Gomantak
MDMK	Marumalarchi Dravida Munnetra Kazhagam

Party type Abbreviation	Party
MNF	Mizo National Party
MPP	Manipur People's Party
MUL	Muslim League
NTRTDP(LP)	Ntr Telugu Desam Party (Lakshimi Parvathi)
PMK	Pattali Makkal Katchi
RSP	Revolutionary Socialist Party
SAD	Shiromani Akali Dal
SDF	Sikkim Democratic Front
SHS	Shivsena
SP	Samajwadi Party
SSP	Sikkim Sangram Parishad
TDP	Telugu Desam Party
TMC(M)	Tamil Maanila Congress (Moopanar)
TUJS	Tripura Upajati Juba Samity
UGDP	United Goans Democratic Party
REGISTERED (UNRECOGNISED) PARTIES	
ABBNS	Akhil Bharatiya Bhrastachar Normoolan Sena
ABBP	Akhil Bharatiya Berozgaar Party
ABDBM	Akhil Bharatiya Desh Bhakt Morcha
ABDD	Akhil Bharatiya Dharmnirpeksh Dal
ABDUP	Akhil Bharatiya Dalit Utthan Party
ABHM	Akhil Bharat Hindu Mahasabha
ABJND	Akhil Bharatiya Jagrook Nagrik Dal
ABJS	Akhil Bharatiya Jan Sangh
ABJVP	Akhil Bharatiya Janata Vikas Party
ABKMM	Akhil Bharatiya Kisan Mazdoor Morcha
ABLTASJM	Akhil Bharatiya Lok Tanatrik Alp-Sankhyak Jan Morcha
ABLTP	Akhil Bharatiya Loktantra Party
ABMSD	Bhartiya Manav Seva Dal

Party type Abbreviation	Party
ABMSKP	Akhil Bharatiya Mahasand Sarvahara Krantikari Party
ABRAHP	Akhil Bharatiya Rashtriya Azad Hind Party
ABRRP	Akhil Bharatiya Ram Rajya Parishad
ABRRP(P)	Akhil Bharatiya Ram Rajya Parishad (Prem Ballabh Vyas)
ABRS	Akhil Bharatiya Rajarya Sabha
ABSR	Akhil Bharatiya Shivsena Rashtrawadi
AD	Apna Dal
AIAHMJKP	All India Azad Hind Mazdur & Jan Kalyan Party
AIDPF	All India Democratic People Federation
AIMIM	All India Majlis-e-Ittehadul Muslimoon
AKD	Ambedkar Kranti Dal
ALD	Adarash Lok Dal
AMB	Amra Bangalee
ARS	Arya Sabha
ATMK	Anaithinthiya Thamizhaga Munnetra Kazhag
BAZP	Bhartiya Azad Party
BBM	Bharipa Bahujan Mahasangh
BCVD	Bhrishtachar Virodhi Dal
BEP	Bhartiya Ekta Party
BHJP	Bharat Jan Party
BHJS	Bhoomijotak Samooh
BJKP	Bhartiya Jan Kisan Party
BJS	Bharatiya Jan Sabha
BJTP	Bharatiya Jantantrik Parishad
BKD	Bahujan Kranti Dal
BKD(j)	Bahujan Kranti Dal (jai)
BKS	Bharatiya Kranti Sena
BKUS	Bharatiya Krishi Udyog Sangh

Party type Abbreviation	Party
BLP	Bharatiya Labour Party
BLPY	Bharatiya Lok Panchayat
BLTMD	Bharatiya Lok Tantrik Mazdoor Dal
BLTP	Bahujan Loktantrik Party
BMRD	Bharatiya Manav Raksha Dal
BMSM	Bharatiya Minorities Suraksha Mahasangh
BNJP	Bharathiya Nethaji Party
BOP	Bira Oriya Party
BPF	Bharat Pensioner's Front
BPI	Bolshevik Party of India
BPM	Bharatiya Parivartan Morcha
BRC	Bharatiya Rajiv Congress
BRD	Bharatiya Rashtrawadi Dal
BRM	Bharatiya Rashtriya Morcha
BRP	Bharatiya Rashtriya Party
BSK	Bharatiya Sarvkalyan Krantidal
BSP(A)	Bahujan Samaj Party (Ambedkar)
BSP(R)	Bahujan Samaj Party (Raj Bahadur)
BSSM	Bharatiya Samaj Sangathan Morcha
BSVP	Bharatiya Samajwadi Vikas Party
CMM	Chhattisgarh Mukti Morcha
COP	Congress of People
CPI(ML)(L)	Communist Party of India (Marxist-Leninist) (Liberation)
DBP	Desh Bhakt Party
EKD(UP)	Ekta Krandi Dal U.P.
ESP	Ekta Samaj Party
FB(S)	Forward Bloc (Socialist)
FOS	Federation of Sabhas
GAVP	Gujarat Adijati Vikash Paksh
GGP	Gondvana Gantantra Party

Party type Abbreviation	Party
GJJP	Gujarat Janta Parishad
GSP	Gareebjan Samaj Party
HJKP	Hul Jharkhand Party
HJP	Hindustan Janta Party
HKMP	Hindi Kisan Mazdoor Party
HNP	Hind National Party
HPP	Hindu Praja Party
IBSP	Indian Bahujan Samajwadi Party
IDP	Indian Democratic Party
IDPP	Indian Democratic People's Party
INL	Indian National League
ISC	Indian Secular Congress
IUML	Indian Union Muslim League
JEM	Jan Ekta Morcha
JMH	Janhit Morcha
JKC	Janata Kranti Congress
JKP	Jharkhand Party
JKP(N)	Jharkhand Party (Noren)
JLPP	Jharkhand People's Party
JMM(M)	Jharkhand Mukti Morcha (Mardi)
JPS	Jan Parishad
JSTP	Jansatta Party
JSWP	Jan Swarajya Party
KCVP	Kannada Chalevali Vatal Paksha
KEC	Kerala Congress
KP	Kannada Paksha
KRD	Kranti Dal
KSM	Krantikari Samajwadi Manch
KVMP	Kisan Vyawasayee Mazdoor Party
LD	Lok Dal
LHP	Lok Hit Party

Party type Abbreviation	Party
LP	Lok Party
LPI(V)	Labour Party of India (V.V. Prasad)
MB	Mukt Bharat
MBT	Majlis Bachao Tahreek
MCO	Marxist Coordination
MCPI(S)	Marxist Communist Party of India (S.S. Srivastava)
MELPHC	Marxist Engelist Leninist Proletariat Health Commune
MKVP	Mahakushal Vikas Party
MMS	Mahabharath Mahajan Sabha
MPKP	Maharashtra Pradesh Krantikari Party
MPVC	Madhya Pradesh Vikas Congress
MSP	Manav Samaj Party
MSS	Manav Sewa Sangh
NDPF	National democratic Peoples Front
NIP	New India Party
NRP	National Republican Party
NVAS	Nag Vidarbha Andolan Samiti
PBRML	Pachim Banga Rajya Muslim League
PDLI	peoples Democratic League of India
PDP	Peoples Democratic Party
PHK	Pavitra Hindustan Kaazhagam
PMSP	Pragtisheel Manav Samaj Party
PPNMS	Political party of National management Service
PRC	Poorvanchal Rashtriya Congress
PSP	Pragati Sheel Party
PSS	Pratap Shiv Sena
PSSS	Proutist Sarva Samaj Samiti
PVP(P)	Punjab Vikas Party (Punjab)
PWPI	Peasants and Workers Party of India

Party type Abbreviation	Party
RAM	Rashtriya Aikta Manch
RBNNS	Rashtriya Bharat Nav Nirman Sangathan
RCPI(R)	Revolutionary Communist Party of India (Rasik Bhatt)
RKD	Rashtriya Krantikari Dal
RKP	Rashtriya Kisan Party
RMEP	Rashtriya Mazdoor Ekta Party
RNP	Rashtriya Nayay Party
RPI	Republican Party of India
RPI(A)	Republican Party of India (A)
RPI(D)	Republican Party of India (Democratic)
RPI(KH)	Republican Party of India (Khobragade)
RPI(S)	Republican Party of India (Sivaraj)
RPPI	Republican Presidium Party of India
RSDP	Rashtriya Samdarshi Party
RSPP	Rashtriya Samajwadi Party 'Prgatisheel'
RSRP	Rashtriya Surajya Parishad
RSSD	Rashtriya Samaj Sevak Dal
RUD	Rashtriya Unnatisheel Dal
SABJAN	Sabjan Party
SAD(M)	Shiromani Akali Dal (Simranjit Singh Mann)
SBHP	Sachet Bharat Party
SDP(MP)	Sarvadharam Party (Madhya Pradesh)
SHSP	Shoshit Samaj Party
SJP(M)	Samajwadi Janata Party (Maharashtra)
SKD	Samajik Kranti Dal
SLI	Socialist League of India
SLP(L)	Socialist Party (Lohia)
SLP(R)	Socialist Party (Ramakant Pandey)
SMP	Satya Marg Party
SSD	Shoshit Samaj Dal

Party type Abbreviation	Party
SUP	Surajya Party
SVSP	Savarn Samaj Party
SWD	Samajwadi Dal
SYP	Satyayug Party
TNHVYK	Tamil Nadu Hindu Vellalar Youth Kazhagam
UIDC	United Indian Democratic Council
UMFA	United Minorities Front, Assam
UPRP	Uttar Pradesh Republican Party
UTNLF	United Tribal Nationalists Liberation Front
VJP	Vijeta party
Independents	
IND	Independent

Note: This is only a list of Parties which participated in the Elections to the 11th Lok Sabha, 1996.

A TALE OF TWO DOCUMENTS: VISIONS UNLIMITED, CHOICES LIMITED

By Rajeev Deshpande

The din of Campaign 2004 lends itself to various labels. But going by Congress replay to the BJP's Vision Document, a clash of visions between the two principal political outfits in the country may not quite be the defining feature of this elections.

The Congress statement on economic policy has lengthy preamble listing the party's role in ushering in reforms with due consideration to social justice. And while suggesting that monsoon and luck had more to do with the current robust GDP figures, the Congress also spins a dream: Of achieving a 10 per cent growth rate.

The much-maligned Mungeri Lal would be justified in feeling a bit bemused as the speech with which his dreams are being appropriated. Congress general-secretary Jairam Ramesh said that he objected to BJP's claim that all the good things that have happened to the economy are the result of the last five years of NDA policies. "All governments benefits from wise decisions taken before they came to office," he said.

If one were to quickly set aside the Congress' bid to run down the NDA record-no political party worth its name would not do so - the prescriptions for a high - growth economy, reduction in unemployment and spurring agricultural growth bear examination.

The Congress promises to create an environment to boost the rate of investment. The BJP says that savings must be directed into entrepreneurship and employment generative investments. The Congress calls for less government while the BJP says that the government's role should be that of a facilitator and creator of the necessary environment for creative energies of the people to find expression.

The Congress calls for ensuring that regulators are in place to prevent private monopolies replacing the government as it withdraws from certain sectors. The BJP formulation is that the government's role in manufacturing and services be curbed except for strategic reasons and to prevent private monopolies.

The Congress initiatives on unemployment are not to different either. Both parties speak of encouraging reforms in sectors like banking and services, there are pledges for urban renewal and support for making inter-state movement of trade and services easier.

APPENDIX III

THE DELHI SOCIALIST CONFERENCE

Annual session, New Delhi, 2nd & 3rd July 1939

Presidential Address

"Ever since the Tripuri Congress, confusion has arisen in the ranks of the Congress Socialist Party," observed *Acharya Narendra Dev*, in the course of his presidential speech at the Delhi Socialist Conference, which was held in the Municipal Hall, New Delhi on, the 2nd. July 1939.

There was great resentment, added Mr. Deo, against the National Executive in certain quarters at its attitude of neutrality as regards the Pant resolution. The leadership was accused of vacillation at a crucial movement and it was said that the Executive, in taking the decision of neutrality, departed from the party line. There was lack of understanding amongst Party members about the Party Line itself. Other groups had taken advantage of this confusion and, as a result, the party was passing through a crisis.

The President admitted that the leadership was partly responsible for the present state of affairs and that sufficient care was not taken in the enrolment of members. "We have allowed other groups to enter the party and these groups function as such within the Party itself. This is against all principle of Party organisation. The Party has thus largely lost its character and has become a platform." Mr. Deo added. "The Party has, by its growing influence in the Congress, also succeeded in correcting the ultra-Leftist tendencies of certain Socialist groups in the country. The attitude of Socialists of all ranks towards the Congress has radically altered during the last five years. It has decidedly become favourable towards the Congress attitude taken by the Congress Socialist Party from the very beginning towards the national organisation."

In order that the Congress Socialist Party should continue to represent this healthy tendency, it is necessary that the Socialists should first set their house in order. All important questions should be thrashed out in the Party and decisions about be taken democratically and every effort should be made to make the Party as homogeneous and compact as possible. Strict party discipline should be enforced in the enrolment of members and they should insist on quality rather than numbers. Certain organisations had got jealous of the growing power of the Congress and they wanted to undermine its influence and prestige. Socialist would protect the Congress from such attack and they should do nothing which might weaken the great organisation to which Socialists belonged.

After explaining at length the reason Why the Socialist Party took a neutral attitude at the Tripuri Congress session on the Pant resolution, Mr. Narendra Deo stated that the Left was weak and divided and at present no section could initiate and lead the struggle single-handed. It had been said that present leadership did not want a struggle in the near future. Ever if that be the case, he asked, "should we not, by energetic action, create an atmosphere in the country which will compel the leader to implement the resolution of the National Demand? Let the so-called Left give proof of its earnestness; let it translate the Congress resolution into action and those who lag behind will soon have to follow suit. Concrete political action alone can move the Congress as a whole towards implementing its own resolutions."

If the slogan of unity for immediate struggle was correct, Mr. Deo observed, their stand of neutrality was the only correct attitude consistent with their policy. Opposition to the Pant resolution, if it had succeeded, would have brought about disunity and they would have been held responsible for it. If there was no unity to-day in the Congress, Congress Socialists were not be blame.

While he criticised the left for its shortcomings, Mr. Deo also did not absolve the Right of its share of blame, and stated that the Right had done nothing to implement the resolution of the National Demand. The resolution had been relegated to the background and steps were being taken which led one to think that the High Command had no other programme except the parliamentary programme to implement. Regarding the working of the Congress Ministries in the provinces, the President remarked that offices were accepted to strengthen the national movement and not to demonstrate fitness for rule. It the Minister found that it was no longer possible for them to fulfil that purpose they should frankly say so and vacate office. "We can hold ourselves responsible for provincial administration," he said "only so long as we are in a position to utilise these new opportunities for strengthening the nation. Such opportunities are every day proving less and less and things have come to such a pass that the parliamentary programme can be fulfilled only by subordinating every other programme to it. If that be so and if we are called upon to make a choice, we shall vote for direct action." Concluding Archarya Narendra Doe said, "There is phenomenal awakening in the country and the international crisis is deepening and one does not know when the world will be involved in a war. Let us not throw away our opportunities. Let those whose vision is clear, formulate a plan of action and by following a correct line and by resolute action demonstrate to the people the immediate necessity of making elaborate preparations for the impending struggle. Let the Congress Socialist Party realise that it has to perform these urgent tasks in conjunction with all those who think and act alike".

Second Day - New Delhi - 3rd July 1939

Mr. ***Jai Prakash's*** *speech*

Addressing the Conference on the next day, the 3rd July, Mr *Jai Prakash Narain,* General Secretary of the All-India Congress Socialist Party explained the aims and objects of the party and denied the impression held in some quarters that the Socialists wanted to create a split in the Congress. Mr. Narain declared that the Socialists had no quarrel with the Congress as a political organisation but they did not completely agree with its programme which, they left, was not sufficiently advanced. They also wanted to counter the growing tendency towards "parlimentarism" among Congressmen. The Congrss Socialist Party had been, proceeded Mr. Jai Prakash Narain, in existence for the last five years and during this period had constantly endeavoured to radicalise the Congress programme and to direct that body along the path of revolution. The only way they could achieve that object was to organise effectively the Kisans and labourers in their own organisations under the aegis of the Congress. The Socialist never cared about the leadership of the Congress - the personalities, in whose hands all the power of Congress was concentrated. They were only concerned with its programmes. It was their conviction that the old Congress programme of attaining Swaraj had outlived its utility; it had become too antiquated to cope with the modern needs. Hence the necessity of a new programme based on full recognition of the greatly changed conditions. Referring to the charge that the Socialists were weakening the parent body (the Congress), Mr. Jai Prakash Narain pointed out that the chief task to which the Socialist Party had addressed itself was the formation of Kisan Sabhas and Mazdoor Sabhas. This they were doing to bring Kisans and Mazdoor in large number into the Congress fold. The harnessing of the tremendous force behind the Indian masses, consisting chiefly of peasants and labourers, could not but greatly strengthen the Congress. The Congress was not opposed to the organisation of Kisans and Mazdoors in their own organisation, and therefore, it could not be said that the Socialists were impairing the forces of the Congress by diverting them into different channels. Mr. Jai Prakash concluded by expressing satisfaction at the progressive consolidation of the forces of the Left, which, he declared, augured well for the future of India. He also opposed the participation of Indians in imperialist wars.

Resolutions

A number of resolutions were adopted by the conference. It urged that more concerted efforts should be made to prepare the country for nation-wide struggle to enforce the national demand and urged that for this purpose a national volunteer corps should be immediately formed.

The conference condemned the policy adopted by the Governments of Bengal and the Punjab against' the Kisan and labour movements in their respective provinces. It also strongly criticised the Punjab Government for enforcing the Princes Protection Act.

By another resolution, the conference welcomed the co-ordination of the activities of Socialists and Communists, which it regarded as the only solid basis for consolidating the forces the Left.

The conference urged the Congress Working Committee immediately to convene a joint conference with the Standing Committee of the All-India States Peoples Conference in order to devise ways and means to resume the struggle in the States with the full backing of the Congress.

A resolution on war was also adopted, requesting the Congress to take up, *inter alia,* active anti-war propaganda on band, especially in the chief recruiting areas. It also desired the Congress Governments in the various provinces to make their position absolutely clear to the British Government that they would resist the working of proposed amendments to the Government of India Act relating to recruitment.

Bibliography

Alexandrowicz, C. H. *Constitutional Developments in India.* Bombay: Oxford University Press, 1957.

Anstey, Vera. *Economic Development of India,* 2nd ed. New York: Longmans, 1932.

Appleby, Paul H. *Public administration in India: Report of a Survey.* New Delhi: Manager of Publications, 1953.

Appley, Paul H. *Re-examination of India's Administrative System.* New Delhi: Manager of Publications, 1956.

Archer, W.G. *India and Modern Art.* London: Allen and Unwin, 1959.

Austin, Granville. *The Indian Constitution: Cornerstone of a Nation.* Oxford: The Clarendon Press, 1966; New York: Oxford University Press, 1966.

Bailey, F.G. *Caste and the Economic Frontier.* Manchester: Manchester University Press, 1957.

Basham, A. L. *The Wonder That Was India.* London: Sidgwick and Jackson, 1954; New York: Hawthorn, 1963. (rev.).

Berkes, Ross N., and Mohinder S. Bedi. *The Diplomacy of India.*

Stanford: Stanford University Press, 1958.

Bouquet, A. C. *Hindusim.* New York: Hutchinson's University Library, 1948.

Bowles, Chester. *Ambassador's Report.* New York: Harper, 1954.

Braibanti, Ralph, and J. J. Spenger, eds. Administration and *Economic Development in India.* Durham, N. C.: Duke University Press 1963.

Brecher, Michael. *Nehru: A Political Biography. New York and London*: Oxford University Press, 1959.

Brecher Michael Nehru's Mantle: *The Politics of Succession in India.* New York: Frederick A. Praeger, 1966.

Brecher Michael *The Struggle for Kashmir.* New York: Oxford University Press, 1953.

Brown, D. Mackenzie. *Indian Political Thought From Ranade to Bhave: The Nationalist Movement.* Berkeley: University of California Press, 1961.

Browñ, D. Mackenzie, *The White Umbrella: Indian Political Thought From Manu to Gandhi*. Berkeley and Los Angeles: University of California Press, 1953.

Brown, W. Norman. *The United States and India and Pakistan*. Cambridge, Mass: Harvard University Press, 1953.

Charkravarty, P. C. *India's China Policy*. Bloomington, Ind.: Indian University press, 1962.

Chaudhuri, Nirad C. *The Continent of Circe: An Eassay on the Peoples of India*. London: Chatto and Windus, 1965; New Your: Oxford University Press, 1966.

Choubey, Jagdish Narain. *Problems of National Integration*. Delhi: National Integration Council, 1961.

Coale, Ansly J., and Edgar M. Hoover. *Population Growth and Economic Development in Law-Income Countries: A Case Study of India's Prospects*, Princeton: Princeton University Press, 1958.

Congressional Record, 85th Congress, and Session, June 6, 1958. Senate Debate on Section 2 of the Mutual Security Act of 1952 as amended (Kennedy-Cooper Proposal "to assist India to complete successfully its current programs for economic development").

Constitution of India, The. New Delhi: Manager of Publications, 1956.

Cormack, Margaret. *The Hindu Woman*, Bombay: Asia Publishing House, 1961.

Cressey, George B. *Asia's Lands and Peoples*. New York: McGraw-Hill, 1951.

Davis, Kingsely. *The Population of India and Pakistan*. Princeton: Princeton University Press, 1951.

Douglas, William O. *We the Judges: Studies in American and Indian Constitutional Law from Marshall to Mukerji*. Garden City, New York: Doubleday, 1956.

Dube, S. C. *Indian Village*. London: Routledge and Kegan Paul, 1955.

Dube, S. C. India's Changing Villages: *Human Factors in Community Development*. London: Routledge and Kegan Paul, 1958.

Embree, Ainslie T., ed. *The Hindu Tradition*. New York: Modern Library, 1966.

Fischr, Louis. *Gandhi*. New York: Signet, 1954. Paperback.

Fisher, Margaret W., and Joan V. Bondurant. *Indian views of Sino-Indian Relations*. Berkeley: University of California Press, 1956.

Gadgil, D. R. *Economic Policy and development*. Poona: Gokhale Institute, 1955.

Gadgil, D. R. *The Industrial Evolution of India*, 4th ed. Bombay: Oxford University press, 1942.

Garratt, Geoffrey Theodore, ed. *The Legacy of India*. Oxford: The Clarendon press, 1937.

Gibb, H. A. R. *Mohammedanism*. Mentor, 1955. Paperback.

Gorwala, *A. D. Not in Our Stars: Through the Eyes of An Indian Critic*. Bombay: Jaico Publishing House, 1958. Paperback.

Gorwala, *A. D. Of Matters Administrative*. Bombay: Popular Book Depot, 1958.

Government of India. *Report on India's Food Crisis and Steps to Meet* It, by the Agricultural Production Team sponsored by the Ford Foundation (Ministry of Food and Agriculture and Ministry of Community Development and Cooperation, April 1959).

Griffiths, Percival Joseph. *Modern India*. New Your: Frederick A. Praegr, 1957.

Harrison, Selig S., ed. *India and the United States*. New York: Macmillan, 1961.

Harrison, Selig S. India: *The Most Dangerous Decades*. Princetion: Princeton University Press, 1960.

Hart, Henry C. *New India's Rivers*. Bombay: Orient Longmans, 1956.

Hutton, J. H. *Caste in India*, 4th ed. New York: Oxford University Press, 1963.

Isaacs, Harold Robert. *Scratches on Our Minds: American Images of China and India*. New York: John Day, 1958.

Isherwood, Christopher, and Swami Prabhavananda, trans. *The Song of God: Bhagavad-Gita*. N.Y.: Mentor, 1954. Paperback.

Kabir, Humayun. *Education in New India*. London: Allen and Unwin, 1956.

Kabir, Humayun *The Indian Heritage*. London: Meridian Books, 1947; Bombay: Asia Publishing House, 1955.

Kalidasa. *Shakuntala*, trans. Arthur W. Ryder. New York: E. P. Dutton, 1928.

Kautsky, John H. *Moscow and the Communist Party of India*. New York: Wiley, 1956.

Kidron, Michaeli *Foreign Investments in India*. New York and London: Oxford University Press, 1965.

Kogekar, S. V., and Richard L. Park, eds. *Reports on the Indian General Elections*, 1951-52. Bombay: Popular Book Depot, 1956. Distributed in the United States by the Institute of Pacific Relations.

Korbel, Josef. *Danger in Kashmir*. Princeton: Princeton University press, 1954.

Kramrisch, stella. *The Art of India: Traditions of Indian Sculpture, Painting and Architecture*. New York: Phaidon, 1954.

Lamb, Beatric Pintney. India: *A World in Transition*, 3rd ed. New York: Frederick A. Praeger, 1968. Paperback.

Levi, Werner. *Free India in Asia*. Minneapolis: University of Minnesota Press, 1952.

Malenbaum, Wilfred. *East and West in India's Development*. Reports on the Economics of Competitive Coexistence (National Planning Association, April 1959).

Malenbaum, Wilfred. *Prospects for Indian Development*. London: Allen and Unwin, 1962; New York: The Free press of Glenlcon, 1962.

Masani, M. R. *The Communist Party of India*. New York: Macmillan, 1954.

Mayer, albert, and Associates, in collaboration with McKim Marriott and Richard L. Park. *Pilot Project, India* Berkeley; University of California Press, 1958.

Mehta, Asoka, "The Political Mind of India," *Foreign Affairs* (July 1957).

Mehta, G. L., "As Others See Us," *Foreign Affairs* (October1958).

Menon, V. P. *The Story of the Integration of the Indian states*. New York: Macmillan, 1956.

Morgan, Kenneth W. *Islam: The Straight Path*. New York: The Ronald Press, 1958.

Morris-jones, W. H. *Parliament in India*. London: Longmans, 1952.

Myers, Charles A. *Labour Problems in the Industrialization of India*. Cambridge, Mass: Harvard University press, 1958.

Nanda, B. R. *The Nehrus: Motilal and Jawahralal*. New York: John Day, 1963.

Natarajan, *S. A Century of Social Reform in India*. Bombay: Asia Publishing House, 1959.

Nehru, Jawaharlal. *The Discovery of India*. New York: John Day, 1946; Anchor Books, 1960 (paperback).

Nehru, Jawaharlal. *Glimpses of World History*. New York: L. Drummond, 1949.

Nehru, Jawaharlal. *India's Foreign Policy*. Publication division, Ministry of Information and Broadcasting, Government of India, 1961.

Overstreet, Gene D., and Marshall Windmiller. *Communism in India*. Berkeley: University of California Press, 1959.

Palmer, Norman D. "India" in George McT. Kahin, *Major Governments of Asia*. Ithaca: Cornell University Press, 1958.

Palmer, Norman D. *South Asia and United States Policy*. Boston: Houghton Mifflin, 1966.

Palmer, Norman D. *The Indian Political System*. Boston: Houghton Mifflin, 1961.

Pannikar, K. M. *Asia and Western Dominance: A survey of the Vasco da Gama Epoch of Asian History*, 1498-1945, rev. ed. New York: Hillary House, 1959.

Park, Richard L., and Irene Thinker, eds. *Leadership and Political Institutions in India*. Princeton: Princeton University Press, 1959.

Parton, Margaret. *The Leaf and the Flame*. New York: Knopf, 1959.

Planning Commission, Government of India. *First Five Year Plan*. New Delhi, December 1952.

Planning Commission, Government of India. *The New India: Progress Through Democracy*. New York: Macmillan, 1958.

Planning Commission, Government of India. *Report of the Indian Delegation to China on Agrarian Co-operatives*. New Delhi, May 1957.

Planning Commission, Government of India. *Second Five Year Plan*. New Delhi, 1956.

Rau, Benegal N. *India's Constitution in the Making*. Bombay: Orient Longmans, 1960; New York: Paragon Book Reprint Corporation, 1964 (2nd ed.).

Rawlinson, Hugh George. India: *A Short Cultural History*. New York: Frederick A. Praeger, 1952.

Rosen, George. *Democracy and Economic Change in India*. Berkeley: University of California Press, 1966.

Ross, Nancy Wilson. *Three ways of Asian Wisdom*. New York: Simon and Schuster, 1966.

Rostow, Walt W. Testimony; U.S. Senate, Committee on Foreign affairs, 85th Congress, 2nd Session, Hearings: "Review of Foreign Policy, 1958."

Rowland, Benjamin. *The Art and Architecture of India*. London and Baltimore: Penguin Books, 1953.

Rudolph Lloyd I., Suzanne and H. Rudolph. *The Modernity of Tradition: Political Development in India*. Chicago: University of Chicago press, 1967.

Singer, Milton, ed. *Traditional India: Structure and Change*. Austin: University of Texas Press, 1959.

Smith, Donald E. *India as a Secular State*. Princeton: Princeton University Press, 1963.

Smith, Wilfred Cantwell. *Modern Islam in India: a Social Analysis*. Lahore: Ripon Printing Press, 1947.

Spear, Percival. India: *A Modern History*. Ann Arbor; University of Michigan press, 1961.

Spear, Percival. *India, Pakistan and the West*, 3rd ed. London: Oxford University Press, Home University Library, 1958.

Stin, Arthur. "India and the USSR: The Post-Nehur Period," *Asian Survey* (Berkeley, California), vol. VII, no.3 (March 1967)

Tagore, Rabindranath. Nationalism. London: Macmillan, 1917.

Talbot, Phillips. "The Second General Elections: Voting in the States." American Universities Field staff, India. PT-6-1957.

Talbot, Phillips, and S. L. Poplai. *India and America*: A Study of Their Relations. New York: Harper, 1958.

Tennyson, Hallam. India's Walking Saint: *The Story of Vinoba Bhave*. Garden Cinty, New York: Doubeday, 1955.

Thompson, Edward John, and Geoffrey Theodore Garratt, *Rise and Fulfilment of British Rule in India*. London: Macmilan, 1934.

Thorner, Daniel, and Alice Thorner. *Land and Labour in India*. Bombay and New York: Asia Publishing House, 1962.

Thinker, Hugh. *India and Pakistan: A Political Analysis*, rev. ed. New York: Frederick A. Praeger, 1968.

Turner, Roy. *India's Urban Future*. Berkeley: University of California Press, 1962.

UNESCO, *India: Paintings from Ajanta Caves*. New York Graphic Society by arrangement with UNESCO, 1954.

Useem, John and Ruth Hill. *The Western-Educated Man in India*. New York: Dryden Press, 1955.

Ward, Barbara. *India and the West*, rev. ed. New York: W. W. Norton, 1964.

Weber, Max. *The Religion of India*. Glencoe, Illinois: Free Press, 1958.

Weiner, Myron. *Party Building in a New Nation*. Chicago: University of Chicago Press, 1967.

Party Politics in India. Princeton: Princeton University Press, 1957.

Wiser, William, and Charlotte Wiser. *Behind Mud Walls, 1930-1960*. *Berkeley*: University of California Press, 1963.

Woodruff, Philip. *The Men Who Ruled India*, 2 vols. New York: St. Martin's Press, 1954.

Zimmer, Heinrich. *The Art of Indian Asia, its Mythology and Transformations*, completed and edited by Joseph Compbell, 2vols. New York: Pantheon Books, 1955.

Zinkin, Taya. *Challenges in India*. New York: Walker, 1967.

Novels And Personal Memoirs

Anand, Mulk Raj. *Collie*. London and New York: Hutchinson International Authors, 1947.

Novels and Personal Memoirs

Anand, Mulk Raj. *The Villages*. Toronto: Nelson, 1939.

Chaudhrui, Nirad C. *The Autobiography of an Unknown Indian*. New York: Macmillan, 1951.

Forster, E. M. *A passage to India*. New York: Harcourt Brace, 1924.

Gandhi, Mohandas K. *An Autobiography: The Story of My Experiments with Truth*. Boston: Beacon Press, 1957. Paperback

Markandaya, Kamala. *Nectar in Sieve*. New York: John Day, 1954.

Masters, John. *Bhowani Junction*. New York: Viking Press, 1954. Mukerji, Dhan Gopal. *My Brother's Face*. London: Thornton Butterworth, 1935.

Narayan, R. K. *The Financial Expert*. East Lansing: Michigan State College Press, 1953.

Narayan, R. K. *The Guide*. New York: Viking Press, 1958.

Nehru, Jawaharlal. *Toward Freedom: The Autobiography of Jawaharla Nehru*. Boston: Beacon Press, 1958. Paperback.

Rajan, Balachandra. *The Dark Dancer*. New York: Simon and Schuster, 1958.

Rama Rau, Santha. *Remember the House*. New York: Harper, 1956.

Index